# Marisella

*A Cinderella Tale*

Marisa DiRuggiero

With D.P. Conway

*From Darkness to Light through the Power of Story*

Daylights Publishing House, Inc.
Cleveland, Ohio

*Only the heart knows the dreams deeply hoped for.*
*Anonymous*

# Contents

# Opening

### Cleveland Ohio
### 1968

Nonna said, "Do not throw the peach seed away, Marisella. Go plant it in the garden."

I ran out the side door to our vast garden and went to the corner, where I dug a small hole and put the remainder of my peach into the ground. I covered it with dirt, then went to the barrel of rainwater my Nonno, my grandfather, kept under the garage gutter. After that, I scooped a ladle of water, carefully carried it across the driveway to the garden, and slowly covered the ground where the seed was.

As the ground turned dark, I felt a sense of hope. Everything else in our vast garden belonged to the family. But this tree, and the peaches it would someday hold, would be my tree.

I would share the peaches with everyone, but it would be something I could call my own. So, I whispered, "Please grow, little tree. I want to see you grow up."

I smiled and added, "And I will grow with you."

# BEGINNINGS

## Madison Avenue

Cleveland Ohio
1963

The morning sun lifted above the horizon of the early 1960s Cleveland eastern sky. It shined directly down Madison Avenue for miles. Small delivery trucks, cars, and people walking to work absorbed the warm rays. It was summer, and by the sun's vividness and the already warm morning temperature, everyone knew it would be another hot day.

No one minded this early morning sun, though. It was the golden time of the morning when the warm golden light made everything look richer than it was. Factories, houses, and red-bricked streets were all glorious in the morning sun. It did not come often in Cleveland, and we all relished it when it did.

Our home on Madison Avenue was a double: one unit up, one unit down, and a shared basement. Most of the doubles were built the same, all designed to fit on forty-foot-wide city lots, with the drive and house taking up just about every inch of the forty feet. The yards were tiny, with over half of them taken up by the two-car garage, one belonging to each unit.

People lived close to that street. When walking along your driveway, you could not help but hear sounds coming through the glass panes or your neighbors' screens. TV and radios were blaring, pots and pans were clanging, or people were talking, laughing, shouting, and even fighting—the sounds of life, you might say.

Near the front of the houses were the porches. These were the more formal places where the sounds of life also happened. At the front porches, neighbors would see each other daily, greet, and talk. People would go up onto neighbors' porches without thinking twice about meeting the neighbor's friends or relatives who might be visiting.

Our double was a typical one. Each floor had two small bedrooms on either side of the bathroom. The modest kitchen in the back led into a small dining room that you had to pass through to get to the living room in the front of the house.

We lived upstairs in our double. There were two doors in the front living room. One was on the sidewall, leading down the steep stairs and out the front door. The other was at the front of the room, next to the windows. It was my favorite door as it led out to the front porch that looked down over Madison Avenue.

Of course, Madison Avenue was named after Madison Avenue in New York, as all Madison Avenues are, but this was not a New York-style Madison Avenue. It was NOT a wide thoroughfare with many lanes of traffic. Instead, Madison Avenue looked down over an old brick street built to accommodate horses and buggies a couple of decades earlier. It was wide enough for two cars to travel in opposite directions simultaneously. Our Madison Avenue had mostly double houses on one side of the street and mostly bustling factories on the other side of the street.

From our porch, you could look down at the fenced-in parking lot and the Marshall Allen Company front entrance. If you looked directly across from our porch, you would see the large windows of the factory's second floor. If you looked up, you could see all five factory floors' windows. The sky was visible, but you had to be sitting close enough to the porch rail to lean over and look up, something I was not allowed to do. You could also see the sky if you sat on the left side of the porch and looked down Madison Avenue, beyond Marshall Allen. This was my favorite spot when I could get it.

Not all houses looked onto a five-story red brick building. Many only had one or two-story factories across the street from them. It depended on which double you happened to live in. The lucky people on the top porches of those doubles could look out at the distant skyline of doubles reaching to the next main street over a mile away.

Most of those lucky people lived across from quieter factories. Our factory was larger, and it bellowed with the noise of machines clanging, and sometimes men shouting or laughing loudly. The sounds went on six days a week, from morning until night. You got used to it after a while, and it became another of the sounds of life.

None of that mattered to me, though. My life was not outside. My life was inside.

# Roots

My father was an immigrant from Italy. He never talked much, but when he did, it was with his hands and his rising voice. His words were slow, drawn out, ascending upward in perfect unison with his hand that would rise up along with the sound of his voice. After that, his voice would fall too, but not melodically. Rather, after his crescendo moment, his hand would go back to his side, and he would look down at the floor, finishing his sentence in a soft, almost imperceptible sound. This rising to a crescendo and falling to imperceptible was probably understood by his mother while he was still in the womb, for she named him Crescenzo.

Crescenzo was born in Coreno, Italy, a few years before the outbreak of World War 2. He was the middle child in a family of thirteen children, three of whom died as infants. As it often goes with middle children of large families, he was a bit lost in the shuffle of the little attention his parents could give. His father drank more than he should, and his mother was always expecting another baby. She was never in great health.

As his brothers and sisters called him, Cris was only five years old when Italy changed sides in the war. As a result, his family had to flee their little farm and hide out in caves for many months. It was a time of little food and scrounging, even for a piece of bread. These hard times and his mother's health cast a melancholy upon my father. I am not sure why it hit him so hard. Perhaps because he was at such a formative age, perhaps he was just more vulnerable than his siblings. But he spent the rest of his life entrenched in that melancholy place. It was a place of the low ebb of quiet, depressed living, looking down at the floor with a slight frown on his face.

His brothers and sisters were not affected as he was. They were all outgoing and friendly. They never noticed the dire poverty they endured on a tiny family farm in the hills of Italy. But once the war hit and the countryside of Italy was ravaged by it, they realized their vulnerability. They realized they had to leave.

After the war ended, they all boarded an ocean liner and came to America. They were warm and friendly people, full of life, and full of the hope that the adventure and opportunity in America gave. They settled on the west side of Cleveland, where Cris's father started a small corner grocery store not far from Madison Avenue.

His closest brother was Tony, who was just two years younger than him.

Tony looked up to his older brother, and he understood him. Tony seemed to have all the outward personality that Cris did not have. It was as if the powers in charge of handing out happiness and personality forgot to give Cris any and instead gave Tony a double portion. I never minded, as I loved them both equally.

My mother's name was Brigida. She was also an immigrant from Italy. Her people were very different from Papa's people. She came from a very quiet, very strong, and proud people on the coast of Italy in a place called Scauri. She was the only daughter of Ernesto and Rosa. The family had a small coop of chickens and raised their own food, primarily olives, grapes, beans, and greens, in the warm seaside Mediterranean climate.

Brigida's father labored day and night, growing and carefully tending acres and acres of olives and grapes. Then, the whole family would turn them into olive oil and wine every year at harvest time. They made more than enough to feed themselves, and they would sell hundreds of hand-bottled liters of wine and olive oil each year to pay for their other needs.

My mother was only six months old when the war came to Scauri and the Germans turned on the Italians. Ernesto dug a deep hole on his property as the family got ready to flee to the mountains. He buried a large barrel of olive oil and dug another hole where he buried a large barrel full of wine.

As they were racing out the door, Rosa told Ernesto to grab the baby. They were a few steps onto the road, with their two sons and cart full of what they could carry, when they realized the baby, Brigida, had not been taken down from the hamper she had been hanging in. Rosa ran back inside and got the baby, and it was not ten minutes later when they heard the bombs falling on their village.

After the war, they could return to their home and farm. My grandfather dug up his barrels of oil and wine, and their income from selling it enabled them to survive long enough for a new season of crops to come in.

~ ~ ~ ~

Eighteen years later, Cris was ready to find a wife. His older brother, Joe, told him the best wife he could find would be in Italy. So, in 1962, at the age of twenty-five, Cris booked passage on an airline and flew to Italy.

He was short and stocky, with a thick band of black hair sitting handsomely atop his head. He looked like Elvis Presley, perhaps the Italian version, only shorter and stockier. When he arrived, he stayed with his Aunt Carmen in Coreno, Italy. They set about visiting relatives and friends from that day, letting them know Cris was looking for a bride to bring back to America. My mom's family, the Zottolas of Scauri, was on the list.

# The Arrangement

Brigida Zottola was eighteen years old on the day her life was to change forever. She was at her house located on the Via Appia in Scauri, Italy. Scauri was a coastal town two hours south of Rome. She was sweeping the wide steps leading from inside the house down to the dirt entryway at the side of the house. An older woman with a short, dashing young man walked up to the open wooden doors.

Brigida heard them approach and turned. "Can I help you?"

"Yes, I know your mother, Rosa. Is she here?"

"She is in the fields."

"Can you call her?"

"Sure," Brigida said. She ran out and into the fields, calling loudly. Finally, Rosa answered and told her she was coming. Brigida went back to sweeping.

As she did, Cris went up to her, smiled, and took the broom from her. He then began sweeping the steps for her. When Rosa came, she recognized the woman.

"Oh, yes, Carmen. Hello. It has been a long time."

"Hello, Rosa. How is Ernesto?"

"He is well. He is up on the mountain tending to the olive trees."

"Ah, yes. He is a hard worker."

Rosa smiled and asked, "Who have you brought with you?"

Carmen said, "This is my nephew, Cris. He lives in America now. Cris is here looking for a bride to take back to America. I told him about Brigida, and he wanted to meet her."

Brigida's eyes widened. She had no idea that was why they were there. No one had ever come to the house for her before. She looked at the short, handsome man from America. He was not looking at her, but looking down at the ground.

Rosa said, "Oh, I see. Well, I will have to talk with my husband."

Cris stepped forward, with a shy smile on his face, and spoke his first words. He said, "I like your daughter."

Brigida's eyes widened further. How could he like her, she thought? He had not even spoken to her yet. He had not even looked at her, except for a glance.

Rosa shook Carmen's hand and said, "Come back in a week."

*** 

The next morning, Cris and Carmen were at the door.

"I'm sorry, Rosa," Carmen said. "Cris insisted we come."

"Let me get my husband," Rosa said.

Moments later, Ernesto came to the door. "Ah yes, Carmen. I remember you."

He looked at Cris carefully, as he had already heard about the visit yesterday.

"Ernesto. Cris has to go back to America soon. He works at the Ford Motor Company. He wanted to see Brigida again."

"She is sleeping."

"May we come back later?" Carmen asked.

"Yes, come tonight."

*** 

When Brigida woke up, her parents told her of the morning visit and that the visitors would be returning. She felt excited all day but completely unsure of what she was supposed to do. Her parents did tell her to be ready to talk to the young man when he came later. She felt very strange, suddenly being the object of such an enterprise. That evening, Carmen and Cris arrived. This time, the entire family was there. Ernesto and Rosa, along with Brigida's two older brothers.

Everyone gathered in the small living room. Brigida sat in her dress on one side of the small room next to her father. She wore her best dress, the best of the two she owned. Cris sat across from her; a kitchen table separated them. Brigida kept looking over at him, but he did not speak and mainly looked at the ground. Rosa and his Aunt Carmen were the ones doing most of the talking. After a while, Ernesto got up and said, "Well, we have to go to bed."

Carmen said, "We will come back."

"Come in about a week," Ernesto said.

Cris smiled and crossed the room. He looked at Brigida and smiled without saying anything. Then, he left.

\*\*\*

The next morning, there was a knock on the door. It was Cris and Carmen again.

Rosa answered the door and asked, "Carmen, what are you here for?"

Carmen shrugged her shoulders. "I'm sorry. Cris insisted we come back this morning. He has to go back to America soon. He really likes your daughter."

Rosa threw up her hands, then looked up at the sky in a moment of private lament. She then nodded, saying, "Come back soon."

\*\*\*

Word came the next morning. The visitors were coming back in the evening. Brigida found it to be very strange that this man from America was so insistent. She ate a piece of bread and oil and went to the land behind their villa to tend to the sheep. One of the lambs darted through a fence opening and ran into the neighbor's land. Brigida jumped the fence and chased it, but it kept getting away, going farther and farther. She had to chase it for so long, and she was so mad at the lamb that she said to herself, "If that man asks me to go to America, I think I will go. I am tired of chasing sheep."

When evening came, Cris and his Aunt Carmen arrived. Cris was dressed in dark plaid slacks with a short sleeve white button-down shirt. He wore black shoes and had his jet-black hair combed back. For the first time, Brigida noticed how handsome he was. She had on her other dress, her only other dress. The entire family gathered in the small living room again. Like the night before, Carmen and Rosa did most of the talking. At one point, Carmen said, "Cris has to go to America soon. He likes your daughter."

All eyes turned to him. He looked up and, with a half-smile, said to Brigida's father, Ernesto, "I like your daughter." He then looked back down.

Silence returned to the room as everyone considered what he said. Brigida wondered why he had not said any more. She looked at her brother with worried eyes.

Her brother then broke the silence. "OK, Brigida, do you want to marry this man? Do you want to go to America with him?" Brigida's eyes widened again, realizing that now was the critical moment.

All eyes now turned to her. She looked at her parents, then over to Cris's aunt and Cris. He slowly looked up at her, seemingly for the first time that evening. He was waiting.

She shrugged. "Yes, I would."

A long exhale came from the entire room, followed by silence. Carmen broke the silence. "Well, we should arrange the wedding soon."

Rosa joined in. "She will need time to gather needed documents to go to America. When does he have to return to America?"

"Monday," Carmen said.

"In five days?" Rosa exclaimed.

Carmen nodded, with her head tilted and eyes hopeful.

Ernesto stood up and walked across the room. He shook Cris's hand, then turned, walked to the other side, and hugged his daughter. He then led her across the room and gave her a chair to sit next to Cris. He said, "They can marry on Sunday after Mass. Then, Cris can go to America. She will come as soon as she gets all the necessary paperwork."

Suddenly, there was silence again.

Brigida's brother stood and said, "Well, congratulations."

Carmen stood, then everyone stood, and congratulated Cris, then Brigida. Brigida turned to look at Cris, but his eyes only met hers for a moment. He looked down, smiling shyly, and she wondered about this man she had just agreed to marry.

So began the love of my parents. They were such different people, and I do not know how much they truly did love each other.

Four days later, they wed at the Church in Scauri. After the wedding, there was a small gathering to celebrate at Brigida's house. She was not allowed to sleep with her husband that night. Ernesto and Rosa feared their daughter could become pregnant, complicating her journey to America. Therefore, the consummation of their marriage would have to wait until she got to America.

~ ~ ~ ~

Six months later, Brigida was driven to Rome to board the ship. She walked up the ramp onto an ocean liner with no family or friends accompanying her. It was a hard crossing in which she got seasick and had to survive on lemons a steward was gracious enough to give her. When she got to New York, Cris was there to meet her.

They stayed the night with Brigida's relatives in New York. Their hosts would not let them sleep together. That would have to wait until they got to their own home. The following day, they drove to Cleveland from New York. It was a quiet drive. Cris did not talk much, and Brigida was unsure what to say. She had never been out of her hometown. In Cleveland, she was brought to Madison Avenue. Cris had just rented the upstairs of a double. His brother Tony lived downstairs.

That was where they began their life, where I began my life, and where our story begins.


## Sounds of Life

From my earliest days, I remember the ebb and flow of the sounds of life inside my home. They were highs and lows, like Papa's countenance. At times, the family would be over, and the noise to a small girl seemed overwhelming. When the company was gone, it was just me, Mom, and Papa. Often, due to their conflicting work schedules, it was just Papa and me. These were quiet times.

Both my parents worked very hard and long hours on opposite shifts. Dad worked at Ford in the foundry and worked the second shift. It was a sweltering place that left men wiped out after their shifts. Mom worked as a seamstress at Joseph and Feis. She was required to work long hours, and if you didn't want to do it, they could easily replace you with some other immigrant who would be willing. So she, too, came home very tired at the end of the day.

On some days, I was taken to a sitter's house. Sometimes though, the sitters were not available. And it was up to my parents to watch me. This was very hard on them. On the days when Papa watched me, he often left me in the crib while he rested from his difficult job at Ford. I spent long hours sitting alone in my crib, watching the sun's narrow beams shedding their light through the narrow gaps on either side of the drawn window shade.

When Mom came home, or when Uncle Tony was at the door, the daunting silence of the house shook free of its cocoon and came alive.

One day, Uncle Tony's voice cried out from the back of the house.

"Cresenz!"

No answer. I smiled, happy to hear he was visiting, but then worried Dad would not get up. I looked at the bedroom door, hoping it would open.

"Cresenz! Are you sleeping? Wake up!"

"Whadda you want!" Dad replied loudly from his room.

Uncle Tony marched through the house. He knocked on Dad's bedroom door. "Get up, Cris. I have news!"

Papa complained, "Just a minute."

I pulled myself up in my crib and looked at the door. Suddenly, it opened, and there was the bright smiling face of Uncle Tony.

"*Ahhh*, Padina! You're here!"

"Uncle Tony!" I said in my broken Italian as I reached my arms up. Uncle Tony was my godfather, and the word Padina was reserved for godchildren.

He walked over and picked me up. "Oh, my little Padina. Oh… we have to change you. Then we will get you something to eat. Are you hungry?"

"Yes," I said.

He kissed me warmly on the cheek. "You are a princess, Marisella. A princess of Italy."

He turned to the door. "Cris, come on. We have to change the baby."

"Shaat up!" came the reply, and the door opened. My dad was dressed in his typical white boxer shorts and white tee muscle T-shirt. Though he was short, he looked like a giant in my eyes. His hair was thick and wild, and his arms were like short stubby poles, covered with dark hair.

"Why are you waking me, Tony?"

"I have news."

"Whadda news!"

"I will tell you in a minute. Let's get this baby changed."

Dad sighed and walked into the kitchen. He took down a fresh cloth diaper and got a wet rag. They changed my diaper and took it to the toilet to shake it out. Then, Dad put the pins on the new one while Uncle Tony took the dirty one and put it in the bucket in the hallway. Mom would deal with those after work.

Uncle Tony went into my room, got a clean shirt, and put it on me. Then, they took me into the living room and let me listen while they sat to talk.

"What is the news?" Cris said with his arm raised.

"I am bringing the lady I am going to marry here!"

Cris shook his head. "Who!"

"Her name is Jean. What time is Brigida home?"

"Not till 4:00 p.m. I gotta go to work."

"Oh," Uncle Tony said, disappointed.

Cris's expression fell, and his brow furrowed. He said nothing.

Uncle Tony said, "What about tomorrow?"

Cris's furrow deepened. "I don't know."

"Do you have to work tomorrow?"

Cris seemed to delay for a moment, thinking, his worried look deepening. "No, I don't."

"OK, then. We will come tomorrow."

Uncle Tony turned to me. "Come here, Padina. Are you ready to eat?"

"Yes," I said, clasping my hands.

He took me by the hand and helped me to walk into the kitchen. He put me in a wooden highchair and opened the fridge. "Cris, what should I give her?"

"I don't know. There is some milk and bread."

"Come in here and help me."

Dad came in and sliced a piece of Italian bread from a loaf. They put it into a bowl and added milk, and a large spoonful of sugar, then cut it up into pieces I could eat.

"Here you go, Padina," Uncle Tony said as he sat down and made sure I ate. Then, he asked, "Cris, when did you say Brigida is coming home?"

Cris looked up at the clock and quietly remarked, "In two hours."

Uncle Tony hugged me once more, then he left.

Dad picked me up and closed the door to the kitchen. He closed the bedroom and bathroom doors and took me into the front room. He lay down on the couch, turned on the TV, and told me to play. Before long, he fell asleep, and I stayed near him, watching the TV, waiting for Mom to come home.

## Jean

The following evening, Mom came home at four o'clock. She opened the door and walked into a dark house. "Cris!" she cried out. She saw him and marched into the front room and opened the blinds. "Where is Marisella?"

"Sleeping," he said.

He sat up while Brigida raced into my room.

"Marisella, look at you, my little girl." She held me up and turned, shouting, "Cris, help me get her ready."

She immediately took me straight into the bathroom and began running the bathwater. She removed my very wet diaper and clothes and put me in the tub.

"Cris, come here and sit with Marisella. I have to start the pasta."

Mom waited for him, then got off the chair and let him sit down. "Here," she said, handing him a small bar of soap.

Mom was excited at the news that Tony was bringing someone he was serious about over. She realized they would become sisters-in-law, and she welcomed the idea warmly. The fact that this girl was an American excited her even more.

After starting the pasta, she took out the leftover sauce and meatballs from two days earlier and got them ready to warm up. Finally, she made a salad. She then hustled into the bathroom, dried me off, and got a new diaper and a little dress to put on me.

There was a knock at the back kitchen door within a short while. Mom dried her hands with a towel and went to the door. I ran and stood by her. As soon as she opened it, I saw Uncle Tony's usually smiling face looking quite reserved and stoic. Next to him was a lady that looked like one of my Barbie Dolls, only her hair was brown.

"Brigida, this is Jean."

Jean stepped right in and lifted her hand to shake my mom's. Her voice was gravelly, and she spoke very quickly, quicker than I had ever heard anyone talk. "Hi, it's nice to meet you. *Ohh…* who have we here?" Jean stooped down quickly. "What is your name, little girl?" She looked up at my mom before I could answer. "What's her name?"

"Marisella," my mom said in her broken English.

"Hi, little Marisella. Are you hungry? I sure am." She stood up as quickly as she had stooped down. "Oh, I have had such a long day. I can't believe it's actually over. How was your day?"

Before Mom could answer, Jean turned back to Tony. "Where is your brother?"

Before Tony could reply, Dad walked in. Jean saw him, stepped beyond my mom, and extended her hand. "Hi, I am Jean."

Dad's brow furrowed, and I could tell he was uneasy.

"What's your name?" she asked.

My mom interjected, in her best English said, "This is Cris."

"Hi, Cris," Jean said enthusiastically. "I heard you work at Ford. My brother works at Ford too."

My dad turned away and walked into the dining room. My mom's face showed her embarrassment at my dad walking away. She quickly said, "Come… let's… eat."

Uncle Tony ushered them in and stopped to scoop me up. "Hello, my Padina. Do you have a kiss for your Uncle Tony?"

I smiled and kissed him, then let him carry me into the dining room, where he set me down in the high chair.

I was so excited to be sitting at the table with all the adults for such an important dinner. Though I did not talk much yet, I understood all. These times when we saw others were my only escape from the silence of most days. I relished every moment. I did not quite comprehend the words Jean was using, though. They were foreign to me.

Jean was seated across from my mom and me. Uncle Tony sat at one end of the table and Dad at the other. No sooner had we sat than Jean began talking again.

"So, Brigida, I heard you work at Joseph and Feis. A girl I used to work with is there. Bianca Corstos. Do you know her?" She turned to my dad without waiting for a reply. "My brother works in the engine plant. Tony Bonacci? He is very tall. Oh, he's too skinny to be working there! I told him to eat more." Her eyes shifted quickly to me. "How old is the baby?"

"Threeeee," my mother said in a flute-like tone, accented by her broken English.

"Oh, you're kidding. She is so small and skinny. Are you feeding her enough? She looks pale?" Jean looked down at the bowls of food. "Everything looks so good. Did Tony tell you how we met? He and my dad met at the police lodge. Can you believe—"

"Jeanna!!!" Cris shouted.

Silence filled the room, and Jean froze with her mouth open. She turned and said, "Yes?"

"Why do you talk… so much!"

"Cresenz!" my mother yelled.

Jean's face was first surprised, then grew cross. "Tony!" she said.

Uncle Tony shook his head with a look of dire chagrin. "Come on… let's eat."

"Aren't you going to say anything?" Jean demanded.

Uncle Tony furrowed his brow and said quietly but firmly, "Jean... let's eat."

Jean's lips pressed together, and her eyes grew narrow.

Mom glared once more at Papa as she simultaneously picked up the bowl of pasta and handed it to Jean. Jean shook off her mood as fast as she talked and scooped a hearty helping onto her plate. They all did, and then Mom placed a portion into my bowl, tied a bib around my neck, and gave me a long fork. I did not eat right away but instead listened, trying to understand the silence of the uncomfortable atmosphere, wondering about Uncle Tony and this lady he wanted to marry.

Right after the meal, Jean wiped her mouth with a napkin, smiled at me, then said, "Well, we have to go now."

"Stay for coffee," Mom said, but Jean looked at Tony, signaling she wanted to leave.

As soon as they left, Mom and Papa began fighting.

"Why did you open your mouth?"

"Because she's crazy," Papa said, raising his arm and with it his voice, loud and high.

"You cannot offend people like that!"

"I will do what I want," Papa replied.

I nervously finished my bowl of pasta and then cried out to be let down. I went into the front room to play with my doll while Mom and Papa silently cleared the table. Mom went to wash the dishes, and Papa got the broom and dustpan and swept around the dining room table, carefully moving all the chairs.

When he finished, he entered the front room and turned on the news.

I sat by him, thinking. I was glad he did not like Jean as I did not like her either.

Mom was right, too, though, as Papa's ways were harsh and sudden and caught everyone by surprise. Especially foreigners like Jean.

## Uncle Joe

A few weeks later, Uncle Joe visited with his sons, Armando and Carlo. Uncle Joe was a man who scared me. He had a long scar coming out of the side of his mouth, reaching like a knife blade toward his ear. I was told that a donkey had kicked him in Italy. I never could understand how a donkey could make a mark like that with its foot.

Uncle Joe had a dark countenance about him and spoke in a low, authoritative voice. The family revered him because he was thought to be the most world-wise of them. He already had two rental properties, doubles like ours, one of them also on Madison Avenue. When he came over, my parents were different people. They looked up to him and honored him in every little way, from immediately and carefully serving him coffee and coffee cake to allowing him to sit at Papa's seat at the head of the dining room table.

When Uncle Joe spoke, my parents grew quiet and listened intently. Their eyes held anticipation of some important tenet of life they were about to learn about life in America.

He was not that way with his sons. When Uncle Joe spoke to his sons, Armando and Carlo, his words were often accompanied by a glare. Like Papa and Mom, Armando and Carlo would grow quiet, but for a very different reason. Their eyes held the remnants of whatever momentary bedevilment was upon them, as well as the look of sudden fear at being called out by Uncle Joe. They were wise too, as their eyes assessed the severity of the warning, which sometimes signaled that they would be harshly disciplined as soon as they got home.

It was one of the reasons I was afraid of Uncle Joe. His authoritative demeanor and perpetual scowl scared me. It often caused me to think of how kind and how opposite Uncle Tony was. I imagined that, like Papa, when the powers that be handed out personality and skipped him, Uncle Tony got a double dose. Those same powers that be, who handed out kindness, skipped Uncle Joe and gave Uncle Tony another double dose. So, Uncle Tony got a double dose from both his brothers, and in both directions.

After the normal greetings, Uncle Joe picked me up. "Mali," he said in his thick, low Italian accent. "You have a kiss for your uncle?" Uncle Joe called me Mali because he could not pronounce my name.

I kissed him at the top of his cheek, not wanting to go near the scar that ran across it. He smiled, and said to Papa, "She is a princess, Cris. You make sure you raise her right."

Papa's eyes lowered to the floor, and a half-smile came across his face as he nodded, taking in his older brother's compliment and advice.

Uncle Joe put me down as fast as he picked me up, with the words, "Go play, Mali."

I obediently went into the front room to play with my doll. They all gathered around the dining room table, and the conversation turned to Jean.

Joe told my parents he did not like Jean and that he had told Tony that.

My mom said, "Tony likes my cousin Anna from Rome. She wants to come here."

Joe nodded. "Yes, I remember Anna. She would be good for Tony." Joe turned to me, "Mali, run downstairs and tell Uncle Tony to come upstairs."

I was excited to be part of the effort, not because of Jean, but because it made me feel important. I ran through the dining room, out the back door, and down the steps and knocked. Uncle Tony answered, looking at me, and then looked behind me, as I rarely was allowed out without one of my parents. "Padina, what are you doing here?"

"Uncle Joe is upstairs. He wants to talk to you."

Uncle Tony's face immediately grew somber. "I'll be right up."

A few minutes later, Uncle Tony walked in. Joe was seated at the head of the table, with his hands folded. He said, "Tony, sit down."

Uncle Tony didn't look at my parents. He already knew they were all there for something related to him.

Joe said, "Tony, we don't think Jean is good for you."

"Why not?" Tony said.

Papa raised his hand, and then his voice. "She's crazy, Tone." My dad often shortened words when he was excited.

"Cresenz!" Mom countered, glaring.

Joe raised his hands, bringing everyone back down. "Tony, Jean, I know you like her. But she is different. Do you remember Anna, Brigida's cousin?"

Tony sighed and nodded. "Yes, why?"

"Because she is looking for a husband and wants to come to America."

Tony seemed surprised, and his whole thinking shifted. His mind was looking across the ocean.

Joe said, "Tony, go to Italy and see Anna. Find out if she wants to marry you and come to America."

"*Hmmm,*" Tony said, thinking. "But what will I tell Jean?"

Joe said, "Tell her your grandfather is very ill, maybe dying, and you have to see him."

Uncle Tony nodded, and the plan was hatched.

~ ~ ~ ~

Three weeks later, Tony found himself in Italy, staying with one of his cousins, enjoying his stay and making every effort to court Anna.

Jean's parents happened to be traveling in Italy. Jean called them and told them that Tony's grandfather was near death, and they had to see him. Of course, it was out of their way, but they agreed.

When they arrived in the town of Coreno, where Tony's grandfather still lived, they were surprised to find him in good health.

They called Jean.

"What!" she said, hanging up the phone. She immediately began calling everyone in Italy she knew, telling them it was a family emergency until finally, she found out where Tony was staying.

She called. Uncle Tony's cousin answered his phone. "Hello?"

"Is Tony there?"

"Tony? Who is calling?"

"This is his girlfriend, Jean."

"Tony! It's Jean."

Tony got on the phone. "Jean, why are you calling over here?"

Jean started talking a mile a minute. "Tony, I'm so upset. Why are you doing this? My parents called me. Your grandfather is fine. He had wine with them. I can't take it, Tony. I am going to do something terrible. My poor parents, do you know they went all the way there. What are you doing there? I can't believe he is fine. My job is going well, Tony. I miss you. When are you coming home? My poor parents. Why did you tell me he was sick?"

"Jean!"

There was silence.

"What?"

"He was sick. He is better now."

"Oh, Tony. I am going to do something. I can't be away from you. I love you so much. Please, come home, and let's start our life. I... I can't take it."

"Jean, I have to—"

"Oh, Tony.... I can't take it anymore." Jean started weeping incessantly.

"Jean, stop. Jean. Jean, I am sorry."

"Please come home, Tony. I love you. My whole family loves you. I need you, Tony. My poor parents. They are heartbroken."

"Jean... I will be home."

"Please hurry. I love you, and I miss you. Oh, Tony." She started crying even louder.

"Jean!"

"Come home, Tony. I can't eat or sleep till I see you. We need each other. You know I love you." She wept more.

"I will be home!" he said.

"You have to... I won't be able to go on without you!"

"Bye," Uncle Tony said as he hung up, feeling frantic at the frantic call.

~ ~ ~ ~

Five days later, Uncle Tony arrived home. He came upstairs and told Papa it had not worked out with Anna. Papa and Mom believed him until Mom got a call from Anna. She said she liked Tony a lot, but he left suddenly.

Within the month, he and Jean walked down the aisle of St. Angela Church.

I was their flower girl.

The family went along as they had to. They welcomed Jean into the family. But, much to Papa's dismay, she moved in downstairs with Tony right after the honeymoon.

# Papa

I sat in my crib on Saturday morning, looking at the branches swaying outside the window. My door opened. It was Papa.

"Mari, get up. We are going to clean the house."

I was happy he came for me so early. He lifted me out of the crib and helped to change my diaper and clothes. I followed him into the kitchen. He opened the closet, took out a broom and dustpan, and then handed the dustpan to me.

He said nothing, but went to the corner of the kitchen and began to sweep. "Can I help, Papa?"

"Watch, Mari. You see how I do it?"

I observed as he did not speak, but kept going around the entire kitchen, moving the dirt closer and closer to the center of the room. He stopped and said, "Hold the dustpan."

I placed it down, and he gently swept the dirt up. Then he walked to the garbage. "Put it in here, Mari. Slow. Don't spill any."

I was ever so careful.

"Come back now and put it down again," he said as he swept up the small remaining pile.

"Good job, Mari. Now let's mop the floor."

I was so proud to have helped him sweep. I could not wait to mop.

We got the bucket from under the sink, and he filled it with water, adding soap. He put it on the floor, then got the mop out of the closet. He dipped the mop and squeezed it tightly, wrapping it around, squeezing out the water with his strong hands. I stood over the bucket, carefully watching. "Can I do it, Papa?"

"Just watch, Mari."

He began mopping. At one point, he stopped and motioned for me to come closer. He lowered the stick so I could grab it and helped me to push the mop and pull it a few times. "When you get older, Mari. I will buy you a mop, and you can help me."

We finished, then went into the bathroom. I watched Papa mop and then dump the water in the bathtub.

I was so proud to have helped him. He got me a glass of milk, took down a few cookies, and went into the front room. He turned on wrestling, and I sat next to him, eating my cookies and drinking, waiting for Mom to come home.

~ ~ ~ ~

The following week, Uncle Tony brought Jean for dinner. Mom had come home from work early and made spaghetti sauce and meatballs. After sweeping the dining room and kitchen floors, Papa seemed anxious and sat in the living room, curled up with his legs tucked under himself, reading the newspaper. I sat on the other end of the couch, watching him and glancing out the window. It was a typical cloudy day in Cleveland. It felt like a long day today, and I wished I had more to do.

"Cris, come and set the table," Mom called from the kitchen.

I watched Papa's face grow cross. It did not have to do with setting the table. He was mad because Jean was coming over.

"Cris!" Mom called again.

"Papa, Mom is calling you."

He looked down at me with a slight scowl, then looked out to the kitchen. "What!" he shouted across the living room and dining room.

"Get up and help me."

He shook his head. His cross expression grew longer, then he neatly folded the paper and went into the dining room to set the table. I watched him until he started, then went over to stand next to him and walk slowly around the table as he set each place. When we finished, Papa went out to the front porch. I followed him out, as I rarely got a chance to go out there—only when I was with my parents. I stared for a long time at the building across Madison Avenue, listening to the sounds of the humming factory. Finally, I stood next to him, went to the rail, and peered over.

"Be careful, Mari," he said.

I stepped back a half step, keeping my hand on the rail, and stood on my tiptoes, trying to see down to the street. Within a few minutes, it started to rain. Papa walked over to the side where he could look down at Madison. He was growing anxious again, I could tell. I followed him over and stepped as close as I could without causing him to tell me to get back.

"Ahhh!" he said, raising his hand. "Stupid rain! Dammit."

I wondered why he was mad at the rain. I liked it. I put my hand out to allow some of the drops to fall on my hand.

"Watch, Mari," he said excitedly. "You're going to get wet!"

I pulled my hand back. "Si, Papa." I looked up at him, watching the concern in his eyes.

"You gotta watch, Mari."

"I am sorry, Papa."

We heard the doorbell ring. Papa grimaced and turned to go into the house. I followed him.

By the time we walked across the living room into the dining room, Uncle Tony and Jean were already in the kitchen greeting Mom. We walked in, and Papa exclaimed, "Ton!" Papa grabbed him by the shoulders and shook him. Uncle Tony smiled warmly, shrinking. Then, after a moment, Papa let him go, and his glance fell to the ground.

Mom said, "Cris, say hi to Jean!"

Papa looked up. "Hellouh, Jean."

Jean half-smiled, clearly still offended by their last meeting. "Hi," she said.

Uncle Tony picked me up. "Hello, Padina. Say hi to Aunt Jean."

"Oh, hi, little Marisella. Here, let me kiss you." Tony held her toward me, and Jean planted a kiss on my cheek. I pretended to like it.

Mom broke the ice, saying, "Come in the dining room. It's a time to eat!"

"All right," Uncle Tony said as he carried me in and put me in the high chair. Jean sat at the side of the table, and Uncle Tony sat across from her. Dad sat at the opposite end, facing the kitchen. Mom came in with a bowl of spaghetti and meatballs. She set them down, saying, "Tony, get started," before returning to the kitchen.

Moments later, she came out with a plate of pork chops. "Oh, I love pork chops," Jean said.

My father's countenance remained fixed, aggravated. He took the pasta and some pork chops, then sat still, too nervous to eat.

Once Mom came in, Jean started the conversation. "Tony, did you tell them about our honeymoon? We went to Niagara Falls. I was so tired. My brother called me when we were there. I don't know how he found my hotel. The food was terrible. We did take the bus to the Falls. It was something." Her face grew concerned. "There was a homeless man on the bus. I didn't like him. What did you guys do after the wedding? Did you have fun, little Marisella? The Falls were so amazing."

"Jean! Slow down!" Papa yelled, his face showing dismay as I had never seen.

Jean looked at him, her mouth wide open as if frozen in time.

"Cresenz!" Mom cried out, slamming her fork down like last time, only harder, and glaring at him.

Uncle Tony just bobbed back and forth and kept eating his pasta with a half-smile on his face. It was as if he had already accepted some fate no one else knew yet.

Papa exclaimed, "Eata, Jean! We talka later!"

Jean tightened her lip and started eating her pasta. Finally, she looked up and said, "Marisella, don't you want some pork chops? Brigida, cut her some pork chops."

"No, thank you," I said as I looked down and put my fork into the pasta, pulling up a few strands, and trying to get them into my mouth.

"She's so skinny!" Jean said. "Is she eating enough?"

Papa put his fork down and looked like he was about to cry. The sadness on his face I was accustomed to was married with deep dismay. Jean bothered him.

During the meal, Jean proceeded to tell us about their honeymoon and her job in the country. Papa did not speak at all.

Once they left, he went to bed in silence.

## Sundays

I knew it was Sunday because Papa, Mom, and I had watched a movie the night before. I was so happy because Mom always made popcorn for us. I had to be careful, though, not to spill any, and as soon as we finished, Papa would get up and put the bowl away, returning with the broom and dustpan. I would help him by holding the dustpan.

I would inevitably fall asleep and be carried into my bed.

Sundays were my favorite day because we went to see my cousins. I was the youngest, and it was always a thrill to see my older and more active cousins. They could do so much more than me, and I wanted to be like them all someday.

Sunday mornings were slow, though, as my Papa and Mom slept in. So, I stayed in my crib alone for a long time, waiting for them one of them to come and get me. I was used to this time alone, which never bothered me.

Today, Mom opened the door. "Marisella! Good morning," she said as she got me changed and put some fresh clothes on me. On Sundays, I wore special clothes, like a small dress. We would not put my shoes on until it was time to go, so I did not get them dirty.

After having a breakfast of boiled eggs and toast, we sat on the front porch while Papa and Mom read the newspaper. Sometimes Mom would go inside and call people she had not been able to talk to during the week. Today we waved and called down to Uncle Tony and Aunt Jean. They were on their way to Mass. Tony went every Sunday to Mount Carmel. Papa did not, and I did not know why they were different.

As lunchtime approached, Mom put my stockings and shoes on, and we all went down the back steps to the car. We got in the station wagon, me sitting in between them, and drove to my Uncle Italo's and Aunt Mary's house.

He was the oldest of Papa's brothers and sisters. We usually had dinner there on Sunday, though occasionally Uncle Joe, who was not the oldest, insisted we go to his house instead. I liked Uncle Italo and Aunt Mary more than Uncle Joe and his wife, Maria. Maria was not mean like Joe, but she was just as stern, and you wondered if she was herself.

As soon as we pulled into the drive, I could see Papa's countenance rise like when he got excited talking. A smile came over his face, and his eyes twinkled. It was because of Italo. Papa would get out of the car, go up the steps, not waiting for Mom or me, and knock on the door. His brother would answer and cry out, "Crescenzo!"

"Italo!" Papa would cry and wait for his older brother, his hero, to open the door and grab him around the shoulder. "Welcome, my brother." Papa would look down, taking in the adulation. Then, always the gentleman, Italo would usher him past and stretch out his arm. "Brigida, come here till I hug you."

Mom would light up, too, like on no other day, as she hugged Italo and let him kiss her on the cheek. I was next and, with my face beaming, would be lifted high above Italo's head as he said, "Princess Marisella. My little princess."

He kissed me on each cheek, then turned and set me down inside the house. It was how I always entered the house. As soon as my feet hit the ground, the bedlam and chaos started. It was like going into another world. The house smelled of sauce, meat, bread, and spices. The table was full of food, with trays of olives, cookies, pastries, and Italian candies. The dining room table was stretched out with another table at its end, covered by white tablecloths and set for at least twenty people. Folding chairs were aligned up and down each side.

The noise of the adults greeting, talking, and laughing was deafening. I would wade my way in, looking up at all the handsomely dressed men and pretty women in their thick hose, heels, and Sunday dresses. Then, after a moment, I caught a glimpse of Armando scurrying from the kitchen between a couple of adults toward the basement steps. I followed him.

Down in the basement, Armando and Carlo were fighting with swords. Standing to the side watching were Italo's daughters, Rosemary and Mary Grace, who were a little older than me, and Italia, who was a year younger than me.

"Marisella!" Rosemary shouted. "Come stand over here with us." I listened, only because that was what you did when Rosemary said something. She was the boss of the girl cousins.

I smiled and walked over, careful not to fall into the battle between Armando and Carlo. Armando shouted, "Girls, move out of the way!"

We all moved. Armando was the boss of the boy cousins, which only included his brother Carlo, but since he was the oldest of all the cousins, he was sort of the boss of the girl cousins too, to the degree Rosemary would allow in any given circumstance.

Rosemary went along, turning to us wide-eyed. "Hey! Let's go play on the swing set." She took off running, and we all followed. I was the last to the steps and struggled to keep up with the others, who ascended the steps quickly. By the time I got out the door, all the swings and slides were taken, so I waited my turn, climbed the slide, and slid down.

The call came from inside to go in, and we all gathered at the table. I loved being there because I was allowed to sit in a real chair. Of course, I had to get onto my knees, but I did not care. We ate and listened to the adults talk for hours until, finally, Uncle Italo said the children could go outside.

Near the end of the day, I heard Mom talking with my Aunt Mary.

"Marisella does not run as fast as the other children. Is anything wrong?"

"No, I don't think so."

"She walks unsteadily. Is it her shoes?"

"No," Mom said, looking sad. I could see she was embarrassed.

"*Hmmm,*" my Aunt Mary said, thinking. She then asked, "Is she potty trained yet?"

"Almost."

"Who is watching her?"

Mom frowned. "I have a sitter, but sometimes she is unavailable, and when I have to work on Saturdays, it is Cris. I don't think he knows what to do. We are eating a late supper by the time I get home, and it's late."

Aunt Mary nodded, not sure what to say.

Mom said, "She has an appointment with the doctor this week. I will talk with him."

Aunt Mary seemed relieved and nodded, smiling. "That's good. They will help you."

Mom nodded subtly, but I could tell something was bothering her. She was worried about something.

By the time the day ended, I was exhausted. We drove home happy and full of the fun of the day. When we got home, I was given my ritual Sunday evening bath, a snack, and put to bed.

## The Doctor

A few days later, Mom came home from work early. She got me dressed in a small red long-sleeved shirt and a yellow skirt. She put on my Sunday shoes and took me down the back steps and we walked to a bus stop. We were going to the doctor. I loved being alone with her out in the world. We seldom went anywhere together, just her and me, and it made me feel important to be riding the bus next to her.

When we got off the bus, we walked a short distance to the doctor's office on Lorain Avenue. I marveled at the big billboard next to the office. It showed a family eating out at the restaurant The Ponderosa. It seemed so strange to me, as it looked so different from my family's images of eating Sunday dinner at Uncle Italo and Aunt Mary's house. They looked happy, though, and I wondered if we would ever go to The Ponderosa.

We walked into the waiting room and got into a short line. When it was our turn, Mom stepped up, and a lady slid a glass window open and spoke with words and sounds I had only heard on TV and never heard another person say.

My mom tried to talk to her with some short and slow words and sounds I had never heard her say. The lady at the desk spoke just as slowly back to her, and she spoke loudly, and she used her hands, pointing, trying to explain something to my mom. From what I could tell, we were to sit down behind us and wait. We did.

As we waited, I sat with my hands folded, fidgeting with my skirt, looking at the other moms and children sitting quietly in the office. Every once in a while, a lady in white with a clipboard would come out and say something. Then, one of the moms and their child or children would get up and follow the lady through a door, where they disappeared.

I looked up at Mom. She looked worried. Soon, I heard the name DiRuggiero called. Mom started and took my hand, then helped me to walk toward the lady. We followed her through a door, and I was asked to stand on a scale. The lady looked down carefully at the number, then looked again, wrote it down, and said something I did not understand. We were ushered into a small room, and Mom put me on a kind of table with a cushion. Then the lady left.

Moments later, a tall man with dark hair, dark eyebrows, and wearing a long white coat with something hanging around his neck came in. I figured he must be the doctor. First, he spoke to my mom in words I did not understand. He then pulled something from his pocket, flashed a light into my eyes, pressed a long flat stick into my mouth, and held my tongue down, looking inside my mouth. Last, he put the thing around his neck into his ears and began poking me with it. I looked at Mom, wondering if it was okay, and she nodded.

He then said something to my mom, slowly and loudly, using his hands. She spoke words and sounds I had never heard, trying to tell him something. His face looked puzzled, and finally, he began nodding.

He took hold of my dangling legs, felt the bottom of them, and then squeezed them just above the knee. Then he took hold of my arms, again, squeezing the bottom of them and then moving up and doing the same at the top.

He took hold of my hands, closed his grip, then pulled. Finally, he motioned me to pull back, which I did forcefully, and he smiled and nodded.

He then proceeded to use his hands and make strange sounds to tell my mom that he wanted me to eat more, and he wanted me to walk more, and play more. At first, she found it hard to understand, but finally, she began nodding. I could see he was relieved she understood. He then held up his hands and pointed to the calendar. He flipped the page, pointed to a day, and said, "Come back."

I understood that, as I had heard Aunt Jean say it, and gathered its meaning.

Mom nodded too, and I saw her wipe a few tears from her eye. Then, finally, the doctor gave her a Kleenex, and he smiled and left.

Mom kissed me, and hugged me warmly, then helped me down. As we reached the bus stop, she took out a plum from her purse and a small bag with two cookies and gave them to me. Then, she took out another plum for herself and we waited for the bus. I could tell she was thrilled she had talked to the doctor.

That night I could not fall asleep. Papa was already in bed, but Mom had stayed up. I sat in the bed listening to her. She had called Italy on the phone. I could only hear what she was saying and not what the other person on the phone was saying.

"Mom, I need you here. Marisella needs help."

"No, she is not sick. She is just…. She needs help walking more. Eating more. That is what the doctor told me today."

"Yes, I took her to the doctor because I was worried. She needs help walking more."

"No, Cris doesn't know what to do. Huh? I have to work. We have bills to pay."

"Mama, there is one more thing. I am expecting another baby. I don't know when."

"A few months, I think. I must go to the doctor, but I think it will be in October. Mama, I need help… What?… Okay, go get Papa."

There was silence, and I wondered who she was talking about.

Mom started speaking again. "Papa, I miss you. Come to America and stay with us. You can work here. There are factories all over."

There was quiet for a while, and then Mom started to cry. "You will! When! Oh my God!" she said through a deepening tear-ladened voice. "Okay. Oh, thank you, Papa. I will find a bigger house right away."

She listened for a while, then started crying again, but I could tell they were tears of happiness. Her final words were, "I can't wait to see you."

She hung up, and I wondered who they were and where they would stay. Would they like me? Would I like them? I hoped they were not like Aunt Jean or Uncle Joe. I hoped they were like Uncle Italo or Uncle Tony.

## Lorain

It was a Saturday morning. I knew because Mom did not go to work. I was still sleeping when I heard Uncle Tony at the door, shouting, "Cris! Wake up!"

Then another voice, Uncle Italo's: "Crescenz! Wake up! We have work to do!"

Then more voices, Aunt Mary's, then Aunt Jean's. Finally, I heard Mom open the bedroom door. "Why are you here so early?"

Aunt Jean shouted, "We brought donuts!"

My door opened, and I saw Uncle Tony's smiling face and heard his warm greeting. "Good morning, Padina. I have a donut for you."

He picked me up and twirled me around. "Today, you go to your new house!"

I did not understand what he meant by that. I knew this was my house, but a new house did not make any sense to me. He took me into the living room, sat me on the couch, and brought me a big donut and a napkin. I was so happy to see everyone.

Aunt Mary came over and kissed me, then Aunt Jean. Then Uncle Italo kissed me and said, "Mary, get Marisella ready, and I will take you and her to the house."

Aunt Mary went to my room, and soon I was heading down the back stairs, a half-eaten donut in one hand and Aunt Mary's hand in the other. We went to the car, and Uncle Italo drove us away. It was not long before we pulled into an alley and drove for several houses. Then he slowed and turned into a drive, pulling past a garage and a yard. Finally, he pulled up next to a house. I could tell it was not a double. Aunt Mary got out and helped me out. Then we walked through a side door.

I was amazed. There were large rooms, it seemed, with nothing in them. I ran from room to room and could see no furniture anywhere. There were a lot more rooms than in my old house. There were stairs too, but not back stairs. These were our stairs, carpeted and comfortable. I ran up them and again through the two small rooms at the top.

Then I ran down. "Is this my new house?" I exclaimed.

"Yes," Aunt Mary said, hugging me. "This is your house, Princess Marisella."

I ran to the front bedroom and looked out the window. There, in front of me, was a whole new world—a bustling street with cars going in both directions. Stores were across the street, and people were walking in and out of them. A fence stood right in front of me, only ten feet away, with a small gate leading to the sidewalk on our side of the bustling street. I was so excited and couldn't believe I was in such a busy place.

Within the hour, the first load of boxes arrived in Uncle Tony's station wagon. Mom was with him and immediately went to work unpacking them and putting the kitchen dishes and other things away.

Aunt Jean arrived shortly after, bringing the donuts. Mom started a pot of coffee, and everyone was filled with a joy I had never experienced. There was nothing I could do to help, so I just kept running into all the rooms and running back outside, exploring the long driveway that went from the front gate on Lorain Avenue all the way to the gate at the back alley. This was my new world, and it was outside of the house. I was so happy. Along the side of the yard, between the driveway and the grass, was a long narrow sidewalk filled with cracks that had grass coming out of them. I walked up and down it, trying to jump over every crack without touching it.

Soon, the loud sound of Uncle Joe's station wagon rang through the air. He had arrived with as much of the furniture and belongings that could be packed or tied to the vehicle. I ran outside and saw Uncle Joe driving, carefully turning the wheel into the drive. Papa was sitting next to him in the front seat with a grim look on his face. I could tell he was nervous.

They opened the tailgate, and we all started unloading. Papa, my uncles, and a few other friends began hauling furniture and boxes in. Inside, Mom directed them where to put everything. Then, Uncle Tony and Uncle Joe took off again with Papa and Italo to go get another load. The next load had many beds, and my crib came with it. Uncle Tony proudly carried it in, announcing to me, "Follow me, Padina." I ran after him, and he set my crib up in the front bedroom, a room I would be sharing with my parents. After that, all was unloaded, and a final trip was made, including stopping at Uncle Joe's to pick up another large bed. This one was set up in the bedroom on the other side of the hall, where my grandparents would sleep when they arrived from Italy within the next two weeks.

# Nonna

On a warm fall day, Mom did not go to work. Papa was home, too, as he usually worked later in the day. After breakfast, Mom dressed me in my Sunday clothes, combed my hair, then told me she would be back soon. Then she left in the station wagon.

Sometime later, I heard the horn beep and ran to the side window. Mom had pulled into the driveway, and two people were in her car. They got out. An older woman with brownish-gray hair and slim brown glasses got out of the front. She had on a long brown coat and wore plain black heels. She immediately began looking around the yard, pointing out things, and giving my mom instructions.

Then a large man with a stoic-looking face got out of the back. His hair was white and short and perfectly straight. He wore plain brown pants, a blue collared shirt, and a tan windbreaker. His hands were large, and his fingers gently curled. He smiled as he glanced around, then walked slowly up the sidewalk along the side of the house with his hands clasped behind his back. He was studying the grass next to the walkway. Finally, he nodded and turned, saying something to the woman. He then went to the car, took out two large suitcases, and effortlessly carried them to the side door.

Mom came in first. "Cresenzo, Marisella, guess who is here?"

Papa came to the door and smiled. "Rosa," he said heartily.

"Ahh, Crescenzo. How are you?" she asked as she hugged him. The man then walked in and set down both suitcases. "Hi, Crescenzo," he said in a deep, strong voice.

"Ernesto, welcome to America," Papa said.

I was standing in the doorway by the living room, watching. Finally, the woman turned to me, and a wide smile crossed her face. "Come here, Marisella. Let me see you."

She bent down onto one knee with stretched-out arms. I walked to her, and she grabbed me, hugging me tightly. "My beautiful granddaughter. I am here to help you. I am your Nonna. You call me Nonna from now on."

I smiled as she kissed me over and over again on the cheek. Then she stood and took her coat off. Underneath, she had on a plain blue dress with stripes. "She is too skinny, Brigida." The woman looked around. "Where are the pots?"

"Under there," Mom said.

Nonna immediately got a pot out, put water in, and started it. "Do you have any chicken?"

"No," Mom said.

"Go to the store and get me a chicken right away. We need to make some soup for this girl."

The man then came over and kneeled by me. I was struck by his strong-set face and gentle smile. He took hold of me with his large hands and said, "Hello, Marisella. I am your Nonno Ernesto." He, too, kissed me on each cheek, but only once.

Mom headed out the door. Nonna walked through the house and looked into their room. She saw the crib. "Ernesto, Cresenzo, come here."

They walked over.

"Tomorrow, I want you to go buy her a small bed."

"Why do we need a bed?" Papa asked, his face growing nervous.

"Because she is almost four. I will pay for it. You two go in the morning."

Papa sighed. Nonno Ernesto patted him on the back. "We will go early, Cresenz."

Nonno Ernesto went into his room with the suitcase. A few minutes later, he came out wearing blue overalls and a flannel shirt. He asked Papa, "Where are the shovels?"

Papa sighed and got up from the couch and took him outside. I ran to the window to watch. Nonno Ernesto took a shovel and carefully examined it, then went to the end of the long walk on the side of the house and began digging and turning the soil next to it.

I watched him for a long time. He moved quickly and steadily, bit by bit, up the long drive and walkway. Eventually, a long wide strip of soil was turned, stretching from the back alley to Lorain Avenue. He then rubbed the sweat from his brow and came in. Mom was home now.

He said, "Brigida, we are starting a garden. Go to the market tomorrow and buy several pieces of garlic and a bag of onions. I will plant the garlic and onions so they will grow during the winter."

Mom smiled widely. "Yes, I will."

I was excited at what that might mean. As I turned to go into the house, I could smell the chicken cooking from the kitchen screen. As soon as I entered, Nonna lifted me up, put me into a chair, and said, "Here, Marisella. Watch how I do this."

She took a long piece of celery and cut it up into pieces. Then she got a carrot and cut it into pieces. Last, she got a pasta bag and put it into the pot with the vegetables. Then she said, "It will be ready in an hour."

That night I sat at the table with Mom, Papa, and my Nonna and Nonno Ernesto. I was as happy as I had ever been. My Nonna sat next to me, feeding me soup by the spoonful. After, she cut up chicken and made sure I ate it all. Then, we all watched a show on TV together, and I fell asleep.

# New Life

The following day was Saturday. Nonna Rosa awakened me. "Come, Marisella, we have work to do."

She got me up, took me to the bathroom, and set me on the toilet. I held on for dear life, looking up at her. She smiled. "You go to the bathroom now, Marisella. I will be back."

She left, and I waited and listened. I could hear her speaking quietly with my Nonno Ernesto in the kitchen. By the quiet, I could tell my parents were still asleep. Then, I felt myself tinkling in the water and was so happy. I waited. After a while, Nonna came back. "Are you finished, Marisella?"

I smiled and nodded.

She smiled wider than before, and there was a twinkle in her eye. She said, "OK, from now on, when you have to go to the bathroom, you come and get me. I will bring you in here and lift you up."

I nodded, feeling like such a big girl.

She helped me down and helped me to get dressed.

After that, I entered the kitchen and saw my Nonno sitting at the table reading the newspaper. He smiled at me and said, "Good morning, little Marisella. Will you help me in the garden later?"

"Si, Nonno," I said.

"She has to help me in the kitchen first, Ernesto," Nonna replied. "We have to get lunch ready for everyone."

I was so excited. Not only did I have one thing to do today, but now I had two! I could not wait.

"Over here, Marisella. Come and stand on the chair and watch me make the sauce."

My Nonno patted me on the head with his large, broad hands. I smiled, crossed to the sink, and climbed up on the chair.

Nonna Rosa pulled down a jar of tomato sauce from the cupboard. Then she got a clove of garlic from the refrigerator. Next, she laid down a cutting board and began crushing the garlic, then mincing it. "You see, Marisella, the garlic has to be crushed so the flavor comes out. Then, and only then, do we cut it up."

I was amazed at being shown something so important.

She then put a pan on the stove and turned on the fire. Next, she pointed and said, "Go get me the oil, Marisella."

I hopped down from the chair and ran to the pantry. Moments later, I carefully walked back with the large oil bottle. Nonna took it and said, "Watch, Marisella."

I climbed back up and stood on my tippy toes. Nonna poured some oil into the pan and then sprinkled the garlic. "Now we have to wait a few minutes, but not too long."

She gently swirled the oil, then opened the tomato sauce. She then got a jar of Contadina Tomato Paste and opened it with the can opener. After glancing back into the pan, she said, "OK, the garlic is light brown. It's time."

She immediately dumped the tomato sauce in, creating a sound of bursting sizzling. Then she filled the jar with water and put that in. Next, she used a knife to pull the tomato paste out of the small can and put that in, too. Finally, she picked up a bottle of wine and poured a small portion in.

"There, Marisella. That is how we make the sauce. We have to keep an eye on it now and stir it often."

I was amazed at what I had just learned.

"Here, Marisella. Get off the chair so that I can move it. Come over here and help me wash the dishes."

Nonna Rosa pulled the chair close to the sink, then began filling the sink with water. Next, she got an apron from the pantry and looked it over. She then took scissors, cut the bottom neatly, and gave it to me. "Here is your apron, Marisella. You wear it when you are in the kitchen with me."

I could not believe how lucky I was to have my own apron. I had only seen my mom and aunts wearing them, and now I had my own.

I leaned over, amazed at the water and suds forming in the sink in front of me. Just then, Papa walked in. "Mari!" he shouted. "You're gonna get wet!"

"Cresenz!" Nonna Rosa replied, turning with a look of chagrin on her face. "She is fine, Crescenzo. She has to learn!"

"She's too little!" he shouted, raising his hand high into the empty air, holding it for a few moments.

Nonna Rosa shook her head and turned to help me.

Papa walked to the refrigerator, pulled out a milk carton, and poured a glass. He then went into the living room.

Minutes later, Mom walked in from work. "Hello, everyone," Mom said, smiling. "Oh, look at you, Marisella. Are you washing the dishes?"

I turned, proud as ever, and said, "Si."

"Oh, look at your apron!" she said as she came over and hugged me. Then she hugged Nonna Rosa and said, "I am so happy you are here."

Nonna Rosa's face lit up. "I am too, Brigida. I am too."

## Mount Carmel

After cleaning the kitchen, Nonna Rosa and Mom took me to the market. There, they bought steaks and greens. When we got home, we immediately began cooking everything. By mid-afternoon, we all sat down to enjoy the sumptuous meal. Then we all sat in the living room together to watch a show on TV.

That first Saturday with my grandparents with us was an exciting day for me. I learned that I was an important member of my family. I needed to help make the sauce, help wash the dishes, help go to the market, help dust furniture, and even help run the vacuum cleaner. By the time I went to sleep, I was so tired. I never imagined doing so much in one day, but little did I know that was much more to come.

***

The following morning, Sunday was the first Sunday with my grandparents with us. The days normally reserved for my parents sleeping in and me waiting in the crib for them to wake up were suddenly in the past.

Nonna Rosa woke me early. "Come, Marisa, we have to make bread."

She took me to the kitchen, got my apron, and we started with flour, water, and yeast, punching up the dough. When Nonna said we had punched it enough, she took a knife and cut the sign of the cross on it. She then covered it with towels and pronounced, "Now we let it rise."

Next, she went to the refrigerator where she had bought ground meat the day before.

She got a large bowl, took down breadcrumbs, eggs, and spices, and began mixing them all in the bowl. "Here, Marisella. Now I need you to help me roll them into meatballs."

A flat pan was laid out, and I was given a napkin with Crisco on it and shown how to smooth it out on the pan. Then we got a bowl of water to dip our fingers into and began rolling meatballs. When we finished, Nonna Rosa put them in the oven and exclaimed, "Now it is time for us to eat."

She took me to the sink and helped me to wash my hands thoroughly, then made me a bowl of oatmeal. After I ate, she told me to go play. We had one more thing to do in a little while before going to church. *To church?* I wondered what that meant. I knew Uncle Tony and Aunt Jean went to church, but I did not remember going.

Once Nonno Ernesto woke, Nonna Rosa took me into our room, and I was dressed in my Sunday clothes: stockings, a tiny skirt, and a maroon shirt. She put my hair in pigtails, and we set off.

Nonno and Nonna took me by one hand and helped me walk the long walk down West 65th street. There were not many people out. I had them all to myself. After a while, I was too tired, and Nonno Ernesto picked me up in his strong arms and carried me.

When we arrived at the church, I was awestruck. So many people, all dressed in nice clothes. Inside, the church was beautiful, with colors and gold and statues of men and women. We sat near the front, and I remember sitting and standing along with my grandparents, following their motions.

Afterward, we took the long walk home. By the time I got home, I was exhausted, and I went to the living room. Papa was up and reading a newspaper. I sat next to him, resting, thinking about church and all the people and things I had seen along the way.

On this first Sunday, with my Nonno and Nonna living with us, we did not visit anyone. Instead, we had a meal together, in which my Nonno Ernesto took the freshly baked loaf of bread and cut a large slice for everyone. It was a sign that he was our patriarch, the leader of our family. It was his way of showing respect to all of us by slicing bread individually. We enjoyed the salad, meatballs, and spaghetti, along with the fresh bread. After the meal, we all rested until the company came. Today, the gathering was at our home. By mid-afternoon, the house was alive with kids running around and adults laughing and talking at the table.

It was a whole new world for me. Of course, my world was still inside my home, but everything had suddenly changed. Suddenly, a new and exciting life was upon us.

## A New Arrival

It was a time of change for Mom, too. Because she was having a baby, her stomach was growing larger. She went to work each day, working the same long hours she always worked, but when she came home each evening, she would be exhausted and have to rest. Papa was tired too, it seemed, as when he was not working long hours at the Ford Foundry, he was sleeping.

~ ~ ~ ~

Late in the winter of that first year, when my grandparents lived with us, Mom had to go to the hospital to have the baby. Papa went with her. It was the middle of the night, and I remember Nonna and Nonno Ernesto getting out of bed to help see them off. I got up and watched from the living room couch as their car quietly pulled out of the driveway onto snow-covered Lorain Avenue. Nonna came and sat next to me. She pulled me into her warm arms and said, "Your mom is going to bring a new baby home."

I smiled and rested my head against her warm flannel robe. It all seemed like a great puzzle to me. Then, the following morning, we received the news. Papa came home from the hospital in the early afternoon. We heard him pull into the driveway, and Nonna and Nonno went to the kitchen to wait. Papa walked in the back door, raised his arm high as a preface to what he was about to say, then proudly exclaimed, "I have a son!"

The joy that erupted in the room between Papa and my grandparents was something I never remembered seeing. The news of a boy being born seemed to make the entire occasion extra special, and I did not understand why. Papa told us his name was Crispino, named after his father.

Five days later, Mom came home with a tiny red-faced baby in her arms. At once, all activity in the house changed. Now, everything was done for Mom and the baby.

My daily duties grew at once.

Things changed in other ways, too, though. I was no longer the center of affection for everyone. Instead, everyone who came in seemed to want to see, hold, or kiss Crispino. I became almost an afterthought. I also had to be quiet, which was not hard for me. I was used to being quiet.

All was fine, and life went on.

I loved being with my Nonna every day, but things changed in many ways. Not only was I Nonna's helper in the kitchen and cleaning the house, but I was now in charge of diaper patrol. Diaper patrol consisted of bringing new diapers to wherever my brother was plopped down to be changed. The first step was to carry away old diapers to the toilet, if necessary, where they had to be shaken out. They were then rolled up and taken to the bucket in the hall by the basement. After they were formally washed by Nonna each day, I was in charge of hanging the washed diapers on the line in the basement or outside if it was a sunny day. If it rained while they were out, I would have to run outside and take down all the diapers. Then, when the sun came back out, I would have to run them all back out and hang them up to dry again. Once dry, the long cloth diapers had to be folded and placed in a neat stack, the very pile which had begun the whole process.

I never imagined so much work would be involved for a single diaper, and I was glad I did not need to wear them anymore. Nonna had taught me that.

# The Fur Coat

A few months after my baby brother was born, a fur shop opened next door to our house on Lorain Avenue. It was not unusual for a store to open next to us, as almost every structure on Lorain was a store or shop. However, there was a store on the other side of our house. It was a masquerade shop, and Papa forbade me from talking to the lady who owned it.

I was not allowed to talk to the lady who owned the fur shop, but it did not matter, as I never saw them. Their building had no windows on our side, and they walked in and out of the front entrance on Lorain. Since I was not allowed outside our fence, I had no way of ever seeing them.

One night, after work, when Nonno Ernesto and Nonna were visiting some friends, Mom said, "Marisella, come over to the fur shop with me."

I was so excited.

When Papa heard, he exclaimed in a rising tone, "No, Brigida. We can't afford those coats."

"Be quiet, Cresenz. I am just going to look. Come on, Marisella."

I ran to the door, took my small brown coat off the hook, fastened my brown leather strap shoes, and waited by the door. Mom put her brown plaid coat on and grabbed her purse.

"Brigida!" Papa yelled.

"Shees! Be quiet!" Mom yelled back as she took me by the hand, and we went out. We walked out the front gate and turned left. It was rush hour, and hundreds of cars were passing us as we walked the short distance to the front door at the other end of the store. As we opened the door, a bell rang, announcing our presence.

A lady came over, dressed more elegantly than I had ever seen a lady dressed. She wore a slim light blue dress with matching heels and a myriad of jewelry adorned her neck and wrists.

"Welcome to Szackas Furs."

"Hi," my mom said. "We wanted to look around."

"Very well. Help yourself." The woman then looked down at me. "Who is this pretty little girl?"

"This is my daughter, Marisella. We live next door."

"Oh, I thought I saw you before. You are always helping your grandmother and grandfather."

I smiled.

"Well, I have some things you may be interested in. Come with me," the woman said.

She took us to a back rack that was marked clearance. She pulled a waist-length light brown fur from the rack and said, "I think this would look beautiful on you."

Mom's eyes widened as she hesitated to take it. But the woman pushed back her hesitancy and helped her to try it on. She then walked her to a mirror, and I watched my mom's face light up with delight. She held it shut, turning, and opened it, turning the other way. The woman looked on just as pleased. Then my mom said, "I don't know if I can afford this."

"It is on clearance. It only costs $45, AND I will knock a little more off since your little girl is so sweet."

I was suddenly on board, knowing I had participated in the price negotiation. Mom looked back into the mirror with hopeful eyes and said, "How much, then?"

"$39," the woman said.

Mom looked down at me, then back into the mirror, and said, "Yes, I will take it."

~ ~ ~ ~

On Saturday night, Uncle Joe and Aunt Maria, along with Uncle Tony and Aunt Jean, came over to visit. The women were at one end of the table. The men were at the other end. As everyone sat around the table, Aunt Jean started talking about the fur shop next door. "I wish I could get one of those fur coats! They're probably too expensive. When did they open? Have you been in there yet? I wish Tony would buy me one."

"Jean!" Papa yelled from the other side of the table, already uneasy, as he had been all week that my mom had bought a fur coat for herself.

"What do we need a fur coat for, Jean?" Maria said, interrupting the suddenly tense moment.

My Nonna Rosa said nothing, and I made eye contact with her. She half-smiled as if she knew what was about to happen.

My mom got up and said, "I have one of them. I will go get it."

"What!" Aunt Jean said, her mouth gaping wide open.

Moments later, Mom came in wearing her fur coat.

"Oh, my," Aunt Maria said. "It is so beautiful."

Aunt Jean exclaimed, "That must have cost a fortune." She looked at Papa. "Did you buy it, Cris? Tony, I want you to buy me one," Jean shouted down the table. "How much did it cost? Maria, do you want one? Ask Joe to buy you one."

"Jean, stop it," Uncle Tony said.

"Why? I want a fur coat too. Tony, let's go there Saturday. You get paid Saturday."

"Jean!" Uncle Tony said louder.

"Don't you want one, Maria?"

"Hey, Jean," Uncle Joe said, not waiting for Aunt Maria to reply. "Maria does not need a fur coat."

"Yes, she does," Jean replied, wide-eyed, turning to Aunt Maria. "Don't you, Maria?"

Aunt Maria shifted in her seat and said, "Well, yes, it would be nice."

"Jean," Uncle Joe said, as his brow furrowed. Then, he turned to Papa, "Look at what you started, Cresenz."

Papa raised his hand high and exclaimed, "I didn't do anything!"

Nonno Ernesto interrupted everyone. "Enough about the coat. Cresenz, Tony, Joe. Come outside and let me show you the garden."

The men all nodded and started getting up as the women watched.

Jean turned to the women and said, "Tony and I are going to go Saturday."

"Jean," Uncle Tony said, his voice rising.

Aunt Jean smiled and waited until the men got outside, then said again, "I am going to have him take me Saturday."

## The Old-World Farm

When the snow melted and the warm weather came, Nonno Ernesto turned his attention outside to the long garden he had dug in the fall. I would go outside with him as he showed me where the garlic and onion plants were breaking through the soil. I was amazed at how many, at least a hundred of each type, and we went out to look at them every night.

When the snow was gone for good and the spring was breaking through, Nonno Ernesto began designating more of the yard as a garden. He would go out in the evening and turn all the soil. Days later, he would take a hoe and break the dirt up to make a smooth patch of soil, ready to receive newborn plants and seeds. Wooden apparatuses were built and affixed up and down the yard from the back alley to Lorain Avenue. Nonno Ernesto told me these would be filled with plants and vegetables in a few months. He told me we were making our land into our own farm. He told me about his vast farm in Italy and promised me he would make our small, long yard on Lorain Avenue into a farm that would be just as beautiful. Every time I looked out our windows, I could not believe what was transpiring outside, and I grew more excited by the day.

Mom arrived home and walked up and down the turned soil, amazed at what her father had done so quickly. Nonno said to her, "Brigida, tomorrow go to the market and buy twenty tomato plants and twenty pepper plants and get me seeds for green beans and cucumbers. We are starting a garden."

Mom smiled widely. "Yes, I will."

***

Early the next morning, Mom and Nonno Ernesto left in the car for the market. When they returned, the entire back of the car was loaded with trays and trays of plants. They carefully unloaded the trays and spread them out across the entire patio. I had never seen so many plants in one small space.

That afternoon, after I had finished helping Nonna Rosa make the sauce and prepare the dough for over five loaves of bread, Nonno Ernesto asked me to come and help him plant. I was so excited and glad he had not started without me.

We got the first tray of plants and walked up the drive to the end of the alley in the back, just inside the gate. We started there. Nonno Ernesto had brought a thick piece of cardboard to kneel on. He knelt and took a thick pointed stick and made a hole. He then showed me how to pick up a single plant and gently pull it out of the single tray, carefully keeping all the dirt around the bottom. I handed it to him, and he placed it into the small hole, carefully pressing it and surrounding it with dirt. He then dug the next hole while I stood next to him, with the small tray of plants at my feet.

I picked up the next one, gently pulled it, handed it to him, and smiled. It was a clean hand-off, the first I had done by myself.

"Good, Marisella," he said as he scooched down a foot, dragging the tray with him.

I slowly moved along the long garden with him. We planted several trays of tomatoes. When we reached the first of the wooden apparatuses,

Nonno told me to go get him the small bags of seeds from the patio. I ran with delight, so happy to be an important part of our family farm.

When I returned, he took a stick out of his back pocket and made three long narrow furrows in front of the apparatus. He then placed the seeds inside each track. Then, he told me to get another tray, and we started a long line of different plants.

It must have been hours later when we had finished. Nonno Ernesto walked over to the patio chairs and sat down. Before us was a pile of empty vegetable trays. "Sit down, Marisella," he said gently. "Rosa," he then called.

"Yes, young man," came the cry from the kitchen window.

"Bring Marisella and me some lemon water."

I felt so honored to be in the seats with him, waiting for lemon water. Just us two, looking out over the vast garden we had made. Nonna Rosa came out and said, "*Ohhh!* Look at the beautiful work you both did. Here. Have some lemon water."

As I took the large glass from her, I could not help but feel like a needed member of the family. I was doing my part to help the adults, and it made me feel very important. I watched Nonna walk up and down the long drive and wander into the side gardens, carefully observing all.

Nonno Ernesto drank his water down, looked at me, and smiled. Then, he pulled me onto his lap and pointed across the yard, saying in his strong, quiet voice, "Marisella, these plants are going to grow and give us lots of food. We have to take care of them now. Will you help me to take care of them?"

"Oh, yes, Nonno. I want to help you."

He kissed me warmly on the forehead. "Good girl, Marisella. I will show you how to take care of a garden."

## My First Spring and Summer

That spring and summer was the first time my world extended beyond the inside of the house. Days were spent in the yard with my Nonna, sweeping and hanging laundry out on the line to dry. I would be allowed to go outside with my Nonno Ernesto in the evenings as we tediously worked in the long garden. He would talk to me as he went from plant to plant, watering, pulling weeds, and tending to each plant's needs.

Even though I was only five years old, I was busy from morning until night. And I was beginning to understand my role in this growing family. During the day, Mom and Nonno Ernesto went to work. All day long, I was by Nonna's side, helping with cooking, helping with cleaning, helping with the baby, and taking care of diaper patrol. Papa usually slept during the day because of working the night before. So, in all we did, we had to be quiet not to wake him. Then, in the afternoon, Papa would get up, shower, eat, read the newspaper, then go to work.

On many evenings, our home would come alive. Because my grandparents were from Italy, Italians from all over the neighborhood would come to visit.

The women would gather inside at the kitchen table. Some of them would bring their own young children. The laughter and talk of kids and husbands and jobs and school would fill the room with wonderful noise inside the kitchen. I would walk around the table, looking up at them, greeting them as they smiled at me, and bent down to hug or kiss me. Often, the other children and I would chase each other around the house. Inevitably, the chase would lead to the kitchen, and we would hastily scamper under the table, crawling on top of the women's feet and bumping past their hosiery-clad legs.

The men would gather outside under the cover of the roofed patio. Of course, they would not be laughing as much, but they were clearly having a great time. When my Nonno Ernesto spoke, it would grow quiet, and all eyes were on him. When the younger men spoke, I could see they would always stay connected to him, keeping their eyes on him as if what they said needed his blessing. I was amazed at the respect they showed him.

Papa was there only on the weekends because of his work schedule, but he was quiet, mostly even when he was. That was his nature. But Uncle Tony was there often. Seeing him, being near him, talking with him, and hearing his strong deep voice gave me a great sense of security and belonging. It gave Papa the same sense of security and belonging. Papa was different when Uncle Tony was around. He was happy, his face bearing a pregnant smile that was never ready to give birth fully. The melancholy he possessed nearly all the time lifted some in the presence of Uncle Tony. It was as if Papa knew there was someone present who understood him and appreciated him.

I did not know why Papa was always sad. His sadness made me feel sad too. It was impossible for me not to feel his moods and often internalize them. So, in these moments or days, when Uncle Tony was around, and Papa's mood lifted some, it lifted for me too, and I had hope for happiness for him and for our family.

## The Beginning of Harvest

The tiny, neat rows of plants in the large garden grew enormously as the summer wore on. Our entire yard suddenly became filled with lush green plants, growing wider and taller daily, with most of them towering over me. Countless strings, ropes, and pieces of wire my Nonno had carefully affixed during the year now kept everything delicately but firmly supported. On their branches, vegetables dangled like hundreds of pouches of gold on the sand of the seafloor. This was our gold, the gold of home-grown vegetables.

Several times a week, Nonna took me with her to a deserted field several blocks from our home during the afternoon. We brought with us two large shopping bags and a knife. Once we arrived at the field, I held the bag while Nonna cut dandelions. She worked her way forward, cutting every dandelion to her right or left. I stayed next to her, holding the bag. Once one was filled, we closed it and set it down, then continued until the other was filled.

When we arrived home, we took them to the sink and washed them thoroughly. Next, two large pots of water were set to boil, and we filled each pot with dandelions. When they were finished boiling, Nonna put them into a strainer to remove all the moisture, then put them into bowls in the refrigerator. These would be our greens for dinner for the next several nights. We made this trip to the field all summer long. No one else was in the fields, and I was amazed that we found something so common and abundant that no one else seemed to notice.

As the summer hit the midway point, the time came when we picked the first pieces. There were three tomatoes, six peppers, and a handful of green beans. Nonno Ernesto placed them in a wicker basket, and we took them to Nonna Rosa for inspection. "Come, Marisella," she said cheerfully. "We have to clean them."

I ran to the pantry and got my apron. I pushed a chair up to the sink and watched. Nonna filled the sink with clean water, then placed the vegetables in. She washed them carefully, rubbing each one, and then allowed me to do several. After that, she then drained the water and filled it again, washing them one more time. "These are what we call First Fruits, Mari. We will not eat them ourselves."

"What will we do, Nonna?" I asked.

She placed them back inside the basket and said, "We will give them to a neighbor."

Nonna put took off her apron and took me by the hand. We walked into the alley and over to Colgate Avenue, where Nonna had recently met another lady from Italy. We knocked on the door, and Nonna gave her the basket of vegetables.

~ ~ ~ ~

Two days later, we went to the garden again. More vegetables were ready. We performed the same ritual, carefully cleaning them, but we placed them on the table to dry this time. Nonna took a bowl down from the cupboard and carefully cut the tomatoes and peppers. It nearly filled the bowl. She then covered it and put it in the refrigerator, proudly proclaiming, "We will eat this tonight with dinner."

She then took the green beans and snapped off the ends, handing me several of them and showing me exactly where to snap them. These were put in a small pan of water and set onto the stove to boil.

"Marisella," she said. "This is what we do on a farm. We harvest what we have planted and prepare it for our meals. This must be done every day. This will be our job until all the vegetables are harvested."

"I see, Nonna."

"Do you like helping me, Mari?" she asked, smiling.

"Oh, yes. I do."

I was so happy to be part of this little farm on Lorain Avenue in Cleveland. It never occurred to me we were a long, narrow city lot sandwiched between a fur shop and a masquerade shop. To me, it was indeed a vast farm filled with the most wondrous delights.

~ ~ ~ ~

On a hot summer day, when the crickets were chirping outside our window, my grandmother turned a page on the calendar. She pointed and said, "Today is the first day of August, Marisella. It was named after Augustus Caesar, a famous Roman Emperor." She then moved her finger down to a block near the bottom of the page. "This day is your birthday, but we have a busy month ahead of us. First, there are lots of vegetables to be picked. Then, at the end of the month, we will also begin getting ready for winter. Are you ready?"

"Yes, Nonna," I said, excited about all we had to do. I realized that one thing led to another on our family farm, and one season led to the next, each with its own importance and duties.

***

The following evening, Uncle Italo and Uncle Tony came over with another man I had never seen. They went down to the basement with my Nonno Ernesto and Mom. I followed them down while Nonna stayed upstairs with my brother Crispino.

They went to the basement's storage area, and the man pulled out a thing that extended in a long, straight line. He was putting it up against one wall, then another.

"What is he doing, Nonno?" I asked.

"He is measuring the wall, Marisella. We are building a kitchen down here."

"Oh, really," I said, excited at what all that could mean. The kitchen was the center of our life. Everything happened in the kitchen. All cooking, eating, talking, laughter, and even arguing happened in the kitchen. I could not imagine why we needed another, but I could not wait to see.

The basement was large and cavernous and lined with tiny windows along the top of the walls. At the bottom of the stairs were a furnace and lots of pipes. Beyond that were the washer and dryer, with two large concrete sinks in between and a drain under them. Across the way were a bathroom and a large area used for storage. Beyond that was a door that led to another room. Again, it was a large and cold and damp feeling with a lone small window on the back wall that barely let in any light.

The men were busy talking, pointing, and measuring. Then, they went into the small, dank room in the back of the basement and measured there too. After that, they left.

~ ~ ~ ~

A few days later, on a Saturday, I was asleep when I heard a noise in the house. I got out of bed and went into the living room toward the kitchen, rubbing the sleep out of my eyes as I walked. As soon as I turned the corner, I saw Uncle Tony's smiling face. He was holding a cup of coffee in one hand and a donut in the other. He turned. "Padina! Come here, my little princess."

I ran into his arms, so happy to see him. Uncle Italo was there too, and so were Nonno Ernesto and Papa. They were all seated, drinking coffee and eating donuts, talking. Nonna Rosa was at the sink washing dishes. Uncle Tony handed me a donut. "We have a big day today, Padina."

"What are we doing, Uncle Tony?" I asked.

"We are building a kitchen."

Papa raised his hand and waved it. "We are making you a new kitchen, Mari!"

I smiled widely, feeling the excitement in Papa's voice. "Yes, Papa!" I replied.

Moments later, a small blue truck pulled into the drive and turned off its engine. Uncle Tony said, "Angelo is here."

The truck door opened and closed, followed by the sound of a knock. Uncle Tony got up to open the door. "Come in, Angelo. Sit down, have some coffee."

"Good morning, everyone. Good morning, Rosa. Oh," he said, looking down at me, "is Marisella helping us today?"

Nonna answered, "She will be helping me to take care of you men. Now, hurry up and drink your coffee, and let's get to work."

Nonno Ernesto smiled. "See, we cannot sit while the women are around."

Everyone laughed, quickly sipped down the rest of their coffee, and went outside. I looked at Nonna, my eyes seeking permission to go with them, and she nodded. I raced outside. The men had already begun lifting wood along with large white boards and carrying them all down to the basement. They carried tools in, and before long, the sound of sawing and hammering and men talking and shouting orders to each other filled the house. I sat on the steps watching them, scooching over every time one of the men had to go up or down to get something.

"Marisella," Nonna Rosa called. "Come and help me make lunch."

I wanted to stay with the men, but I went upstairs and helped her. Nonna had made the sauce and meatballs the day before. Now, she put a large pan of water to boil. She then took down a salad bowl, placed it on the table, found some vegetables from the counter, and put them next to it. "Go to the garden, Marisella. Get me four tomatoes and four peppers."

I raced outside and came in. Nonna was already cutting up the salad. She motioned for me to wash them, which I did and gave them to her. She cut them up, and the salad was done. Once the pasta was boiled, we drained it, put some sauce on to keep it moist, then filled two large gravy boats with more sauce and scooped the meatballs into a large bowl. Then Nonna and I stretched a large tablecloth over the table. She took a large stack of dishes and set it on the corner of the table. My job, I already knew, was to place them around. "How many places, Nonna?" I asked.

"Six," she said. "We will eat after the men eat."

After I finished setting the table, Nonna told me to sit down. She put together two pieces of bread covered with squeezed tomato and olive oil. "Here, Mari, let's enjoy this snack so we are not hungry. After the men eat, we will have pasta and salad."

We enjoyed our snack, and then Nonna Rosa shouted downstairs, "Mangia!"

Shouts of happiness could be heard downstairs. I ran down to the steps to watch them as they joyfully put down their tasks and went to the large wash basins to clean their hands. One by one, they walked by me up the stairs, into the kitchen, and the feast began.

Nonna and I walked around the table during the meal, making sure everyone had what they needed. The men talked quietly, concentrating on eating. I could feel the overwhelming feeling of energy and strength from these men, their clothes covered with sawdust and their necklines and backs of their shirts dampened with sweat. It felt wonderful to be around them, to be part of such an important event.

The basement's block walls were hidden behind the tall white boards by the end of the day. The entire basement now looked like a giant room.

~ ~ ~ ~

Throughout the week, the men returned in the evenings. By the end of the week, a long counter sat on top of three cups, and three more cups hung above them. There was a large space next to the counter. The following night, the men carried a stove and refrigerator in on dollies. The men then built a long wooden table that was larger than our kitchen table. One of the last steps was in the damp room next to the storage area. Inside that room, shelves were built from floor to ceiling, taking up every single wall. Finally, the following Saturday, Uncle Tony and Papa swept and mopped the basement. Once it dried, the entire basement floor was painted gray.

Two days later, we all went down to admire the transformation. Nonna and Mom were so happy, and I could see the possibilities the space represented to them. I peered inside the damp room and asked, "What will we put on all these shelves, Nonna?"

"You will see soon, Marisella. That is our cellar, and many wonderful things will be stored there."

# Birthday

The daily harvest and tending to plants went on for all of August. At the end of August came my fifth birthday. Nonna made a large cake, three tiers high, with vanilla pudding between one tier and fresh strawberries between the other tiers. After we ate dinner, I helped Nonna and Mom clear the table. The cake was set in the middle, and a pot of coffee was put on. I was very excited. I did not remember having a birthday party before that. Soon after, Uncle Tony and Aunt Jean arrived at our home. Uncle Tony carried a gift in his arms.

"Uncle Tony!" I exclaimed, smiling, as I ran into his arms. He was my guardian angel always, and to see his broad smile and the gift he bore made me feel happier than I ever imagined.

He picked me up and kissed me. "Hello, Padina," he said. "I heard it was someone's birthday. *Hmmm*…. I have this gift for them. *Hmmm*… Is that you?"

"Yes," I said, laughing.

He put me down, and Aunt Jean hugged me tightly and kissed me on the cheek. "Happy Birthday, Marisella."

Nonna Rosa said, "Sit down, Sit down."

Papa was at the head of the table, and I could already tell he was getting nervous. I was in the middle, standing on a chair so I could reach the table enough to blow out the candles once they were lit. Everyone else sat down.

Aunt Jean started speaking right away, "Oh, my gosh. My brother wants to send his kids to public school. I told him, are you crazy? When I have children, they are going to Catholic School. Oh, Brigida, my father is upset. There are not enough people going to the lodge meetings. Ernesto, you should come. You would like it. Anyway, he has to decide about the school tomorrow. I yelled at him. Ernesto, do you want to come to the lodge meeting?"

"Jean!" Papa yelled, bringing silence to the room.

"What!"

Papa raised his hand. "We gotta sing, Jean!"

"Oh. Anyway, I told him—"

"Jean!"

Mom stood up and lit the candles, smiling. "OK. Happy Birthday, Marisella."

Right away, Uncle Tony stood up and, in a wonderful, deep, operatic voice that seemed to belong on TV, started singing, "Happy Birthday to you! Happy Birthday to you! Happy BIRTHDAY, Marisella…. Happy Birthday to you!"

Everyone began to clap. I leaned over and blew out the candles.

Mom brought me a package, which I opened. It was a red dress and a pair of black buckle shoes. I loved them. Nonna gave me a gift, too. It was a new blue apron she had sewed for me by hand. Then Uncle Tony put his wrapped box on the table. As I unwrapped it, I saw a green slate and a small box of chalk.

Aunt Jean said, "Now you can write things on the slate and erase them."

I was so amazed. It was the best gift of all.

# La Scuola

The day after my birthday, my mom told me I would have to start going to school. I did not understand what she was talking about. I remembered hearing Aunt Jean talking about school, but I did not understand what she meant, and I did not think it had anything to do with me.

"What is school?" I asked.

"It is a place where boys and girls go to learn."

"Where is it?" I asked, starting to feel anxious.

"It is close by. I will take you there tomorrow."

"Oh, we are going tomorrow." I felt a tinge of fear, and I did know why.

"Yes, and after school, you have to walk home. The other boys and girls will be walking home too. I will show you. It is very close by."

Upon hearing this, I suddenly felt very afraid. I had never been outside the yard alone in my whole life. What if I got lost? What if I got kidnapped? I could not imagine how I was going to do this. The whole night I laid awake, afraid of what might happen to me.

*** 

The next morning, Mom helped me to dress. She put on my Sunday clothes, then brushed my hair and put it in two pigtails. Then we went into the kitchen, where Nonna was making some oatmeal. Nonna Rosa smiled at me. "Are you ready for school, Marisella?"

I smiled. "Yes, Nonna."

"Here, sit down and have some oatmeal."

Nonna watched me for a moment, then said, "You will learn lots of things in school, Marisella. We want you to do your best and make our family proud."

I nervously sat down, not at all excited at being thrust into this new thing. I wanted to stay with Nonna today, like I did every day. But somehow, her words made me realize that this was another part of my role in the family. I was to go to school to make them proud.

As I ate my oatmeal, Nonna put a small brown bag on the table and said, "I packed you a sandwich and an apple for lunch."

I tried to offer a fake smile and glanced behind me to see Mom gathering her purse and jacket. It looked like she was getting ready to go.

"OK, Marisella. Let's go."

Nonna Rosa came over and gave me a big hug. "Have a wonderful day, Marisella. I will be waiting for you when you come home."

Mom and I walked out the side door, down the long walk, opened the gate, and stepped onto the sidewalk on Lorain Avenue. There were already other children walking, all in the same direction. We followed. In a short time, we came to W. 65th Street. We turned left and walked two blocks. Suddenly, a massive, towering church with a large old brick building next to it stood before us.

Mom stopped me and pointed. "That is St. Coleman." She pointed back from where we came. "You see Lorain Avenue. When you get out, go there and go to the right. Our house is two blocks down. Will you remember?"

I looked back to the corner of Lorain Avenue, my mind in hyper gear. *Go there and turn to the right. What is right?* I tried to understand, then said to myself. *Turn that way.* I could see the way I was supposed to turn, and I was desperately trying to memorize it.

"Do you understand? Marisella?"

I swallowed, nodding.

Mom stooped down and fixed my hair, looking into my eyes. "You will be fine. There will be lots of other children."

We waited for the light and crossed 65th Street with the other children. Soon, we were in front of a large building with large glass doors. As soon as we went inside, we had to ascend a wide staircase. Children were hustling up and down, some with parents, some alone. The noise was something I had never imagined hearing. It was like stepping inside an entirely new world, with high ceilings and wide halls and the constant loud noise of children talking, shouting, and laughing. We walked out of the stairway into the first vast hallway, filled with children and adults. We got into a line, and soon we approached a lady with a clipboard.

The woman said something.

My mom replied in a flute-like tone, "DiRuggiero."

The woman smiled and scanned down her list. She then pointed and said something that I did not understand. My mom looked, then pointed for assurance. The woman nodded, and off we went.

As we walked, I saw doorway after doorway. Inside each one, children were sitting at desks. There was a large desk with a woman sitting or standing next to it, facing the children.

I was scared.

We stopped in front of one of them, and Mom walked in with me. The woman by the desk said something I did not understand.

Mom said, "DiRuggiero."

The woman looked at a piece of paper on her desk, smiled, and pointed down a row to an empty, smaller desk. Mom let go of my hand and pointed. "Go, sit there, Marisella."

I looked up at her, then the woman. They were both smiling, but I was terrified. I bravely walked down one of the rows to the desk, nervously glancing at the other boys and girls already seated. I had trouble getting in when I finally got to my desk. I was a little short for it, but I hopped up and sat there.

Mom waved, then left.

The woman said something I did not understand, then went around her desk and sat down, folding her hands, watching as more children came in. She pointed each one to their seats, talked with some parents, then kept waiting.

I looked around the room at all the children. I had never seen so many. They had all different kinds of colored hair, too. Most of the children I knew had dark brown hair. Most of these children were different from me. Most of them looked bigger than me, perhaps older. Not by much, but I noticed the difference. One girl in front of me turned around and said something. I could not understand her, so I just smiled. Then, a boy with blond hair sitting next to me put his head down and started to cry. I looked at him, wondering why no one was helping him, but it was so loud in the room that I don't think anyone noticed.

I walked up to the teacher and waved. She smiled and said, "Yes?"

I waved again, then pointed to the boy at the desk, crying. She immediately got up and went down the aisle to console him. I was glad I could help, and I quietly went back to my desk.

Suddenly, a bell began ringing loudly. My eyes widened, and my gaze darted about the room. What was I supposed to do? Was I supposed to follow someone out? Who would I follow home? I was so scared.

Then, as quickly as it started, it stopped, and the woman walked to the front of the room and turned to face us all. She said something, pointing to herself, and said, "Mrs. McChrystal. I am your teacher." She then said again, "Teacher." I did not know what it meant, but I kept saying it over and over in my mind, trying to memorize it.

Next, she began calling out names, and one by one, the other children stood and said something to her. Finally, she called a name that sounded only a little like mine. I thought maybe there is another girl in the class with a similar name. The teacher looked at me. I realized I was supposed to stand and say something like the other children, but I did not know what they were saying. I was afraid she would think I was dumb and send me home. My Nonna's words, 'Make us proud,' ran through my mind. I stood and just smiled. The teacher said something and waited for me to answer, but I did not understand her, so I just shrugged. The other children laughed, and I sat down.

The time went very slowly. I could not understand what the other children were saying to me. Crayons were passed out, and we were all given a piece of paper with a picture on it to color. I loved using crayons. I had only used them a few times before when we were visiting another Italian family.

At one point, I had to go to the bathroom. So I went up to the teacher, curtseyed, and pointed at my hips. She asked me something. The word sounded like Bano, so I nodded. She then asked me something else. But I did not understand. I said in Italian, "Io devo andare al bagno."

She looked at me, smiled, and called another girl. The teacher said something to her and pointed for me to follow her. Moments later, we walked into an enormous room with lots of doors hanging a foot off the floor. The girl pointed to one. I reached up to grab the handle and swung open the door. I could not believe it. It was a bathroom inside. I went to the one next to me and looked. There was one there, too. I realized there were over ten bathrooms in that room. I went inside, closed the door, and hopped up. Moments later, I got down and then went over to wash my hands. I could barely reach the water.

Shortly after I got back, someone knocked on the classroom door. The teacher's face lit up like she saw someone she knew and waved them in. A tall man carrying a crate walked in. He set it down on her desk, said something to her, then left.

The teacher said something, and the children stood next to their desks. I quickly hopped down into the line. Then she said something else, and the first row walked up and was handed a small carton from the crate. When it was my turn, I was given a straw and a small carton of milk, but it was not like milk I had ever seen. The outside was brown.

I went back to my desk and noticed the other children opening and drinking with looks of satisfaction on their faces. I opened mine and smelled it. It smelled like chocolate. I sipped it. It was milk that tasted like chocolate. At first, I only had small sips and then decided I liked it and drank it all down. Once I finished, I decided that I had never drunk anything so delicious.

During the rest of the day, the teacher kept looking at me. At one point, she said my name and waved for me to come up. She gave me a book with pictures in it. I looked at it curiously, and she gently took it back, then opened to the first page. There was a picture of a cat. She pointed to the large letters at the bottom and said aloud, C A T. She pointed to the picture and said, "Cat."

I nodded and smiled and said, "Gatto."

She nodded and said, "Gatto is cat."

I did not understand completely, but I knew I had to learn in order to make my Nonna proud, so I memorized that C A T meant Gatto.

She then turned the page and pointed to a picture of a woman, and a man, and a boy. There were three words on the bottom of the page. M O M, D A D, B O Y. She pointed to the woman first. I said, "Mamma!"

"Yes," she said excitedly, as she pointed to the woman, then down to the word M O M.

Next, she pointed to the man, then looked at me questioningly.

I smiled and proudly said, "Papa!"

She nodded and said, "Yes, Papa is D A D."

I was a bit puzzled, and my mind tried very hard to understand what she meant. Finally, I gave a small nod, not wanting to seem dumb.

She then gave me the book, turning the pages, motioning that I should go through them. I could not believe I was being given such a special book. I held it close and could not wait to get home to show my Nonna.

Soon the day ended, and the bell rang. All the children lined up at the door. When another bell rang, we marched outside. Once outside, I began to become frightened. I looked to my right and panicked. Then I looked to my left and saw Lorain Avenue in the distance, with people and cars whizzing in both directions. I noticed children walking that way, and I ran and walked behind them. As we neared Lorain, I remembered I was supposed to turn. I was afraid to see what I would find when I did. But some other children were turning too, so I followed them.

It got very loud as I turned the corner, and nothing looked familiar. I began to cry and started to walk faster, but then I saw the doorway of the fur shop in the distance. I ran to it, then looked beyond, and saw our yard full of tall plants. I saw our house and the front gate. It all looked so different from the sidewalk. I opened the gate, dried my tears, then ran into the house.

Nonna was at the sink. She turned, and I dropped my book and ran into her arms. I was so happy to see her. I had been so afraid, but now I was safe.

"Welcome home, Marisella. Come, I made you a special treat."

Nonna sat me down at the table, then took out a fresh piece of Italian bread. She cut a half tomato and squeezed the juice and seeds up and down the bread. She then drizzled fresh olive oil, sprinkled light salt on it, and gave it to me. I was so happy, hungry, and relieved to be back in my world.

Nonna watched me eat, then said, "Go get out of your dress. We have to go out and hang laundry. Then we are going to clean up the vegetables for dinner. Would you like to help me?"

"Oh, yes, Nonna. I want to help."

That night I lay awake thinking of the day and wondering what tomorrow would be like. My mind was full of questions, and I was trying to figure it all out.

# To the Farm

During the first week of school, I walked there every morning alone and returned every afternoon alone. Each day I was afraid, but the feeling grew less and less. However, my anticipation of returning home to Nonna did not lessen each day. She was waiting for me every day, wearing her apron already stained with the day's chores. Her face always bore the same smile—a smile that gave me the courage to say that we were a team and had work to do. Her warm hug and kind words always brought me back home to our farm and where I belonged.

"Marisella, go get changed and put your apron on. Then I will slice you a piece of bread and squeeze a tomato."

This was music to my ears, and within minutes the world of school faded, and I was sitting in our kitchen eating my favorite snack. Nonna would ask me about the school, but I would not have too much to say. I was slowly learning words that were not my own and belonged to another world. It was painful to feel afraid all day, worried that I would be found out and kicked out and forced to return home at any moment. I prayed a lot, asking God to help me make my family proud. It was all I could do. No one understood what I was going through. There was no one to talk to except Him.

When I finished my bread, tomato, and olive oil, it was time to get to work. Our first task would be going out to harvest from the garden. After that, we would hang any newly washed laundry or take in and fold any dried laundry. These were our preliminary chores. During this time, I would see Papa and greet him. He was usually at his best around this time. He was well-rested and ready for work. He liked going to work, and I think he liked it better than being home. Nonna always prepared lunch for him to eat before he left and had a packed lunch waiting for him to take with him.

"Hello, Marisella," he would say as he hugged me. His hugs were warm, like a bear, in his muscle-style T-shirt, his strong arms covered with dark hair lifting me high. His Old Spice aftershave was always pleasant, and he would kiss me on both cheeks, then set me down with the words, "Go play, Marisella." The word was foreign to me, as my playing was helping Nonna, but I knew what he meant.

***

"Marisella. Marisella. Wake up."

My eyes stirred, but kept shut, as I raised my arms above my head and stretched. It was Mom.

"C'mon, Marisella. We have to go to the farm."

I opened my eyes. "Good morning, Mom."

"Get dressed, Mari. We have to go to the farm today."

"Why are we going to the farm?"

"We have to pick tomatoes."

I did not understand what she was saying. We picked tomatoes every single day. Finally, I got out of bed and dressed, wondering what she meant. When I got to the kitchen, Nonna was washing some final dishes. She turned to me with her warm, familiar smile. "Come, Mari. I made you oatmeal and toast."

I smiled and sat down. The screen door was open. Outside, I could see Papa and Nonno Ernesto loading up large baskets into the back of the station wagon. After the final baskets were loaded, Papa closed the station wagon door and shouted, "Brigida! Let's goooo!"

From the back bedroom, I heard Mom shout out the window, "Cresenz, stop yelling. You will wake the neighbors."

"We have to goooo!" he replied just as loudly.

"Hurry up, Mari. We have to leave," Nonna said, as she poured me a small glass of milk.

Within minutes, I had finished my oatmeal and toast and drank down my milk. Moments later, I was in the back seat, sitting between Nonna and Mom. Papa was driving, and Nonno was in the front seat. We slowly pulled out of the driveway, then slowly turned onto Lorain Avenue.

The street was quiet and felt strange to me. I wondered where all the people were. We drove down Lorain for what seemed to be the longest time. At one point, Mom said, "Cresenz, why are you driving so slow?"

"Be qui—" he said.

"Go faster!" she scolded.

"I am going faster!" he shouted.

Nonna Rosa patted me on the legs, smiling. "Your Papa is a careful driver, Mari."

Ten minutes later, Mom said, "Cresenz, by the time we get there, all the tomatoes are going to be gone."

"Be qui—" he said again.

But Mom insisted, "Cresenz! Pull into that gas station. I want to drive."

"No, Brigida!"

Nonno Ernesto turned. "It's OK, Cris. Let Brigida drive."

Papa grimaced and put on his turn signal. He came to a near stop, then slowly pulled up into the driveway of a gas station. Everyone switched seats except Nonna and me. Nonno sat on my other side while Mom drove, and Papa sat in front of her. We pulled out.

We were going faster now, but it still seemed like forever. Mom and Nonna Rosa talked while I just listened. Every once in a while, Nonna Rosa would pat me on the legs and would smile at me or speak to me. Nonno Ernesto was quiet, concentrating as if he did when he worked in the garden. Papa was silent, too, as he usually was.

Soon we were out of the city and driving along a road with endless fields. I marveled at how vast the world was. Soon, through the rhythm of seeing field after field, I fell asleep. I was awakened by the feeling of the car coming to a near stop and turning. I opened my eyes to see we turned off the road and traveled down a long dirt road. Then, we entered a lot where there were more cars, all parked. People were getting in and out of them. Everyone had baskets like ours, some filled with tomatoes, going into cars, some empty, sitting behind the cars. Finally, we stopped, and all got out. The sun was warm, and the sky was deep blue. There were no clouds anywhere. The parking lot was lined with bushes open only to a single walkway which I could not see down.

In the corner of the lot was a long hut. There was a large window with a counter in it. Two older people were standing within. They were taking money from some of the people who had tomatoes.

Nonno Ernesto went up to talk with them. He then waved to us.

We unloaded the large baskets and two large containers filled with water to drink. As we walked from the car to the opening of the bushes, I felt hot. I was so excited and wondered how we were going to get so many tomatoes, like some of the other people seemed to have in their baskets.

We stepped through the opening in the bushes and suddenly found ourselves at the start of an immense field that stretched forever. Hundreds of rows of tomato plants stretched as far as the eye could see. They were taller than me, but none had tomatoes on them. We walked down the walkway and soon saw some people to our right. They were in the middle of the plants, some thirty feet off the path. Nonno said, "Keep going," and we all continued. At one point, Nonno stopped and looked out. "Here. Put the baskets down on the path. Everyone, take one. Marisella, you come with me."

We placed the baskets on the path. The adults each took one and spread out about five feet apart. I followed Nonno Ernesto. We walked out through the jungle of tomato plants, careful not to knock any down. Each plant seemed to hold at least ten bunches of tomatoes. Though I could hear the others, I could barely see them. At one point, Nonno said to the group, "Start here, and work back to the path."

Nonno set down the basket and bent over. He quickly began scooping and snatching vine tomato after tomato, gently placing them in the basket. "Start there, Marisella," he said, pointing to a plant.

I began pulling down the tomatoes and placing them with his. I had to hurry to keep up with him, as the basket was moving faster than the tomatoes I could pull. When the basket was filled, Nonno picked it up and said, "Rest, Mari. I will go get another basket."

He lifted the basket, almost overflowing with tomatoes, and carried it high above the plants as I waited and looked around. For a moment, I was afraid. If I got lost in these tall bushy tomatoes, I might never find my way out, but then I heard Papa. He was nearby, bent over, pulling tomatoes. I then heard someone on the other side and peered through. It was Nonna, working her way through the plants back to the path, dragging her basket with her. I felt comforted knowing they were there, and within a moment, Nonno trudged back through with a new basket.

We kept going. I was so tired and hot that I felt like lying down in the dirt and sleeping. "I am tired, Nonno," I said.

He chuckled. "We will be done soon, Mari. Just keep thinking of how delicious the spaghetti sauce will taste."

It seemed like forever, but soon we had filled eight baskets. Nonno and Mom went to the front and brought back two small wagons. We loaded up eight baskets, took them to the car, and headed for home. All the way home, the adults talked about what we had to do next. I understood we would make jars of tomato sauce as I helped Nonna open jars every week. Still, I could not understand how we would turn the tomatoes into the sauce, nor did I understand why we had so many.

When we got home, Nonna called me into the kitchen. We immediately put our aprons on and began boiling water for pasta and setting the table for lunch. Mom, Papa, and Nonno carried the baskets of tomatoes down the basement.

"Mari!" Papa yelled from the basement.

"Yes, Papa?"

"Go get me the newspapers."

I ran into the living room, picked up a handful from the stack of papers he had read, and carefully carried them down the basement steps. Papa took them from me and said, "Go get more, Mari."

By the time I came back down with another bunch of papers, I could already see what they were doing. The entire kitchen table and counters all had newspapers carefully laid out on them. Mom was taking out the tomatoes and filling the counter. Nonno Ernesto was emptying a basket onto the table and filling it up. Papa was laying newspapers carefully on a section of the floor.

I watched them until I heard Nonna Rosa call me, "Mari, I need you."

I sighed and ran upstairs. "Yes, Nonna."

"Go see if there are any more peppers in the garden." I smiled, so happy to be so needed in the epic day. I retrieved six peppers and gave them to Nonna. I immediately went back downstairs. By now, almost all the baskets were empty. The entire basement was filled with tomatoes neatly spread out on top of newspapers. There was only a narrow pathway to the kitchen.

Nonno Ernesto then went over by the furnace and uncovered something. It was a metal machine nearly as tall as me. He picked it up, set it on the table in the only open spot, and carefully maneuvered it near the edge.

"Mangia!" came the call from upstairs, and everyone smiled. Finally, we were done for the day.

"What are we going to do with the tomatoes, Nonno?" I asked.

"We have to wait a few days, Mari, until they are ready. As soon as they are, we are going to make the sauce."

He watched me carefully as I nodded. I could tell he had more to say, so I kept my gaze on him. He then added, "But we cannot wait too long, Mari, or they will spoil. So when it is time, we have to do it right away."

I nodded again, glancing around at the hundreds and hundreds of tomatoes. Finally, he patted me on the head and said, "Good job today, Marisella. Let's go eat."

## Canning Season

On Sunday afternoon, Uncle Tony and Aunt Jean came over for the Sunday meal. We all sat at the table together, including my little brother, who sat next to me in his high chair. A large bowl of salad, a bowl of meatballs dripping with sauce, a bowl of pasta, a plate of olives, two loaves of bread, and two bottles of wine adorned the neatly set table. Papa, sitting silently at the head of the table with a worried look on his face, was his nervous self. He was made worse not only by the hundreds and hundreds of tomatoes covering the entire basement but also by Aunt Jean's presence.

The meal began slowly and quietly, as Aunt Jean did not seem to be her normal self. Her face bore a look too, but not of worry, rather of being upset. At one point, Uncle Tony broke the silence, "So, what day are you planning on canning the tomatoes?"

Nonno Ernesto shrugged. "We are watching them, Tony. I think maybe Wednesday after work."

Uncle Tony said, "I am on second shift this week. I won't be able to help."

Aunt Jean grimaced and started in, "Tony, why don't you call in sick? I want some jars of tomato sauce."

"Jean!" he said, his face bearing an immediate look of chagrin, which spoke of more than this moment. "I cannot call in sick."

"Why not! I do when I have to!"

"Jean! You want me to lose my job!"

Jean leaned forward as if talking privately to my Nonna Rosa across the table from her. "I don't know why he thinks he is going to get fired. I call in sick all the time."

Nonna Rosa raised her eyebrows to appease them both, then raised her hand. "You both work it out."

Mom interjected, "Jean, if you want some tomato sauce, then come and help us."

"What!" Jean said, her face frozen in surprise.

"Yes," Uncle Tony said, with a half-smile. "You come and work with them, Jean."

She looked around the table, her face as lit up as I had ever seen. "I don't know how to make tomato sauce!"

"We will teach you," Mom said, unengaged, as she reached for a slice of bread, keeping her gaze fixed on her plate.

Uncle Tony quickly followed with, "There, Jean. You can have tomato sauce."

Aunt Jean's eyes widened. "What!" She looked around for a moment, then her face changed to one of concern. "I have to work overtime this week. Oh, my boss. He is giving me such a hard time about my work. I don't know what's wrong with him. My brother is crazy too. He sent his kids to public school. I'm so upset." She leaned forward again, this time in Mom's direction. "I'm talking to his wife, though. I almost have her convinced." She leaned back with a devious smile, relishing the memory, then leaned forward and looked down at Nonno. "Ernesto, did you think about coming to the lodge? My dad would love to have you. Oh, my sister-in-law has her hands full. I think it's a sin my brother won't send the kids to Catholic School. Anyway, I have to work overtime every day. I'm worried about my dad. He is—"

Papa slammed down his fork. "Jeannna! Stop it!"

Jean scowled, and there was not a sound to be heard.

Papa sighed, his gaze slightly rising to the ceiling in deep frustration.

Jean glared at Tony, as she had since they arrived. "Are you going to let him talk to me like that?"

"Jean," Uncle Tony said in a descending tone, meant to bring things to a close.

Aunt Jean huffed, then seemed to forget about the whole thing.

"How is school, Marisella?"

My eyes opened wide, suddenly feeling everyone watching me, their expressions still reeling from what had just happened.

"I like it, Aunt Jean," I said, putting my glance down at my plate.

Aunt Jean began eating her spaghetti, as did everyone else. Nothing more was said until the end of the meal, when Aunt Jean announced that they had to go see her dad. And in a whirlwind moment, she and Uncle Tony left.

~ ~ ~ ~

Over the next few evenings, Nonno Ernesto and Mom went to various stores and returned with boxes, boxes of glass jars, and four brand-new large pots. Last, a large apparatus was carried in and taken down to the basement.

It was a metal thing, over a foot tall, with a large funnel on the top and a chute that extended outwards. Attached to it was a handle that was supposed to be cranked. It was set on the table in the basement, and a chair was put next to it. One of the new pots was placed underneath the chute on the chair.

On Wednesday, when Nonno Ernesto came home from work, he went directly down to the basement. I followed him and watched him carefully walk around and through the fields of tomatoes lining every inch of our basement. He smiled and called upstairs to Nonna, "Young girl! We are ready to start."

"I will be right down, young man!" Nonna said.

I felt the excitement building. Finally, Nonna came down and put one of the large pots onto the floor. "Come, Mari. We have to put the tomatoes into the pot."

I ran over and kneeled next to her, and we carefully began picking the tomatoes and placing them in the pot. "Look for any bad spots. Give those to me."

I found one, and Nonna cut it out, then put the rest of the tomato in. Within a short time, we had nearly filled the large pot. Nonna picked it up and lifted it onto the stove.

"What do we do now, Nonna?"

"We wait for it to boil."

We went upstairs and prepared dinner. Mom came home, and Nonno Ernesto sat down too. He was wearing old clothes and had a special tan-colored apron on. As we ate, Nonna kept going down to the basement to check the progress.

After eating, we all went downstairs. Nonno lifted the heavy pot of boiled tomatoes and placed it on the table next to the metal apparatus. We all watched as he took a large scoop and scooped several clumps of tomato into the funnel. He then began turning the crank, and the tomatoes oozed downward. Moments later, a river of tomato-colored slurry slid down the chute, dropping into the pan waiting on the chair. Nonna stayed by his side while Mom got a fresh pot and called me over to gather another pot full of tomatoes.

Once Nonno had emptied the first pot and filled the second with the slurry, Nonna added a handful of salt from the Morton's Salt container and carried it to the stove for the second cooking.

We kept going like this for hours. Finally, as the third full pot of cooked slurry was getting near done, Nonno Ernesto said, "Brigida, Rosa, set up the jars. Mari, go upstairs and get more newspapers. Then go outside and pick a bowl of basil from the garden."

I looked around. A whole section of our basement was now empty of tomatoes. But there were still lots to go. When I returned with the basil and newspaper, boxes of jars were emptied and waiting on the table. Nonno Ernesto got another funnel and began filling the jars with the hot liquid sauce using a special smaller scoop.

As soon as they were filled to the top, Nonna put a fresh piece of basil on top and sealed them with special lids. After making sure it was tight, she turned it upside down. The entire basement was swelteringly hot, and Mom said we could not open the windows because we did not want any flies to come in.

We continued for over an hour until we had filled and sealed over sixty jars. They looked like an army of finely clad soldiers, ready for their mission.

Last, the pans and the metal apparatus were taken to the sink. All were washed and carefully set onto towels on the table to dry. We all marveled at our accomplishments. However, as I looked around, I realized we had a lot more to go.

\*\*\*

The following afternoon after school, Nonna and I went down to the basement and into the small room at the back. We dusted the shelves and lined them with newspaper. Then, one by one, we neatly stacked the jars right side up onto the shelves.

That night, we did another batch, and by the third night, the final batch. Nonno Ernesto counted and proclaimed we had done over 170 jars. I felt like we were the richest family in the world at that moment. All around me was something so beautiful and precious that we had made as a family.

~ ~ ~ ~

Two days later, on Saturday, we all went back to the farm again. But this time, it was a different farm. This time, we picked baskets and baskets of peppers. They, too, were lined up in the basement, though not nearly as many as the tomatoes. More boxes of jars were brought in, and several days were spent around the table cutting them into strips and putting them into jars that were filled with water and vinegar.

~ ~ ~ ~

Mid-week, in the evening, we drove out to another farm. This time, we picked eggplants. These took much longer to process, as after they were cut into slices, we gradually squeezed the water from them until they were ready for large jars filled with oil. The next night Nonno Ernesto came home from work late, bringing with him two large cases filled with olives. These had to be spread around the table. Sticks were put on all edges to prevent them from rolling away. That night, we sat around the table, each with a hammer, hitting the olives, one by one, to open them to their core. Only then could they be thrown in the brine.

~ ~ ~ ~

The following Saturday, late in the afternoon, we went to yet another farm for pears. We drove out to a different farm a few nights later to get peaches. Every farm was different, and yet so much the same. They all had a beauty about them. Each place was born of the hard work of the farmers, as well as the people coming to harvest the produce. Every night between our trips was spent around the basement table, talking, laughing, carefully peeling, cutting these delicacies in half, and placing them in jars.

Our basement seemed like a factory, with more and more coming in and more being readied for the jars. The small room I once disdained had become our treasure chest. Hundreds upon hundreds of jars, all like standing armies from different countries, with different colored shiny uniforms, awaited the command of their leaders. The canning of these foods was our way of capturing the warm, healing months of summer sun and placing them into glass jars that would sustain us for the coming winter. They were like gold to us. They were medicine to us.

Every morning, I went to school exhausted yet filled with fond memories of our laughter and accomplishments of the night before. I was part of the team; an important part of the team that ran our little family farm.

# The Land

On the third Saturday of our harvest season, Nonno Ernesto, Mom, and Papa went to another farm. I was to stay home and help Nonna Rosa. First, Nonna took me down to the basement, and we filled the large basin sinks next to the washer machine with water. Next, I lifted large gallon-size glass bottles, one by one, up to Nonna, who washed them and set them on the table to dry. Two hours later, Nonno Ernesto and the others arrived and beeped the horn. Within minutes, they began carrying down cases and cases of grapes, stacking them against the wall. There were over twenty cases, and the entire basement air was bursting with their flavor.

"Nonno," I asked, "what are we going to do with these?"

In his warm, gentle, hearty voice, he bent down and peered into my eyes, smiling. "I am going to teach you how to make wine and vinegar, Marisella."

I knew what wine was, and I did not like it, but I never imagined it could be made from boxes of grapes.

***

The next morning, Nonno and Nonna took me to church at Our Lady of Mount Carmel. It was a long walk, one that we made every Sunday. My parents always stayed home, and I never understood why they did not come with us. By the time we turned the corner onto Detroit Avenue, we could hear the church bells ringing loudly through the neighborhood. Families were coming out of their houses from all directions, with moms frantically straightening their children's hair or clothes, making sure they were presentable.

Once inside the church, I marveled at the beautiful pictures and statues lining the walls and the altar. I felt at home, at peace, and special, as it was my alone time with my Nonno and Nonna.

After Mass, I quietly held my Nonna's hand while she and Nonno talked with other people. Children were running around, playing, and chasing each other, but I was not allowed to do so. Nonna kept a tight hold on me, and I knew it was because we were so close to the cars going back and forth on Detroit Avenue. She held me just as tightly on Lorain Avenue, and it was because of all the cars, too.

When we arrived home, Nonna and I started making lunch. Mom and Papa were still asleep in their rooms. Uncle Joe and his wife Maria came over when it was time to eat, along with my cousins, Armando and Carlo. We all enjoyed a delicious meal of pasta, meatballs, salad, cooked greens, wine, and fresh bread. After the meal, Armando and Carlo went out to play. I did not want to go outside with them. Carlo was fun, but Armando was too bossy. He and Rosemary always tried to make the rest of us cousins do what they wanted. It was no fun playing with them. So I stayed at the table.

I watched Uncle Joe and wondered again how he had gotten such a bad scar across his face. It made him look very different from Nonno and Papa. He looked mean or mad, and I did not understand why. As I was listening, Uncle Joe began talking about the land in Italy.

"How is your land doing?" Uncle Joe asked Nonno.

Nonno shrugged. "I have hired someone to take care of the grapes and olives."

"Are they going to make oil and wine?"

Nonno's face saddened some as he said, "*Heh*, no. They are going to sell them."

Uncle Joe nodded. "When will you go back?"

Nonno looked out the window as if he were looking all the way to Italy and said, "I cannot now. Brigida needs us."

It was quiet as the men looked down at their coffee. Then, finally, Nonno asked, "How about you, Joe? Are you going back to your land?"

Uncle Joe looked at Papa and then raised his hand. "We do not have much land to work, Ernesto. Only a few acres, next to the large stone mountain. The mountain is on our land, but it is only the mountain, and what can you do with a mountain? Hey, Cris, isn't that right?"

Papa smiled and nodded. He always deferred to Uncle Joe.

It was quiet again when Joe said, "I don't think the land is worth much, but we should maybe keep it somehow. My wife's brother, Mariano, lives nearby. I pay him to keep an eye on it for us." He raised his hand, shaking it. "Hey, Cris, it is costing me a lot of money to watch our land."

Papa only half-smiled this time, and nodded. Then, he said, "Mariano is my half brother."

The women were listening, and Mom asked, "What do you mean, Cris?"

Papa raised his hand high and said in an escalating voice, "His mother nursed me when Mariano and I were both babies."

"Why didn't your mother nurse you?" Mom asked.

"She was sick!" Papa said with raised hand and voice.

Uncle Joe nodded. "Yes, she was always sick, it seemed."

It was quiet again, as the men were still contemplating the land. Uncle Joe then said, "It would be easier to let the land go. But for our mother's memory, I will make sure we hold onto it. Hey, Cris?"

Papa nodded, his glance down; his way of deferring to Uncle Joe.

The meal ended right after that. Uncle Joe went to the door and shouted for Armando and Carlo to come. He said goodbye, and he and his wife Maria left.

I was glad they were gone. I did not like how Papa never talked when Uncle Joe was around. It seemed that he was not as important, and I knew he was not mean like Uncle Joe.

After we cleared the table and did the dishes, Nonno, Nonna, and I went down to the basement. Nonno brought the cases of grapes over to the large sinks by the washer and dryer. He pried each case open and dumped them into the water-filled sink. Nonna got a stool for me, and I stood next to her as we plunged the bunches of grapes up and down in the water, then transferred them to the other sink to dry.

As they dried some, they were lifted out and placed into several large half-barrels lined up at the table's far side. By the time the afternoon was fading, we were finished. I went upstairs and saw Papa reading the newspaper. I sat on the other end of his couch and eventually drifted off to sleep.

## The Final Harvest

As the warm summer nights began to fade away, giving way to the crispness of fall in the air, our family farm's time of harvest began to fade. One day, as I arrived home from school, Nonna told me to get out of my school clothes because we had work to do in the garden. Nonna carried a basket with her as I followed her to the far end of the garden. It was a cloudy afternoon, with the cool wind kissing my cheeks. We carefully rummaged through the leaves and branches of each plant in the garden, picking the last remnants of hidden vegetables. She handed them to me, I placed them in the basket, and we continued along the entire length and depth of the garden. We had two baskets filled with vegetables by the time we were done, most not yet ripe.

"That is the end of this year's garden, Mari," Nonna said, smiling.

We took the baskets inside, washed everything, and set them on newspapers laid out in front of the kitchen and dining room window. Here, they could take their time to ripen, safe from the coming cold weather.

That night, after supper, Nonno asked me to come outside with him. He, too, took me to the far end of the garden, but he did not bring baskets. Instead, he brought large black garbage bags. I held one of the bags open as he leaned forward like a drawbridge and used his large hands to pull plants out of the soil. He bent them up and stuffed them into the bags until, over an hour later, all the plants were gone from the garden. We had collected four bags of them, all neatly tied up, all ready to go out in the trash.

And so ended, it seemed, my first season on our family farm, located on a narrow city lot in the middle of Cleveland.

The work did not stop, though, and neither did my struggles at school. Now that the weather was colder, my walks to school were more difficult. In the classroom, I was beginning to understand bits of the language and words of the other students and my teacher. But it was a constant challenge, a constant worry that they would kick me out and send me home one day. Every moment was a struggle. Were it not for the kind smile of my teacher and the special attention she gave me at moments throughout the day, I may have simply put my head down and cried.

At home, no one knew what I was going through. At home, I was expected to get changed out of my school clothes and help Nonna with whatever she was doing. I never minded this, as Nonna was my life. She was the person I looked up to more than any other. She was the person in the house who loved me and understood me more than any other. I wanted so much to please her, and I always did my best to be attentive to what she wanted me to do.

After our harvest was over, our attention turned to tasks that had to be done in preparation for winter. Nonna began making homemade pasta. It was very fun but hard work. After school, when we made pasta, we would make a special dough and roll it out with heavy wooden rollers, creating a flat yellow mass on the table. Then Nonna would cut it into long strips. I had to peel these up and hand them to her as she then fed them through a grinder-type machine that cut them into further refined strips. Papa would get mad when we made homemade pasta because it made the kitchen and dining room a mess. There would be wide strips of pasta, ready for the grinder, hanging all over the dining room and kitchen chairs.

~ ~ ~ ~

Some weeks later, when the leaves had almost all fallen down, Nonno Ernesto brought home several large boxes filled with pork. He also brought bags with long slimy things they called the casings. Immediately, these long white casings were placed in the kitchen sink filled with hot water. Salt was added, and Nonna and I began the task of washing them thoroughly.

When we finished, they were kept moist in a plastic bag and brought downstairs. Nonno Ernesto set up a meat grinder and began running the pork through it until he had filled a large pan full of ground pork. Next, he and Nonna added special seasonings. They dug their hands in, turning it over and over to mix it all together thoroughly. Finally, the casings we had cleaned so carefully were affixed to the end of another machine. Nonno put the ground sausage in and cranked, pushing the sausage into the casings, making large, long sausages. They would be carefully taken off and laid on newspaper in a large circular pattern. Hours later, when we finished, the sausages were hung on large crossbars in the cellar room, where the rest of our food was neatly stored on the shelf walls.

Now, the room was filled with hundreds of jars, and over twenty long sausages hung down in the center, making it nearly impossible to see out the window.

~ ~ ~ ~

As our life moved indoors for the coming winter, my little brother, Crispino, learned to walk and run. My job was now not only to help Nonna watch him, but to make sure he did not get into trouble. I was constantly running ahead of him to close the bathroom or bedroom door or pick something up quickly to ensure he would not touch, spill, or even break it.

Soon, Christmas time came, and we set up the first Christmas tree I remember in the living room. With Crispino running around now, my job became even more difficult. In addition to feeding him, burping him, and changing his diapers, I now was constantly trying to stop him from grabbing the bulbs or tinsel that hung from the tree. Papa grew even more upset in those days, as Crispino's constant threat of toppling himself or something else over made Papa very nervous.

Christmas came and went, and with it the joy the holiday naturally brought. Our little family now settled in for the long winter. But, deep down inside, I knew it was going to be difficult.

## The Days, the Years

The cycle of life repeated itself on our small family farm, located on a tiny city lot on Lorain Avenue in Cleveland. When I finished first grade, I was six years old and spent the summer planting, tending to the garden, and tending to my brother. When I turned seven and second grade began, we were as busy at home as ever. Then, the annual ritual of canning projects began, lasting well into October.

This year, though, was going to be a special one for me. It was the year I was going to make my first Holy Communion. It was not until the end of the school year, of course, but the talk and the planning and the constant reminders to me of how important it was began in earnest.

I was an adult now, though I never knew the difference between what an adult and a child were. I worked alongside the adults day and night. I was in charge of my brother more than my mom was.

The only reprieve I had from this world of constant work and the constant effort to keep my brother quiet so as not to upset Papa was when company came over. My cousins and I would play in the basement in the yard or in the winter. If we were at their houses, it would be the same. None of our houses or yards were much different, so it never mattered where we were at. All that mattered was that we were together.

At the end of every visit, though, either we would leave, or they would leave, and my quiet, responsibility-driven life would resume. Often after these visits, Papa would be overly anxious. If we had visitors over, he would be a nervous wreck that the house was a mess once they left. So, the cleaning up would begin at once. Papa was always yelling, and Mom could do nothing but try to keep him calm. Fortunately, Nonno and Nonna gave us the buffer we needed to hold it all together.

Papa was nervous if we were just coming home from visiting someone else, especially if Crispino was acting up in the car. Papa would yell loudly, "Be quie!" not finishing the whole word, to which Mom would immediately chastise him, and he would reply softly, "Shaat up!" Which would cause her to chastise him further, often accompanied by a glare. The whole thing would take several long moments to settle back down. This was usually Crispino's cue to start up again, and it all would begin once more.

# Pierced Ears

One day, after canning season, my Nonna told me about something new. "Marisella, we are going to pierce your ears soon."

"What is that, Nonna?" I asked innocently.

"Oh, let me show you. Come with me."

I followed Nonna into her room. She opened a jewelry box and took out a pair of earrings. It looked like two small pearls. Nonna put them into her ears, careful to show me how the small wire went through the tiny hole in her ear. "Do you see how beautiful they are?" she asked.

"Yes, I like them."

"I am going to buy you a pair, just like these."

"Really?" I said excitedly. I had never imagined having something this beautiful.

Nonna hugged me tightly. "You are a beautiful little girl, Marisella. They will look very pretty on you. And… they will match your First Communion dress."

"Thank you, Nonna," I said. My First Communion was before me again. I wondered what marvels it held.

Nonna took the earrings off, then said, "I have something special to show you." She reached into her jewelry box again and took out a small, wrapped piece of cloth. She carefully unwrapped it, took two larger gold earrings, and put one in each of her ears. She smiled and turned to face me, saying, "Nonno Ernesto bought these earrings for me long ago. Do you like them?"

I reached up and touched the gold, and it twirled and swayed. I said, "Yes, they are very beautiful, Nonna."

She then took them off and stood me before her, facing the mirror. "Here," she said. "Let's see how they look." She held the earrings up to my ears so I could see them in the mirror. "Someday, when you grow older, Marisella, your husband will buy you beautiful earrings. Would you like that?"

"Yes, Nonna," I said with a tinge of trepidation. The idea that someday I would have a husband was new to me. Of course, I did not understand what it meant, but I knew Nonna had Nonno, and Mom had Papa, and so it was with all the adults. Still, how that would happen to me seemed a million miles away. But still, I marveled at how beautiful they were, and the idea that my husband would someday buy me beautiful earrings was exciting to me.

"When are we going to do it?" I asked.

"In a few weeks," Nonna said.

~ ~ ~ ~

On Halloween morning, I sat at the kitchen table, listening to the rustling of the falling leaves being blown around outside our door. My brother Crispino was still asleep. And I was alone in the kitchen with Nonno and Nonna. Nonno Ernesto was sitting quietly, drinking his coffee, and eating a piece of toast. Nonna was by the stove stirring a pan of oatmeal. I always loved being alone with these two, and only in the mornings had the opportunity. They were both quiet in the mornings, periodically exchanging bits of information about their day. There was quiet trust and quiet acceptance in their words to each other. It was almost as if they had their own language. Yes, I understood what they were saying, but the way they spoke and listened was intimate and showed the deep love and connection they had for each other. Mom and Papa did not talk this way, and it was probably why it seemed so special to me.

But this morning, I was barely able to contain my excitement. The lady at the masquerade shop next door had made me a small crown and a pink dress. I was going to be a princess tonight, and I could not wait.

Nonno Ernesto left for work at a local factory where he got a job, and soon after, my mom came in to have coffee. She, too, was getting ready to go to work. She told me, "Marisella, before we go out to trick or treat tonight, Nonna is going to take you to Asunta's house to pierce your ears."

"Tonight?" I said, surprised.

"Yes, after I get home from work."

I did not know what it entailed. After all, the tiny holes in Nonna's ears were tiny. But I was immediately worried that whatever it was would take too long. Tonight was the first night ever that I was going to be allowed to walk to the neighborhood houses to get candy. The previous year, I had been only six and told I was too young.

I looked at Nonna, and she smiled, saying, "Don't worry, Mari. We will go before dinner and be back in plenty of time."

I trusted her, as I trusted everything I was asked to do, and put the matter out of my mind.

All day long in school, I could think of nothing except my princess costume. During school, all the kids traded little heart candies. We were also given small chocolate bars by some of the teachers. I felt rich, seeing all the candy and chocolate bars in the small bag I had been given. I had never had so much candy, as we never bought candy in our house. When I got home, my Nonna took the candy and told me she would give me one piece each day. She told me we had a few things to do before Mom got home. So, I donned my apron and began helping her get ready for dinner.

When Mom arrived, she took over watching my little brother, and Nonna grabbed her coat and her purse, and we left for Asunta's house.

Asunta Valentino lived a few short blocks away. She and her husband were also from Italy, and we were just getting to know them. Asunta was much older than my mom. She reminded me more of my Nonna than anything else. For some reason I did not understand, I did not like her husband, Domenic. Domenic Valentini was a sophisticated man with a long, brown, curved mustache. He was a fast talker and very well-spoken, and I don't know why I did not like him. The Valentinis had a large family with seven children in all. Most of them were older than me, but their second youngest boy, Rudolph, was my age. My favorite was their oldest daughter, Maria, who was nineteen years old and very beautiful. I knew someday when I grew up that I wanted to be as beautiful as Maria.

When we arrived at Asunta's home, she greeted us warmly, hugging me tightly. Asunta possessed a soft kindness that permeated her entire being. Her home reflected this too. I saw a towel laid out on the counter with a large needle, string, cotton, and alcohol when we came in. I immediately began to feel tense.

Asunta's daughter, Maria, came in and hugged me. "Hello, little Marisella. Are you ready to get your ears pierced?"

"Yes," I said, trusting her.

Three of Asunta's sons came into the kitchen from upstairs to say hello. Asunta told them, "Boys, go downstairs and play."

"But we want to watch," Rudolph said.

Nonna and Asunta laughed, and Asunta said, "No, boys. This is not for you. Now go." She shooed them away.

Within minutes, I was sitting in a kitchen chair that had been pulled from the table. A large towel was draped over my shoulders, and my hair was pulled back and tied up with a ribbon. Asunta pulled up a chair on one side of Maria and me on the other. I felt my knees starting to tremble. Maria rested her hand on my leg. "It's OK, Marisella, it will only hurt a little bit."

I looked at her with fear in my eyes. "Are you sure?" I asked.

"Oh, yes. We have all had our ears pierced. Look how nice," she said, pointing to her earrings. They were truly special looking, especially on her.

"OK," I said, but the trembling now reached into my stomach. Nonna picked up the needle, and all grew quiet. I could now hear the sounds of the boys playing downstairs. It distracted me for a moment.

Nonna dampened a cotton ball with alcohol and cleaned my earlobe. Then she put a piece of string through the needle. I could not imagine why she was doing that. All I was worried about was the needle. It was very large, and I could not imagine how that was going to make just a tiny hole in my ear. To me, it seemed as large as my ear itself.

Nonna stepped in front of me, and Asunta and Maria each took hold of my arm.

"Turn your head to the side, Marisella," Nonna said, adding, "Put the needle in the fire!"

I closed my eyes tightly and began to shake, turning my head.

"It's OK, Marisella," Asunta said gently.

Suddenly I felt my earlobe pinched, then pulled, and suddenly explode in pain. I screamed.

Immediately Maria and Asunta held me firmer, and they all began speaking to me, "It's OK, Marisella. It's OK."

I screamed louder and began shaking and crying while Nonna pulled the needle all the way through. She then cut the string from the needle, leaving the string in my ear. She took both ends of the string and worked it back and forth. I peered out of my eye, saw the blood on the towel by my shoulder, and started crying more.

Asunta hugged me. "It's OK, Marisella, you did great."

The basement door thrust open, and the boys came in. Asunta yelled, "Get downstairs! Now!"

"But we want to watch!"

Maria jumped up and chased them downstairs.

I sat crying as the pain lingered in my mind. Nonna said, "You did fine, Mari. Let's hurry and do the other one."

Maria sat back down, and I gritted my teeth and turned my head the other way. Moments later, the pain exploded in my ear again, and I screamed, louder this time, as I was ready for the pain and to scream. I cried and cried, even though they tried desperately to reassure me. The boys came up and were chased away again.

Finally, I was allowed to get up. Nonna thanked them, and I left with two pieces of string dangling from the blood-stained holes in my ears. I cried all the way home, squeezing Nonna's hand tightly. She was quiet, and I could tell she was sorry that I had been hurt so much. When we got home, I sat in the kitchen while Nonna put ice in a towel and had me hold it to my sore ears. She tried to cheer me up by putting on a robe with a mop on her head for a wig. I tried to laugh, but I could not. Still, I knew she meant well.

Right after dinner, I was allowed to put my princess costume on. I was too traumatized to enjoy it, as the pain and memory of what I had just gone through stayed with me the whole night. My mom took me out into the dark, chilly night, and we walked down the alley and over to Colgate Avenue, where the city street was lined with homes.

## First Communion Ready

Right after Christmas that year, Mom told the family that she was expecting another baby. Even though I had my hands full with my brother, I was as thrilled as anyone. The thought of new life coming into our home yielded a natural excitement to all. Then, we were a family, and we did everything together. Now, we were a growing family.

Going to school at this time of year was very hard. I was cold all the time, mainly because of the Catholic School uniforms we had to wear. My parents bought me boots to go over my shoes, but they did little to stop the cold wind from blowing through me every day. But Nonna always had a bowl of hot soup for me when I got home, and I would look forward to it all day long.

St. Patrick's Day came and went. I knew this because there were many Italian kids in the school. There were even more Irish kids. They knew how to celebrate, and I envied them. Around this time, papers were sent home that I gave to my mom. She informed me there was a meeting regarding my upcoming First Communion. I remember the night she was going to the meeting because I was in charge of keeping my brother occupied. We were playing school downstairs on the green chalkboard. I was seven and a half, and he was almost four years old. I pitied his teacher when he went to school because he was wild and would never sit still.

After the meeting, Mom came home and said we had lots to do, including sending out invitations and planning the menu, which we would make at home.

~ ~ ~ ~

A week or so later, my mom gave me the great news. "Tomorrow night, Mari, Aunt Mary, myself, and Nonna are going to take you out to get your First Communion dress."

"Really!" I exclaimed. We had talked about this event for months and months. Now, suddenly, the day was here. All night long, I laid awake thinking of how beautiful my dress would be.

The next day I rushed home from school, ate my soup bowl, and helped Nonna prepare dinner. My mom arrived home from her job, and then the phone rang. Mom answered. It was Papa's work. "Cris," she yelled. Moments later, Papa came out of his room. He had just returned from work a little earlier. He got on. "Ello."

"OK, I will come now."

He hung up and said, "I gotta go to work."

"Cris, can't you get a ride?" Mom exclaimed.

"From who?" he said as he went into his room to get dressed. We only had one car, which the entire family had to share. Papa's job was the most important in the house, so if he had to go to work, nothing could be done.

Mom turned to me, and I could tell she could see the disappointment on my face. I looked down. Mom said, "We will go next week, Marisella. Don't worry."

I was so disappointed, but I knew that we were a family. We had to work together and sacrifice when we needed to. It was how a family of immigrants like ours survived in America.

***

The next day, on the way home from school, I stopped at the masquerade shop next door to our house. The lady that owned it was named Nancy. She and I had become friends, as I stopped there often to say hi. Over time, I looked forward to seeing her.

Nancy made all of the costumes in her shop by herself. When I would come into her store, she was often just inside the back room, busy in her material cutting and sewing area. Her shop was busy all year long. She sold very skimpy outfits for what she called Go-Go dancers. I did not understand how a lady could wear such an outfit, nor what Go-Go dancers really did. But Nancy told me they needed the outfits to earn money and that it also helped her keep her store going.

When I entered the store, the bell on the door jingled. A moment later, Nancy peeked around the corner, then quickly gathered something from her cutting table and put it under a pile of material. Finally, she came out into the front store to greet me. "Good afternoon, little Marisella. How are you doing today?"

"I am OK," I said.

"Did you get your dress yesterday?"

"No," I said, lowering my glance to the floor.

"What happened?"

"Papa had to go to work. So he needed the car."

"Oh, you poor little thing. I wish I could make you a dress."

I smiled. "Thank you. We are going next week."

"OK," she said. "I have a gift for you."

"You do?"

"Yes, but I will give it to you on your Communion Day."

"Thank you," I said, excited. "I have to go now. Bye."

~ ~ ~ ~

The following week, the day to go get my dress approached again. While I was excited, I held my breath, knowing the phone might ring and Papa would have to work. I came home, ate my soup, and waited. Papa was in the back room, already asleep from working the early first shift. Finally, Mom came home and said, "Let's get ready. We will pick up Aunt Mary."

Nonna quickly grabbed her coat and purse, as did Mom. My little brother began acting up, crying that he wanted to go with us. Mom took him by the hand and walked him over to the bedroom door. She knocked. "Cresenz. Wake up!"

"Whadda you want!" came the cry from the room.

"Watch Crispino. We have to go get Marisa's dress."

"I can't! I'm sleeping!" he said loudly, adding, "I gotta go in early tomorrow!"

My brother began crying, whining more loudly, and pulling at my mom's dress.

She knocked louder. "Cris!"

Nothing.

She grabbed my brother and picked him up. "He's coming with us."

He immediately stopped crying, but I felt like crying. I suddenly knew this was going to be no special shopping trip.

In the car, I felt the dread of knowing my brother was going to cause havoc at the store. He sat perfectly quiet and still, happy he was with us, but I knew it would not last. So, we picked up Aunt Mary, and the five of us drove downtown to the May Company. We parked in the parking garage and went in.

Inside the store was a different world of lights, clean carpets, tile floors, and racks upon racks of brand-new clothing. There were hundreds of people too, men and women dressed in all manner of clothing, walking in every direction, many pulling children along with them.

We walked onto the large escalators and began the journey down. This was when my brother got started. Though my mom held his hand tightly, he still managed to go down and up, and down and up, almost getting his foot caught in the final shrinking step.

We went into the midst of the clothing, toward the back wall, until we were finally at the place where row after row of girls' clothes greeted us. Eventually, after going up and down a few of the vast aisles, we found the communion dresses. I could not believe how beautiful they were. Nonna and Aunt Mary started rifling through the dresses, talking, glancing at prices, holding them up to me to check the size.

Before long, three were chosen, and Mom took me to the dressing room. I took off my bell-bottom pants and put on the first dress. I then put on the white leotard and white shoes. The dress had a shimmering cross necklace that came with it, and I gently slipped it over my neck. Finally, I put on the veil. I looked in the mirror and smiled. I had never seen such a beautiful dress in my life. I marveled at how pretty I looked in it. I was so excited.

"Mari, are you ready?"

"Yes," I said. I stepped out.

Mom, Nonna, and Aunt Mary all smiled widely. Mom said, "You look beautiful, Marisella."

"Thank you, Mom," I said.

Nonna pulled me in, hugging me.

Suddenly, we heard a lady scream, followed by a baby crying. Mom turned, her lips clenched, and shouted, "Crispino!" Crispino was nowhere to be seen. I stood on my tippy toes and saw the lady looking crossly at the ground in the next aisle. She held the crying baby in her arms, trying to calm it down. In the next minute, my brother ran back through, under the dresses, into our aisle. He then started running away from us.

"Crispino!" Mom yelled. "Get over here now!"

Mom, Nonna, and Aunt Mary all turned away from me and ran to get him. Mom grabbed him by the arm, and they all walked back toward me, each of them glaring at my brother. I knew something like this was going to happen. Mom said to the woman, "I'm sorry." Unfortunately, it did not appease her, as she turned away in a huff.

Finally, with Crispino firmly in Mom's grasp, they all turned their attention back to me. I was still standing there just outside the dressing room. Finally, exasperated, my mom said, "OK, Mari, go get dressed. We will get that one."

When we got home, Mom hung my dress in my closet, carefully laid my white leotard across the hanger, and hung the veil. The whole thing was covered in sheer plastic to protect it. My white shoes were placed on the floor in their box. As we closed the closet door, I saw my brother standing in the doorway, with his black hair and innocent brown eyes, watching us. Now I had to worry about him getting into it. I glared at him, and he ran away.

# The Land in Italy

On Easter Sunday, we all gathered at Uncle Italo and Aunt Mary's house. All my uncles, aunts, and cousins were there, and everyone was dressed in their Easter clothes. I remember how handsome the men looked with their dark suits and ties. The women looked beautiful too, with flowery dresses, matching shoes, and bonnets. Everyone was there, and Aunt Mary had laid out countless trays of delicious pastries. When it was time to gather for the main meal, there were twelve adults at the main table. In addition, almost seventeen children were seated at the long folding table set up to extend the dining room table. We had pasta, meatballs, salad, and bread to begin the meal. This was the same meal we had every Sunday. But today, after those foods were consumed, a plate full of lamb was passed around. I did not like it, as I did not like most meats, but it was a treat for most of the others, especially the boys and the adults.

Late in the afternoon, I was tired of playing and went and sat near the men gathered under the grape arbor on the small patio outside. Papa was there, along with Nonno Ernesto, Uncle Italo, Uncle Joe, and Uncle Tony. When Uncle Tony saw me, he called me over and hugged me. "Here, sit by me, Marisella."

Uncle Italo said, "Angelo DiMassi told me that they found the marble in one of the mountains outside of Coreno."

Coreno was the town in Italy that Papa's family had come from. Their land was situated outside the town, nestled in the small mountains that surrounded Coreno.

Uncle Joe raised his hand, replying, "He's probably exaggerating."

"He is your friend, Joe."

"*Ehh*, yes… he is. But he likes to tell tales sometimes."

"Maybe we should look into it," Uncle Tony said.

I could tell Uncle Joe was upset. His face always showed how he felt about things.

Joe swayed for a moment, thinking, then said, "I'll call my brother-in-law tonight and ask him to look into it."

"Who?" Italo asked.

"Mariano, Maria's brother. He lives there, still."

"Oh, yes," Italo said. "I forgot about him." Italo thought for a moment, then said, "I can check with Tomaso too. He still lives there."

*"Ehh,"* Joe said, raising his hand high. "We can't have the whole town running around checking for marble."

I looked at Papa. He was listening to his two older brothers, nodding with approval. That was Papa's way when he was around them. He never talked much, but deferred to them in all.

Uncle Tony asked, "What are we going to do with the land?"

Italo was about to answer, but Joe replied with hand raised, *"Ehh,* what can we do? Who has the money to take care of the land? Who has the money to go over there? Our life is here."

Italo answered now, "Maybe someday we will have the money, and we can take care of it for the family. Then, maybe, we can someday let our children go there and see where we came from."

Uncle Tony smiled. "That would be nice, Italo."

Papa nodded.

Moments later, I heard Aunt Jean's shrill voice. "Tony! Tony!"

Uncle Tony grimaced and looked up. "What, Jean?"

"C'mon. I want to go see my parents."

"Wait! Jean."

"Tony!" she cried out louder as she came around the corner.

"Jean, give me a few minutes," he lamented.

"Well, hurry up. I am going to fix them a plate. I want to leave now."

"OK, Jean."

She left, and Uncle Joe chuckled. "You better go, Tony, before you get in trouble."

The other men chuckled too, and Uncle Tony's countenance fell, but only for a moment. Then, he smiled, and I could see the love these brothers had for each other.

# The Preparation

We cooked and cleaned the house for the entire week before my First Communion Day. When I left for school on Friday morning, the dining room table was filled with trays of homemade Biscotti, Guanti, SalePeppe Cookies, Brownies, Cherry Strudel, and one Tortano. Only one thing was left to be baked: the Cassata Cake. Nonna told me that she would start it while I was in school and bake all three sections. When I got home, we put the layers of whipped cream, strawberries, and vanilla pudding together. It was carefully put into the refrigerator on Friday afternoon.

Papa and Mom came from the market and carried in two large baskets of peppers, announcing, "OK, it's time to cut the peppers."

"What are we making, Mom?"

"We are making sausage and peppers."

Papa, Mom, Nonna, and I sat at the table and began cutting peppers into long strips and putting them into two large baking pans. We were halfway done when the doorbell rang. A moment later, the door opened, and Uncle Tony and Aunt Jean came in.

"Marisella!" Jean started. "Are you ready for your big day? Oh, Brigida, I just came from work. There's big trouble down there. My boss got fired today. Everyone is so upset. What are you making? It smells good. He was having an affair with his secretary, and they fired him. They didn't fire her, though; we don't think that's fair. I told my father, and he is upset too. Marisella, are you ready to receive Jesus?

"JEANNA!" my father yelled, his face showing his despair at seeing her.

"What?"

"Sit down!"

Aunt Jean sat down, folding her hands, smiling. "Anyway, I am glad they fired him. It serves him right."

It seemed like Dad's eyes were vaulted to the ceiling, and Mom broke the mounting tension this time. "Jean, why don't you help us cut some peppers?"

"Oh, I can't. I just got my nails done." She held them out. "Do you like them, Marisella? Brigida, are you getting Marisa's nails done tomorrow? You should. Oh, you can't believe the trouble we had. It was…"

Papa got up and walked into the dining room, holding the pepper knife in his hand.

Uncle Tony said, "Jean. Let someone else talk."

"What? We are talking."

Jean leaned across the table. "Are you ready for your big day, Marisella?"

"Yes, Aunt Jean."

"Good." She looked at the clock. "Tony, come on. I want to get to Higbee's before they close."

"Jean, we have to help."

"They have plenty of help!" she said, getting up. "Let's go, Tony."

They left as fast as they had sat down. Papa returned, and we finished cutting the peppers, then retrieved several pieces of dried sausage from the basement and baked them all together into a savory dish. Afterward, we carefully put them into trays in the fridge. We were all ready.

Now, we waited for tomorrow's big event to come.

It was my First Communion Day.


## First Communion Day

All night long, I thought of this day and its importance. I was told it was a milestone in my life and an initiation, a step toward adulthood. Why? Because our culture said that I was no longer a child once my First Communion Day arrived. I was now responsible for my own actions, thoughts, and deeds. My actions had consequences. We called it the Age of Reasoning. I had made a vow to stop making childish remarks or blunders because I was receiving the Body and Blood of Christ.

In the morning, I rose early, excited as ever. Today was like my mini wedding day. I went into the kitchen, where Nonna was having coffee alone.

"Come here, my beautiful granddaughter."

I went over, and she hugged me tightly.

"I am very proud of you, Mari. I love you."

*I know, Nonna.*

"What would you like for breakfast?" she asked.

"Oatmeal and toast, please."

"OK. Sit down. I will make them for you."

After breakfast, a professional hairdresser arrived. She was Italian and lived in the neighborhood. We went down to the basement, and she set up a chair and covered me with a gown she had brought. It took almost an hour for her to cut, curl, and dry my hair, and then put gel in and dry it again. Finally, she was done, and she kissed me on the cheek and waited for Mom, Nonna, and Aunt Mary to come downstairs and marvel at how beautiful my hair was. From the moment I got out of the chair, I had to walk around, keeping my head nearly perfectly still to avoid messing it up. I also had to keep far away from my brother, who I was sure would find some way to disturb it.

Next, Aunt Mary came upstairs to help me get dressed. We went to my room, and I put on my new full-length slip. I was not used to wearing such a thing, and I really did not know why I had to. But once that was draped over my head, I stepped into my white leotards. Next, came my beautiful dress. I was almost ready. I twirled around smiling at Aunt Mary, then walked to my closet to look for my new white shoes.

They were gone.

I knew who had taken them.

I ran to Crispino's room. "Where are my shoes?"

He only shook his head, pretending he did not know.

I ran downstairs. "Mom, Nonna, Crispino took my shoes."

"Crispino!" Mom shouted

"I didn't take them!"

Mom charged upstairs. "Where are her shoes?"

"I don't have them!" he said convincingly.

I went into my room and began to look under my bed. Suddenly, the entire house was in an uproar, everyone looking for my shoes.

Papa was yelling downstairs, getting nervous.

Suddenly, we heard Crispino yell, "I found them!"

Everyone sighed with relief. He ran into my room a moment later, holding an old pair of my black tennis shoes. He set them down, and I kicked them away, shouting, "That's not them, and you know it." Now I was worried I had tilted my head too much and messed up my hair.

The uproar began again as we all started looking again.

Finally, I looked again under my bed and found them. I had already looked there earlier, so I knew my brother had snuck them in when no one was looking.

Shoes were found, I put them on, and we all went downstairs and got ready to leave for the church. We piled into our station wagon. I sat in front, in between Mom and Papa. Crispino sat in the back, in between Nonna and Nonno, with strict orders from Nonna not to touch my hair.

When we arrived, I went to the hall where the boys and girls were gathering. Everyone looked so wonderful in their clothes. When it was time, the nuns had us line up. We marched from the hall across the parking lot to the front of the church. Then we processed in. I remember seeing so many faces that I knew from my family and the Italian community. Everyone was there, dressed nicely, with their faces beaming.

When it was time to receive the Body and Blood of Jesus, I was so nervous. I walked up to my place on the kneeling rail and waited with my eyes closed. When I was given the small wafer and drink from the golden chalice, I remember thinking that this was the moment in my life when everything would change. I was no longer a child, but an adult. I closed my eyes, praying, asking Jesus to be close to me, as the nuns said we should pray.

The service ended, and we got home.

Now, the hard work began. First, I had to go to the front door and stand there to greet all the guests while Nonna and Mom and some of my aunts got all the food out and began heating it up.

The celebration began. Family after family arrived, congratulating me. Each one gave me an envelope that I had to put in a special box I was to keep behind me.

It was all exhausting. Finally, I was able to sit and eat. All eyes were on me, and everyone was telling me how pretty I looked. After eating, I went out to play in our driveway and courtyard with all the kids. But I quickly realized I would get my dress dirty, and since I didn't want to, I went back inside to the kitchen where all the women were gathered. I sat for a while, listening to their laughter, but then decided it was too noisy. So I went outside to sit by Papa, who was gathered with the men under the patio. I liked sitting by them and kept quiet, just like Papa, listening to them talk. They were much calmer than the women, and it suited me.

Near the end of the afternoon, Nancy from the masquerade shop came up to me and handed me a wrapped box, saying, "Here's your gift."

My eyes widened. Everyone else had given me an envelope.

"What is it?" I asked.

"Well, open it."

As I started to unwrap it, Nancy said, "I know how hard you work around here for your family, and I wanted to give you something just for you to enjoy."

I opened the box. There was a doll with a beautiful dress on it. With it were two other dresses. I could tell Nancy had made them. This must have been what she had been hiding from me.

It looked so beautiful to me. I had never had a doll before. I started to cry.

"Oh, Marisella," Nancy said, hugging me. "You are going to make me cry."

"Thank you, Nancy," I said, wiping away my tears.

Nancy left then almost right away, and my cousins ran over, wanting to see my doll. I felt bad, because I didn't want to give it to them. I was afraid they would ruin it. But I also knew I was an adult now and had to be responsible for my actions. So, I let them hold it. But I was very worried, especially that my brother would get hold of it. Sharing, like I was supposed to, did not make me feel any better, and I realized being an adult was going to be very hard.

The party ended, and my doll and its three dresses all stayed intact. Once everyone was gone, we all worked together to clean up, then we went to bed.

The ordinary days on our family farm on the tiny city lot in Cleveland were again before us, and the cycle of life, with its seasons and duties, would resume in the morning.

# Italo 1969

It was a long and hot summer that year. Mom was sick all the time. Nonna told me it was because she was expecting her baby. It meant that she had to lie down a lot after work. I not only had to keep my unruly brother from getting into trouble so Papa would not get mad, but now I also had to keep him quiet so Mom could sleep. All summer, I helped Nonna around the house, helping her cook, clean, wash, dry, and fold clothes. When it rained or was too cold to go outside, Nonna would also mend socks and other clothing. My job was to be her helper in everything, including this. She would get seven needles and cut seven pieces of thread, some white and some black. My job was to put the thread through the needles for her to do the job quickly. I would have the needles lined up and watch as Nonna took the sock or garment, chose the appropriate needle, and then quickly sewed it. I marveled at how fast she was and was proud I could help her go fast by lining up the threads in advance.

In the evenings and on Saturdays, I would spend a long time in the garden with Nonno. By now, I knew how to weed and was a much better helper for Nonno Ernesto. I was able to go into sections of the garden myself and pull all the weeds from around the plants. Since it was such a hot year, we had to spend extra time watering, so we were outside longer. It was a very tiring, hot summer.

~ ~ ~ ~

Very early on a Saturday morning, the phone rang. It woke me, and I looked into the living room. I saw Mom, still in her nightgown, walk from her room to answer it. It was unusual to see her not fully dressed. None of us ever came out of our rooms unless we were fully dressed. I listened.

"Hello?"

"What? Oh my God. No!" Mom started to cry. "Cresenz!" she called out.

She turned to the phone. "What happened? Oh my God. Oh, my God."

I was scared. I could hear the fear in her voice. Then, she cried out again, "Cresenz, come here quickly."

Papa must have known it was serious. He did not complain, but ran to the phone. "What happened?"

"Italo is dead!" Mom shouted mournfully.

Papa grabbed the phone. "What happened?"

"When?"

"No! Who did it?" he shouted.

Then, he handed the phone to my mom, stumbled backward toward the couch, fell down on it, and started to cry.

Nonno and Nonna got up and went into the living room. I followed them. "What happened?" Nonna asked excitedly, her eyes filled with fear I had never seen.

Mom replied between sobs, "Italo was shot. He died last night."

"Who shot him!" Nonna asked in a frantic tone.

"It was a robbery. When he was closing his store."

Papa shouted at the ceiling and began cursing. Nonna looked at me and called me over. She hugged me tightly. It still did not register with me. *Uncle Italo dead? Shot? How?* What did it all mean?

## Italo Wake and Land

That evening, we went to Uncle Italo and Aunt Mary's house. When we walked in, the house was already packed with people. Mom told me to go to the dining room table with the other children. I could not see it, but I knew where it was. I walked over, looking at the countless shoes of the men and women crowding the home. My cousins were sitting at the table coloring. No one said a word. I remember looking at my cousins and wondering what they were thinking about their dad being killed.

I stayed with them coloring until I saw Uncle Tony go out the side door. I slipped down from my chair and followed him out. "Uncle Tony, wait!"

He stopped and, through tear-stained eyes, tried to smile. Finally, he bent down, "Come here, Marisella."

I ran to him. He hugged me tightly, and I felt secure for the first time since hearing the news that morning. "Uncle Tony, I am sad."

"I know, Padina. We are all sad."

"Is Uncle Italo going to come back?"

"No, Padina. He is not coming back." Uncle Tony looked into the sky and pointed. "But he is in Heaven now. Someday, we will see him again."

I peered into Uncle Tony's warm eyes. He was trying to be strong for me, but I could see water pockets forming in his eye wells. Finally, he stood up, and I took him by the hand. We walked back to Aunt Mary's patio in the back, where a number of men were gathered.

I sat next to Uncle Tony. I could see Papa across from me. He looked at me, nodded slightly, then looked down at the ground, his face fixed in grief.

One of the men asked, "How did they find him?"

Uncle Joe answered, "The side door of the bar found him. He had been shot twice, and his body was draped over the iron fence." Joe wiped his eyes and stared down at the ground. "Dammit! All for some damn money."

"Was it a robbery?" one of the men asked.

Uncle Joe replied, "Yes, it was."

Uncle Tony said, "I don't understand it, though, Joe. The bag of money from the bar was sitting next to the fence, not that far from him. I don't know how they did not see it."

Uncle Joe said, "Yeah, Tony, I don't either. But they went through his pockets. They stole his wallet and however much money he had. They robbed him."

"It sounds to me like they were waiting for him. But I don't understand why they did not take the bag of money."

Uncle Joe raised his hand high in the air, shaking it. "Aye, how do you… we know why they did anything? They killed my brother. I will find out who did this… and…" He glanced at me, then at the other men, and just nodded.

Papa raised his hand in the air, and with his voice rising, said, "Italo called me!"

"What?" the man next to him said.

With his voice rising even louder, Papa said, "He called me!"

"When?" Uncle Tony asked.

"Friday after work. He said he was coming tomorrow to tell me something very important. Some good news, he said."

Uncle Joe grew quiet.

Uncle Tony asked, "What news, Cris?"

Papa began grimacing, cursing at the ground, shaking his head.

Uncle Joe asked, "What did he say, Cris?"

Papa did not reply.

Uncle Joe's face tightened. "Cresenz! What did Italo say to you?"

Papa exclaimed even louder, his voice still rising, "I don't know."

"He didn't say anything?" Joe asked.

"No, he just said it was good news for the whole family."

Joe looked at everyone. "Hey, we will never know now."

I wondered what Uncle Italo wanted to tell my dad. Did it have to do with the land they had talked about a few months earlier? Of course, no one brought that up, but it was a question in my mind.

***

The next night, we were brought to the wake. It was the first time I was ever at one. All the women were crying or talking in mournful and quiet voices. The men were mostly silent. We got into a line that began outside the door. It took a very long time to get to the front of it. There, Aunt Mary stood with her daughters seated on chairs next to her. Then, not far away, I saw Uncle Italo lying in the casket. I almost screamed. I had not expected to see him, and the more I looked at him, the more afraid I was that he would suddenly sit up.

He looked so normal.

The rest of the night was a blur. Seeing Uncle Italo had really shaken me up. I could tell it shook up my brother, too. He did not say much the rest of the night. All I wanted to do was go home and go to sleep.

# A Quiet Year

That summer went very slowly. Papa was not his nervous self, and I actually missed it. He was very quiet, carrying the weight of losing his oldest brother. Papa had always looked up to Italo. Italo was everything Papa wanted to be. He was funny, outgoing, likable, and a good talker. Papa was none of those things, and I think that is why he looked up to Italo so much. Losing him was devastating to Papa.

At the end of summer, I turned eight years old and started third grade. The harvest time came, and with it, weeks and weeks of difficult work. It was all made harder this year because of the grieving the whole family was going through, especially Papa. But we went on and did what we had to do, canning the tomatoes, peppers, eggplants, olives, and making the sausage. By late October, we had finished. The necessity of our small farm in the city distracted us from the deep void of missing Uncle Italo.

The winter passed uneventfully, colder than I had ever known. My Aunt Mary and her five young daughters were immersed in grief and shock for the entire winter. In the spring, life returned with the time for new planting. Nonno Ernesto led the way. He was the strong man in our family, the patriarch, the quiet rock who led us now into the new seasons of the year.

Another summer rolled in, with all its chores surrounding our family farm, came and went.

~ ~ ~ ~

The start of the school year was perfectly aligned with the start of the harvest season. So, every year, the first two all-important months of school were also the months I had to work night and day with the other adults in my family to finish the work of our tiny farm in the city.

No one at my school, even my cousins, could understand this. It was my secret world, away from the world of normal boys and girls at school, where I spent my life.

## Bruno and Giacomo

That year, just after the early November winds swept the rest of the leaves off the trees in the city, we received the news. Uncle Giacomo and Uncle Bruno were coming to America to live with us. Giacomo was the second oldest son of Nonno and Nonna. He was twenty-one years old and had decided to give America a try. Bruno was the youngest son of Nonno and Nonna. He was only fifteen years old. He had wanted to stay in Italy when his parents first came to America, but now he, too, wanted to find out what it was all about.

Papa and Mom argued briefly about how we would fit them in the house, but Mom insisted that they had to live with us. Finally, it was agreed that Giacomo, Bruno, and Crispino would stay in one room. My parents would stay in their room, and Nonna and Nonno kept their room. I was to sleep on the sofa fold-out bed just inside the living room.

I was excited at this chance. It felt like a great adventure to me. Finally, I got to be in the wide-open room that could see all three bedrooms. I could not wait for them to arrive so I could begin sleeping there.

Within the month, they arrived. It was a time of great joy and excitement for us all, especially for Nonna, who had not seen her sons in over two years. I had never met either of these uncles from Italy either, and I immediately liked them. Both of them were very kind and gave me someone to talk with besides my little brother. They also spent time talking with him and chasing after him, which gave me some relief.

Suddenly, our house was bursting at the seams, and a new baby would be coming soon.

## Robin Hood Flour

Within a short time, Giacomo and Bruno found jobs. Now, the needs of our family grew, as did my duties. We now had five people going to work every day. Lunches for all five had to be made and carefully packed in the refrigerator the night before. That meant bread. Lots of bread.

Nonno Ernesto immediately constructed a five-foot-long, handmade wooden box. It reminded me of a coffin, which scared me, but only at first. The box held twenty-five pounds of Robin Hood Flour. I liked seeing the Robin Hood Flour logo as Nonna poured the flour into the casket-like contraption to knead the dough. The yeast was next to be put in. Nonna carefully poured the melted yeast into a hole in the middle of the huge mound of flour. It looked like a bird's nest. The nest would allow the yeast to be gradually mixed through the flour. Next, the salt was added by pouring Morton's Salt in Nonna's cupped hand until the salt overflowed, spilling over into the trough so as not to waste any.

I asked Nonna if we should measure, and she smiled, saying, "Measuring is not the Italian way, Marisella. You have to learn how much to put in by using your hands. This way, we keep it simple."

Now the hard work of kneading the dough began. It was very hard for me because I was very thin and petite. I did not have the strength needed, and no matter if I stood on the floor or on a chair, I did not have the stature to reach the bottom of the wooden trough. It took us a long time, standing over the long trough, punching and turning the dough, adding water and flour, until finally, we had the perfect texture. Punching the dough gave me a rare opportunity to get my frustrations out. As the oldest daughter, who was now nine years old, and an adult, who needed to think like an adult, there was no chance for me ever to complain. Punching the dough was my way of taking the air out of the balloon.

After that, we covered it with towels and folded tablecloths to allow the first rise. During this time, we had to be quiet to avoid disturbing the process. Once it rose the first time, we had to punch it down again, then cut it and roll it into the baking pans. Those, too, had to be covered and allowed to rise. It was my job to make sure my brother stayed away. This was hard because he wanted to peek under the coverings to see if it was rising.

We made bread every Saturday morning, usually fifteen loaves. Then, Nonna would say to me, "Mari, when the dough finishes rising, I will give you your own little piece, and we will make your own loaf of bread and your own little pizza." This was always the reward for my hard work, and it made the hours pass quickly.

Feeding eight people was an enormous job, and bread was the main staple of our diet. Each night at dinner, we would have at least a loaf, which Nonno would cut into slices and pass out. After dinner, Nonna and I would cut ten thick slices of bread and make five large sandwiches. These were carefully wrapped and put into bags in the refrigerator for tomorrow's lunches.

The entire house would smell of the delicious scent on Saturdays when it came out of the oven. Everyone would be stopping in, no matter if they were coming or going, to slice the fresh bread and cover it with butter.

The bread was never wasted. At the end of each meal, Nonno would scrape the bread crumbs from the table into his hand and crumble them up. He would then take them out the side door and scatter them for the birds. And at the end of the week, on Friday afternoons, if bread was left over, we kissed it first and gave it to the birds outside. If the bread was not properly stored or forgotten and left to harden, which happened if someone forgot to wrap the bread properly, we would take the hardened bread and make La Zuppa di Latte—my favorite pauper's meal.

It was hardened bread broken into pieces and boiled with milk with sugar on top. The concoction was so so tasty. My family never bragged about it because it was a staple food of the poorest of the poor in Italy. Nevertheless, I am not afraid to write about this recipe because it is what we ate.

Another fine meal was hardened bread at the bottom of a bowl, covered with ladles of cooked cannellini beans, lentils, or white navy beans, and topped with cooked salted dandelions. But my favorite meal with bread that was fresh or hardened, was with tomato squeezed over it, so the juice and seeds of the tomato covered the bread. I used to have this every day in the summer and fall when the tomatoes began ripening in the garden.

## Lite Brite

At Christmas time, Uncle Tony and Aunt Jean visited. They gave me a wrapped square box. I had never received such a large gift. "What is it?" I asked.

"Why don't you open it, Padina?"

"OK," I said, as I carefully unfastened the wrapping paper. We never wasted wrapping paper if we could. Nonna had a place in the pantry where we kept folded pieces of it, along with salvaged ribbons and bows for future use.

I slowly opened the box and the words Lite Brite appeared. I marveled at it, wondering what it was.

"What does it do?" Mom asked.

Aunt Jean remarked, "You can make pictures out of lights."

"Really?" Mom said.

Jean's eyes widened. "My brother's kids have one. They love it. Oh, I hope he doesn't send them to public school. It's a big mess over there, Brigida."

Papa scowled at her, then looked at the floor, deeply troubled.

Uncle Tony got up. "Come with me, Padina. I will show you how it works."

We went into the living room, and Uncle Tony said, "We need a dark place."

"In the pantry," I said.

"Is there an outlet in there?"

"Yes," I said as I ran to the pantry. Our pantry was a walk-in kind. There were rows and rows of shelves filled with all kinds of foods stretching from floor to ceiling. I showed him where the plug was. Uncle Tony plugged it in, and the bright light came on. He then put a black piece of paper with a pattern printed on it over the grid. I started placing the tiny colored bulbs, punching each one into the matching holes along with the pattern into the grid. My eyes lit up. I had never in my life seen something more beautiful.

"Do you see how to do it, Padina?"

"Yes," I said excitedly. I could see the beginnings of an image I was forming.

Uncle Tony went out, and I kept putting the little colored bulbs into the paper holes. Finally, when I was done, a beautiful clown face appeared on the screen. It was the most fantastic thing I ever saw, and in that small little dark pantry with my Lite Brite, for the first time, I felt I had a hiding place, a hiding place that belonged all to me.

I enjoyed the Lite Brite and often went into the food pantry to enjoy the little time I had for myself. I relished my Lite Brite time alone with no interruptions.

The shelves above me were filled with stuff like extra flour, sugar, crackers, and snacks. I would occasionally get hungry and get up and climb up on the counter to reach the shelf with my choice of snack that was available to me.

Being alone in the dark panty, lit only by a picture of light I was creating, gave me peace of mind, an escape from whatever was happening around me. When I finished my "masterpiece," I quickly and quietly took all the colored pegs out and put my Lite Brite carefully back into the box. This would be where I would come when my energy waned or was zapped by my family; Lite Brite provided an outlet, and I looked forward to the next time.

For the rest of Christmas vacation, whenever I had a free moment, I would go into the pantry and lock the door, so my brother could not come in and play with my Lite Brite. It was very special to me because it was all mine and because I would make beautiful colorful designs with it.

Our pantry, where I played alone with the Lite Brite, gave me hope when I felt despair. When I was hurt, offended, or punished with the tree branch, the Lite Brite was my anchor.

## Another Baby

In the deep of winter, right after Christmas, Mom felt pains and said she had to go to the hospital. We had just finished dinner. Papa drove her while the rest of us took a break from the normal evening chores and turned on the TV, anxiously waiting for the news. The next morning there was none, so I went to school, and Nonno, Giacomo, and Bruno went to work. I wondered and prayed that everything would be OK all that day in school. I don't know why I was taught to do that. I was never told anything about having babies, and I did not understand it, but somehow, I knew that I had to pray.

When I got home, there was still no news. Then, finally, the phone rang as we were getting ready to sit down for dinner. Nonna signaled to the rest of us that she would answer. She went over to the only phone we had in the dining room.

"Hello?"

"Cresenz. What is the news?"

"A son! Congratulations!" Nonna said heartily. She held the phone to her chest and turned to us. "They have a son."

Nonna listened, then asked, "How is Brigida?"

"Oh, good." She turned to us again. "She's OK!"

Nonna was quiet, then asked, "What is his name?"

"What?"

"Daniel? Oh, why Daniel?"

"You don't know either? It's OK, Cresenz. That is a good name. We will call him Danny."

When she hung up, she came into the kitchen. We were all smiling. Uncle Giacomo said, "Congratulations," to his parents. "You are grandparents again."

"Thank you," Nonna replied. She turned to me.

"Marisella, Crispino, you have a brother now. Congratulations to you!" She raised her hand, shaking it. The long and terrible days of taking care of Crispino came to mind suddenly. And I knew that along with the joy of new life, a lot of work would come for me.

## Taking Care of Baby

Once Mom and the new baby came home from the hospital, changes began again inside our small city home. Papa and Uncle Tony set up the crib in my parents' room. Mom had to rest for a few weeks, which only meant that Nonna and I had to work harder because we had to take care of her during her recovery.

At first, only Mom nursed the baby and changed the baby. He was beautiful, and now that I was nine years old and an adult thinker, I saw him differently than I had seen my brother Crispino as a baby. I was starting to understand how a family grew and grew up.

These mysteries and ideas stayed with me each day when I was at school. Because I was a visual learner, I had to memorize everything. Because I still spoke only the Italian language at home, and English was very new to me, I had lots of time to think and daydream. My life and its difficult work ethic made the school the place where I would think about everything I had to do and endure.

About a month after Mom came home, she returned to working full time in early February. Now, Nonna and I had to take care of the baby. My duties helping to feed, burp, and change his diapers began in earnest. Diaper patrol also began, launched by placing a bucket down the basement to hold the dirty cloth diapers. Dirty diapers had to be emptied into the toilet and brought into the basement. Since it was still winter, once they were washed, we had to hang them up on clotheslines in the basement to dry until they could be folded. I was familiar with the entire process and routine, but when I was only five, the task did not feel as daunting as it did now. Now, it was another duty added to the already strained daily tasks of helping Nonna take care of eight people.

This was a hard winter for me, and in the moments I could find, more so in the evening than any other time, I would sneak away into the pantry to my hiding place and my Lite Brite.

## Uncle Mario at Easter

During the week before Easter Sunday that year, we had more news. Papa's sister from Connecticut was coming to visit with her husband, Mario, and their three children. Immediately, the preparations began in earnest. The house was cleaned from top to bottom. Foods were purchased, and meals were planned. Blankets were taken down from the closet shelves so the visitors could sleep on the couches. Of course, they would stay with us, as they were immigrants, just like us. Immigrants did not stay in hotels.

Aunt Theresa, Uncle Mario, and their three children pulled into the driveway near lunchtime, beeping their horn. Immediately, the fun began. I did not remember ever meeting my Aunt Theresa, but she had met me. She was my godmother. Uncle Tony was my godfather.

Aunt Theresa's voice was soft, slightly pitched, and fell upon you like a blanket of flowers. Her demeanor was kind and warm, and gentle. Her husband, Uncle Mario, was very different. He spoke with a deep Italian accent, filled with confidence and ladened with a perpetual sense of humor. I liked him right away. He said my name in a way no one else ever did, with a deep roll on the "ll's."

"Marisella!" he would say. "Come over here and tell me about how bad your brothers are." Everyone would chuckle, and I would go over and play along. Uncle Mario was taller than any of the other men and broader. He was a landscaper for wealthy people in Connecticut and New York. He was an immigrant from Italy, too, though not from the same places Mom or Papa were from.

Uncle Mario immediately began teasing my brother. "Crispino!" he called out through the living room. "Come over here so I can pull your nose."

Not ever having had his nose pulled, Crispino ran up to him. Uncle Mario put one hand on the back of his head, and the other hand took hold of Crispino's nose. "Do you want me to pull your nose? It's too short, but I can fix it for you."

Crispino only scrunched his face and turned slightly, with his eyes widened, as if beckoning the audience if he should allow it. Everyone laughed again, and Uncle Mario gave a squeeze to his nose.

"*Ow,*" Crispino said, running to the room's other side.

Within a half hour, an extravagant meal was on the table, and we all gathered around. My new cousins and I tried to play, but it was too cold outside, so all we could really do was go down to the basement or sit around listening to the adults talk and laugh.

Uncle Mario announced as soon as we finished eating, "We are all going to the movies. My treat."

Immediately, the whole room erupted in fun. We rarely went to the movies, except for going to see Italian movies on Saturday afternoon at the Italian theater. This was not what Uncle Mario was talking about, though.

"What are we going to see?" Mom asked.

"*Ehh,* we can pick when we get there. But the theater I saw had *The Poseidon Adventure* showing when I drove here. I heard it's a good movie."

"The what?" Mom asked.

"It is about a big boat that turns upside down."

Aunt Theresa chimed in, "Mario, do you think they will like it?"

"I don't know, but let's go see." He turned to Crispino. "Crispino, you sit by me at the movies so I can pull your nose!" Everyone started laughing, and we all piled into the cars and drove to the movie theater.

Going inside the giant theater felt magical. The plush carpeted aisles felt soft on our feet, and walking downward caused us all to go faster. The screen was black and enormous. This was very different from the small neighborhood Italian theater we visited.

When the movie came on, we all sat silent and spellbound—even Crispino. Except for Mom having to step out to change or feed the baby, no one made a sound. Never had I seen something so amazing that moved my emotions. I cried many times during the movie, wanting to see the people live, as so many died.

When we came home, all the talk was about the movie. The pot of sauce and the pan of meatballs were taken from the refrigerator and set to warm. A large pot of boiling water for pasta was started, and Mom, Nonna, and I began making a large salad.

When we were about to eat, there was a knock at the door. Papa nervously got up. I could see he was growing anxious that so many people were crowded in the kitchen. To Papa, that meant that there would be a mess, and Papa could not handle messes.

The door opened. It was Uncle Tony and Aunt Jean.

Immediately, the joyful reunion began. Uncle Tony and Aunt Theresa were very close in age and had been best friends when they were younger. They had not seen each other in a long time.

After a while, everyone sat back down as Papa nervously took his place at the table.

Aunt Jean started in, "How is the baby, Brigida? I haven't seen him in a while? Is he growing?"

Mom put her fork down. "He is sleeping right now, Jean. As soon as he wakes up, you can hold him."

"Oh, that sounds nice. How is New York, Theresa? My father says that New York is going to the birds. Too much crime. He has a cousin who lives there. They talk about it every week, and the stories get worse. Oh, hi, Marisella. How are you doing with your little brother?"

"We live in Connecticut, Jean. Not New York."

"What!"

"Anyway, Annette is starting school soon. Tony wants to send her to public school. But I don't want to. My brother's kids are ruined by them. I'm still mad at him. My father is too. It's big troub—"

"Jean! Stop!" Pappa yelled.

Everything grew quiet.

I don't think Uncle Mario or Aunt Theresa had seen Aunt Jean in action in a long time.

Uncle Mario turned to Crispino and said, "Crispino, Jean reminds me of a lady on TV in Connecticut who talks a lot and has a big nose."

Everyone started laughing.

Jean's brow furrowed, and she nudged Tony and whispered something.

"Jean!" Tony said. "He is only joking."

"You should see this lady!" Mario continued. "She is a commentator on the news. If the camera turns even the littlest bit, her entire nose falls off the screen."

Crispino put his head down and started laughing.

Nonna said, "Mario, leave Jean alone. Let's eat!"

The meal resumed, but I knew from that moment that Mario did not like Jean and that Jean would never like Mario either.

The laughs, fun times, trips to go out for pizza, and all Uncle Mario's treat, continued for five days, and then they went home. It had felt like a vacation to me, and I longed for the days when they would return.

***

Spring planting and another long hot summer spent caring for the garden came and passed. As the end of August approached, I got ready for my ninth birthday and for the start of fourth grade.

With all its excitement, the start of a new school year, including now the boys and girls beginning to notice each other more, could never settle upon me. The home was my main life. Taking care of my brother Crispino, who was five, was difficult. Taking care of Danny, just a baby, was even more difficult. My duties and responsibilities with Nonna were also demanding.

It was often late at night when I could try to do the homework I had been given that day. Tired as I felt at times, I knew I had to keep going as I was expected, along with everyone else, to do my part in helping our immigrant family.

# Book Bag

I was nine years old and nearing the end of fourth grade. It was early May and the middle days of spring when school began to get hot inside, and all of us children began thinking of it ending and going home for summer. For me, that would mean spending endless days as Nonna's helper and taking our free time to play in the driveway and patio area with my six-year-old brother.

My cousins and I all attended the same grade school, though we were all in different grades. Being close in age and living in the same neighborhood, we saw a lot of each other.

One day, after drinking our chocolate milk, my favorite, at recess, we ran outside in the school parking lot to get some fresh air. Uncle Joe's oldest son, Armando, was picking on my older cousin Rosemary and wouldn't stop.

Rosemary began to shout at him and started to cry. Her voice sounded like a whistling train getting louder to announce the departure.

We had all been taught a long time ago that boys did not pick on girls. I was mad at Armando. Yes, his dad was, in a way, the new head of our family now that Uncle Italo was gone. What made me even madder was that Rosemary was Uncle Italo's daughter. Armando should be showing her respect.

Recess ended, and we went back to our classrooms.

After school, the bickering between Rosemary and Armando picked up what where it left off, while Carlo and I watched and tried to tell them to stop.

I had been to the gym for my last class, so I wore my tennis shoes and had my thick, black-soled school shoes in my bookbag. I stood near Rosemary as she yelled at Armando. Carlo, of course, stood by his brother. Suddenly, Armando lurched forward and pushed her down in the parking lot.

He stepped forward and was not watching me. So, I twirled my boot bag in the air and thrust it at his head. The heel of my shoe inside the bag hit him near his temple, just above his eye.

Armando began crying, and a small stream of blood began to trickle down his face.

Momentarily, I felt relieved that he was crying like he made Rosemary cry. But in the next moment, I realized I was in big trouble. So, I ran all the way home, quietly put my apron on, and began to help Nonna.

During dinner, the phone rang. Mom got up to get it. I felt a pit fall into my stomach. I nervously began eating my food, pretending not to listen.

"Hello?"

"Aye, Maria. Hold on. Slow down. What happened? Stitches! How many? Who? Marisella!"

There was quiet. I swallowed my food and put my fork down. I looked up at Nonna. She was watching me with curiosity.

"Yes, yes. I will talk to her. Yes, I will make sure she is punished. Yes, you can tell Joe."

Mom hung up and turned to face the kitchen. "Mari, come over here."

I quickly got up and went into the dining room with my head down, listening to Papa behind me shouting, "What happened?"

Mom shouted into the kitchen, "Armando has some stitches. He's OK."

When I got into the dining room, Mom pulled me into the living room so everyone could not hear us. I told her the story, leaving nothing out. She was quiet for a moment, then said, "Mari, I have to punish you. Uncle Joe and Aunt Maria are very upset. You should not have hit him with your bookbag."

I started to cry. Mom stood up and went outside. She returned with a tree branch and told me to come down to the basement.

I heard my Nonno say, "Brigida, what's going on?"

But Mom only replied, "Marisella has to be punished for something."

I mournfully followed her down the basement steps.

"OK," Mom said. "Stand here." She pointed nervously.

I stood there, shaking, and was beginning to cry.

"Now bend over," Mom said.

"No, Mom, please."

"Mari, bend over. You have to be punished."

I nervously bent over, now crying harder.

Suddenly, I heard the whoosh and felt the sting on my legs. I screamed and jumped.

"Stand still, Mari. Now bend over."

I obediently stepped back into position.

*Whoosh!*

"Mom! Stop!" I screamed.

Mom said, "No, one more time. Now bend over."

I bit my teeth together and bent down once more.

*Whoosh!*

I cried and cried. I turned to look at Mom and saw a tear in her eye. She had not wanted to do this. All I could think about was Uncle Joe and the scar on his face.

# Tooth Fairy 123

Not long after Uncle Mario and Aunt Theresa left, I suddenly had a loose tooth. In the past, Nonna would help me over a few days to wiggle it out, but since Uncle Giacomo now lived with us, he got involved. Uncle Giacomo was a very handsome young man with tan skin and a warm smile that disarmed everyone. You could never be mad at Uncle Giacomo.

"Marisella, we have to get the Italian Tooth Fairy involved."

"Who is that?" I asked.

"He is very practical. He gives you money for your tooth. Then he gives it back, so you can bury it. This brings good luck."

"He does?" I asked, confused. "How does he give it back?"

"He takes it from your pillow and hides it somewhere. So, we have to find it. And the best part: he is rich and leaves more money than the American Tooth Fairy. Now, let me see your tooth."

I opened my mouth as the fear of the pain I was about to feel mounted.

Uncle Giacomo said, "Say *Ahh.*"

"*Ahhhhhhh.*"

"Oh, I see, *hmmm*. This will be a tough one."

He gently placed his finger on the top of the tooth. "*Hmmmm.* I think this one is almost ready. Say '*Ahhhh*' again."

*"Ahhhhhh."*

"OK, wiggle it with your tongue."

I swallowed and began to wiggle the tooth.

"OK, I think I can take it out. Are you ready?"

"Yeth…." I said with mumbled words.

"OK, 1, 2, 3."

I closed my eyes tightly. Nothing. I closed my mouth. "Did you pull it?"

"No, I didn't think you were ready," he said with his warm, gentle smile. "OK, let's do it again. Say *'Ahhhh.'*"

I shivered and swallowed, trying to be brave. *"Ahhhhhhh."*

I felt his finger on the top of the tooth. He said, "OK, 1, 2, 3. Oh, wait a minute. I am not ready."

I closed my mouth and sighed.

"Let me take one more look. Say *'Ahhhhh'.*"

*"Ahhhhhh."*

He placed his finger on top of the tooth. "I think this is ready, Marisella. Are you ready, though?"

Before I could answer, I felt the tooth snatched away.

"Ow!" I said.

"Oh, look at here. It practically jumped out on its own. Are you OK?"

I held my lips tightly together, nodding.

"Now, I will contact the Italian Tooth Fairy, and tonight we will put it under your pillow."

***

The next morning, I found two dollar bills under my pillow. I could not believe it. Of course, I knew it was make-believe, but it didn't matter. The Italian Tooth Fairy Uncle Giacomo introduced me to was my new favorite tooth fairy.

Later, Uncle Giacomo came to me and told me he had found my tooth. So we took it down to the basement and put it between the cracks in the basement wall. It was our way of bringing good luck.

# Piano Lessons

Right after Easter time, Mom told me she would meet me after school for a surprise. All day I wondered what it would be. When I got out, she was standing in front of the school. She smiled and greeted me, then took me by the hand. Instead of walking home, we walked the other direction from school, further away from home, down W. 65th Street, a busy street lined with small storefronts and homes.

"Where are we going, Mom?" I asked.

"I am signing you up for piano lessons, Mari. Would you like to play the piano?"

"I would like that."

"Good. You can come here after school two days a week. But you have to come right home after."

I immediately began to grow nervous and quickly looked behind me to see the now-distant school. My mind was on overdrive, trying to memorize how to get there and, more importantly, how to get home. I was paying little attention to where we were going and more to where we had come from.

We reached a storefront that had a sign in the window. "Piano Lessons."

Mom bent down and turned me around. "See, Mari, there is the school. You walk there and then go home the normal way."

I looked nervously down the street. She was right. St. Coleman could be seen, not too far. Still, I felt fearful.

Mom rang the doorbell, and an older woman, with glasses, and brown and gray hair, wrapped up in a bun, answered. "Hello, Mrs. DiRuggiero. Come in."

She was wearing a thick blue dress and plain brown shoes. She walked slowly and led us to a small room with a piano. There were three plain wooden chairs next to it and a long wooden bench in front of it.

"Please, sit down," she said, pointing to the chairs.

I looked around the room, with its worn green wallpaper and single window looking into an alley behind her shop. Her shop was clean, with a faded light brown tile floor. A special light was on top of the piano, pointing at the place where books were opened over the keyboard. I was excited.

The woman started, "Is this Marisella?"

"Yes," Mom replied.

"Hello, Marisella, I am Mrs. Dembeck. I will be your piano teacher."

I smiled as my dangling feet gently kicked back and forth in the chair.

"Did you come right from school?" she asked.

I nodded.

"Well, would you like a cookie?"

I hesitated for a moment, then said, "Yes, I would."

She went into another room and returned with a small plate of chocolate chip cookies. I was so happy. I rarely got to eat normal cookies, only the Italian kind we made ourselves for dipping in coffee. Besides, I was starving, as Mom had not thought to bring a snack.

She told me to take a few, then offered some to my mom. After eating them, she had me sit on the piano bench while Mom watched.

I could hardly reach the keys. Mrs. Dembeck said, "Oh, I think you need a boost."

She got a telephone book, set it on the bench, and I sat on it. "OK, now sit up straight, and keep your chin lifted."

She sat next to me and began showing me which keys were which.

After a while, the lesson ended. Mom thanked her, and Mrs. Dembeck said, "OK, Marisella. You come here right after school on Tuesday and Wednesday each week. I will have some cookies for you, and we can get started."

"Okay, Mrs. Dembeck. Thank you."

Mrs. Dembeck then asked, "Will she have a piano at home?"

Mom sighed. "I am talking to my husband about getting one. But our neighbor has one she can use to practice a few days a week."

"Okay, good." Mrs. Dembeck bent down, peering into my eyes. "Practice is very important, Marisella. I will go over all that with you in our first lesson tomorrow."

I was so excited. I could not believe I would learn how to play the piano.

# Party Line

Our telephone was in a central location in our home. The red chair had an arm-shaped desk and a space underneath the arm for the telephone book.

Now that Uncle Giacomo and Uncle Bruno were with us, the use of the phone went up. Still, even if the phone was free, you might not be alone. Many times, someone else would be on the phone. I had no one to call, so I only noticed that my parents and the other adults in the family would pick up the phone to make a call and have to say, "Sorry, I will try later." It was called a party line. Party lines meant we had to share. Party lines meant we had to be patient. Party lines meant we knew what, who, when, and where someone else in the neighborhood talked to or talked about. It was a very public forum.

But to us, as an immigrant family in America, when the phone rang, all else stopped. "Answer the phone!" someone would shout, hoping that whoever was near the phone would get to it before it stopped ringing. So many days, the phone would ring when Nonna and I were down in the basement doing laundry or seeing to the cellar. Since we were the only people home, she would say, "Wait here, Mari," and take off running all the way upstairs to reach the one phone before it stopped ringing.

We had strict rules for the adults. No one was allowed to be on the phone for long. That was our rule. It didn't matter to me, but it was central in our home, and so was the entire drama surrounding it.

# Kick Ball

Near the end of the school year, we went out at recess to play kickball.

The bases were set up, and the teams were chosen. As usual, I was the dead last person to be chosen. However, it didn't bother me because I was one of the smallest children and was neither very coordinated nor strong. In other words, I was not of much use to either team.

Because of this, I played in the outfield. Usually, my team had another player next to me, also playing my part in the outfield. I was also the last one up to kick. When my turn finally arrived, we found ourselves in the position of having two runners on base and two outs. It was now up to me to kick the ball for a hit, so the other runners could come home. I felt the nervousness in my stomach as I walked up to stand behind home plate. In a moment, the boy rolling the ball in would send it to me. I would have to run up, kick it, and run to first base.

The children next to me were cheering me on, "Come on, Marisella. Just run up and kick it hard. You can do it."

Suddenly the red rubber ball was rolling across the pavement toward home plate. I began to feel my legs shudder in fear. Then, finally, I broke free, took two awkward steps forward, and let my foot fly. I hit the top of the ball, sending it spinning toward the pitcher and sending me twirling and landing, twisting my ankle. I lay still on the ground and then started to cry. My ankle was throbbing.

Just then, the recess bell rang, and the kids ran toward the doors. One of the girls in my class, Maria, helped me up. I was in tremendous pain. I held her shoulder and hopped into school. My classroom was on the ground floor, so I did not have to go up any steps. My immediate fear was I was going to get in trouble. Papa would kill me if he found out I got hurt playing kickball. Girls were not supposed to play sports.

I hopped into the classroom before the teacher came in. We had a few more classes, and then she dismissed us for the day.

I carefully limped out of the class with Maria's help. My teacher was busy talking with another student and did not notice. From there, I held Maria's shoulder and began hopping again. I was sure I had broken my ankle, and now I worried about what I would tell my parents. If I had to go to the hospital, it would cost a lot of money, and Papa would be very angry.

I hopped from the school side door to Lorain Avenue with Maria's shoulder as my crutch. Once we got to Lorain, Maria had to go the other way. She was already in trouble for taking too long to get home. From there, I turned and hopped, holding onto the buildings on Lorain until finally, I reached Nancy's Masquerade Shop, the store before my home.

I usually stopped there every day, just for a few minutes, to say hello. Nancy always smiled at me, encouraged me, and asked me how I was doing. I felt like my own person around Nancy. So, I popped my head in. "Hi, Nancy. I hurt my ankle," I said with a hop. "I cannot visit today."

"Why not?" she asked, peering down at my one leg while I stood in the door.

"I twisted my ankle," I said, cringing and holding onto the door.

"Oh, let me see," she said as she got up from her desk and walked to the door. She held open the door and said, "Hold onto me." She bent down and looked at my now black and blue ankle. "Marisella, why didn't they help you at school?"

"I didn't tell anyone," I said as tears welled up in my eyes.

"Why not?" she asked, as her hands gently felt around the foot and ankle.

"I am afraid to get in trouble," I blurted out, then I started crying.

It was then a customer came out of the back costume room. Nancy stood up and told the customer, "I will be right back. I have to walk this little girl next door."

Nancy helped me to hop the rest of the way to my side door.

She knocked, and Nonna answered.

Nancy said, "Rosa, Marisa hurt her ankle at school. She will tell you. I have a customer waiting." And she hugged me and left.

As soon as Nonna helped me in, she started with a million questions, chief among them pointing up at the clock and wanting to know where I had been. I tried to explain to her, but she kept going on. I had really scared her by not being home on time.

I hobbled over to the red chair in the dining room, the only chair next to the only phone we had in our house. I sat down. Finally, my long journey that started when I twisted my ankle was over. I would not be able to help with any of the chores Nonna needed to have done. My brother, Crispino, came running up, wanting to know what happened. I told him nothing, but just asked him to stay back.

Nonna went and got a pan of warm water and put Epsom salt inside it. I was unable to set the table, which was one of my chores daily before supper and necessary for family harmony. I had a sinking feeling in my stomach. I blew it. I knew I blew it, and on top of that, I had a headache because Nonna had interrogated me. I never wanted to disappoint my best friend in the world, and I saw clearly that I had.

Nonna got an ace bandage and wrapped my foot. I had to hop around the house for the rest of the night and sit in the living room. Luckily for me, Papa was at work, and I would be in bed before he came home. Still, every other member of the family, including Mom, Nonno, Uncle Giacomo, and Uncle Bruno, had to personally find out from me what happened. And I told the story over and over.

Their responses were all the same: "Sports are not for young girls!" Mom even told me, "Marisella, you are trying too hard to make friends with the other children. You don't have to be like them when you should try to just be yourself." They all also wanted to know why I didn't tell anyone at school. I was afraid to tell them it was because Papa would get mad. If I told them that, it would only start an argument between my parents.

My reasoning was more, though. We only had one car. Who was going to pick me up? I knew this, but I did not tell them the obvious.

*** 

The next day, Mom told Papa she needed the car for the day. She drove him to work, and came home, and drove me to school, along with picking me up after. By the next day, I was able to walk again.

## The Valentinis

That summer, we were getting very close to the Valentini family who were the family on the nearby street we visited occasionally. They were the ones who had helped me pierce my ears. My Nonna was good friends with the mother, Asunta. But that year, Domenic, Asunta, and their children visited us more often. Domenic liked my Nonno Ernesto a great deal, and he respected him tremendously. Every time they sat around, I could tell that Domenic would be in awe of my Nonno. It did not surprise me. Many people were in awe of Nonno Ernesto. He was strong, built like a bull. It seemed his hands were permanently curved and stained light brown from a lifetime of being a master farmer of acres and acres of land in Italy. He was from the old days, and Domenic loved this.

Domenic did not have so much respect for Papa, and this was why I did not like him. He talked much faster than Papa. Papa may have been able to keep up in his mind, but when it came to speech, he was slow and somewhat clumsy, relying on his highs and lows and hand gestures. Domenic often laughed at him; when he did, I felt my blood begin to rise.

But the children were very nice. One boy, in particular, Rudolph, was my friend. We were the same age, and when the Valentinis visited, I was allowed to go out and play with Rudolph. By the end of summer, the adults occasionally mentioned as they sat around the table: 'Wouldn't it be nice for Marisella and Rudolph to grow up and get married someday?'

I thought they were all crazy. I was only nine, and Rudolph felt more like a brother to me.

But the Valentini that I admired most was the beautiful Maria. And much to my excitement, my Uncle Giacomo took notice of her too. She was light and airy around him. I marveled at how easily he talked with her and how easily she talked back with him. They laughed together often, and it seemed like they had their own language, known only to each other.

By the end of summer, Uncle Giacomo had asked Domenic for Maria's hand in marriage. Of course, with Uncle Giacomo being Nonno Ernesto's son, there was no objection. And the wedding was set for the fall.

# Italian Day

At the end of summer each year, we went to a marvelous day of the year—Italian Day at Geauga Lake Amusement Park. Nonno and Nonna would not come, so only Mom, Papa, me, and Crispino. Since Danny was only two, we left him at home.

The night before, we packed sandwiches and other delicacies into the refrigerator. In the morning, Papa would go get a bag of ice, and we would fill the silver metal cooler with whatever we could fit in. That was all we would have to eat all day. As immigrants, we would not be allowed to buy anything.

We would crowd into the station wagon and take the hour-long drive.

The park on Italian Day was alive with life. Large families walked into the park, led by men with thick black hair, most wearing white muscle tee shirts, allowing their muscles and hairy chests to protrude. The Italian women were also dressed to the hilt, the amusement park hilt, with short shorts, well-fitting blouses, sunglasses, and complementary shoes. Most had ribbons of some sort in their thick black hair.

There were tons of children, and the focus of every incoming family was getting the cooler from the parking lot through the gates and into the picnic areas, which seemed to be at least a mile from the gates. The oldest sons would help their fathers carry these, while the women would keep their children rounded up and heading toward everyone else.

Once we arrived and found our picnic area, the difficulty began. Papa would lead us around to rides. Though I was turning ten years old within a week, I was still very skinny and not very tall. On over half of the rides, my brother was measured with a stick. He was tall enough. But when they put it to me, I did not measure up. I had to wait. This meant that Papa or Mom had to stay with me and wait for the other two to go.

It was an exciting day to see all the families, but at the same time, it was hard. Papa would get increasingly nervous as the day wore on, and by the time it was evening, we emptied the cooler, took the long walk back to the car, and then went on the long ride home. Crispino and I would be out within minutes and wake to find ourselves in the dark of night in our driveway, dreamily led into the house to bed.

# Italian School

It was decided that, in addition to attending regular school, my little brother, now six years old, and I, would have to attend Italian School on Saturdays. It did not make sense to me. Italian was the only language I spoke fluently. My brother was not that way inclined, and neither were my cousins, who deferred to English in their homes long ago. But because they were going, I had to go.

The classes were held at Our Lady of Mount Carmel Church and taught by one of the priests, Fr. Arcangelo. He was a husky priest with heavy cheeks. His accent was deep-throated, and his smile was ever on his face. He was very kind to us, and the way he spoke words in Italian was like a song. He could also be stern, though, and his smile would lessen as his face grew slightly cross.

I loved hearing him teach us, even though I knew almost everything. The class was from 10:00 a.m. to 11:30 a.m. in the basement of the church.

My cousins were there too, but they mostly joked, goofed off, and never fully completed their assignments. I, on the other hand, wanted to learn. I loved the Italian language for what it was: beautiful. It was not a respite for what was occurring at home, but rather just a time adjustment. Saturdays were still days of cleaning, chores, baking bread, shopping, and getting ready for the evening meal, after which we would visit our cousins or they would visit our house.

## Joe Peep's Pizzeria

Joe Peep's Pizzeria was across the street from our home on Lorain Avenue, directly across from the United States Postal Office. The owners were Julia and Joe Peeps—a grand couple who were always kind and gracious to my whole family.

Nonna's friend, Pasqualina, got a job in the wintertime. Pasqualina was Italian with dark brown short hair and a beauty mark on her cheek. She did not smile much, but when she did, she looked cheerful. But I rarely saw her smile, as she had a serious demeanor. Her personality was one of sadness, very much like Papa's. Her husband died at the dinner table years earlier, and she witnessed him dying. Since her husband's death, Pasqualina was a sad widow. She told my Nonna, who she called by her name, Rosa, that it was good for her to have the job, explaining that it helped her to get out of the house.

The next week, Pasqualina visited Nonna and told her of a job opening. Within minutes, she had convinced her to come work there too. Nonna worked there on Friday and Saturday nights, from 8:00 p.m. until they closed at 11:00 p.m. Though we had rarely ordered pizza there before because we made everything from scratch, now Nonna always came home with at least one pizza. People would order and not pick up, and these pizzas were given to Nonna and Pasqualina as a fringe benefit of working there.

It was the ideal job for Nonna, because she did not drive, AND, she got to work with her friend. But, about three months after starting, during the month of April, something happened.

~ ~ ~ ~

It was a Friday night, and they had just sent the last orders out for delivery and were preparing to close up the shop. Pasqualina mopped the front entrance while Nonna was behind the counter wiping everything down when a customer entered.

Without looking up, Pasqualina kept mopping and said, "We have closed. No more pizzas for tonight." Nonna looked up and froze. The customer was actually a masked gunman, holding a gun and pointing it at Pasqualina. Pasqualina, of course, did not see him as she was busily mopping. She repeated again, saying, "No pizza for tonight! We are closed." The gunman made no response. Nonna started, "Pasqualina, Pasqualina."

"One minute, Rosa, I am almost done."

"Pasqualina!"

Pasqualina stood up. "What do you want... Oh my God. *Ahhhhh! Ahhhhhh!*"

Pasqualina dropped the mop and ran into the back of the shop and out the back door.

Nonna turned to watch her, then turned to see the gunman shaking his head. He now pointed the gun at my grandmother. "Open the register and give me the money."

Nonna looked to the back door to see if there were any signs of Pasqualina, then opened the cash register and gave the gunman the money.

He took it and left.

Nonna went next door to the house of Joe and Julie Peeps. Pasqualina was already there.

They called the police, and Nonna came home.

After that night, Nonno Ernesto would not allow Nonna to go to work anymore. I was glad.

# Learn from Marisella

One Saturday evening, we had the Valentini family over and Uncle Tony's family, including his two daughters, joined us. The noise level in the house was louder than I ever remembered. All the adults sat around the table in the kitchen, talking, telling stories, and laughing. In the living room and down in the basement, the Valentini younger children, Uncle Tony's daughters, and Crispino and I played.

At one point in the evening, Nonna brought out a special cake she had made, and all the kids gathered around to get their piece. I naturally went to Nonna's side and started to help her by holding the plates and handing them to the visitors, along with a fork and napkin, as she scooped each slice up onto the plate.

Uncle Tony remarked to his daughter, "Annette, learn from Marisella, so you can learn how to raise a family someday."

Domenic said, "Yes, Marisella is special. Whoever marries her will be a lucky man."

"She's a good girl," Asunta added. "You have trained her well, Brigida."

Mom smiled. "Her Nonna is the one who has trained her."

"She is going to be a good wife and mother someday," Uncle Tony added, closing off the momentary admiration as they seemed to move into a collective silent reflection.

I felt very uncomfortable, and I knew that my cousin Annette did not enjoy being told to emulate me. There was nothing I could do, though. This sort of thing happened often. I was very different from any of my cousins, not because I wanted to be. I think I would rather be free, like they were, to do more American things. But my life was as it was. There was no other way, at least none that I could imagine.

Aunt Jean broke the silent reflection. "I think she should be allowed to play more."

"Jean," Uncle Tony chided, as if she were disparaging my achievements.

"Well, she's only a little girl."

Papa raised his hand, and his voice ascended gradually, "Jeanna! What do you know?"

Nonno Ernesto, who rarely spoke, raised his eyes from the table and spoke, his voice like an anvil dropping onto the unfolding drama. "No more talk about Marisella. She is our princess and we are raising her to know the old ways."

Everyone settled into a quiet, and Domenic broke the ice, asking for another piece of cake.

Later that night, after everyone went home after we cleaned up the house, I lay awake in bed looking at the lit sign of Zsackas Fur Shop. Our house on Lorain was one of the few actual houses on the street. Lorain Avenue was a vast, miles-long commercial strip with mostly stores on it. We were sandwiched between the masquerade shop and Zsackas Furs. I would often fall asleep looking at this sign, as it was the only thing I could see out my window while lying in bed.

Uncle Tony's words ran through my mind. *Learn from Marisella so you can take care of your family someday.* This sounded odd to me. I had no family. Yet, this was not the first time I had been put on a pedestal. I was always held up as the model Italian daughter who would someday be the model wife and mother, but so many contradictions ran through my mind. For one, I was only ten. To make matters worse, I never imagined getting married. How could I? I was too busy taking care of the family and was never allowed to really play with the other children.

I knew they wanted me to marry Rudolph, but how? He was only ten, too! I wondered why I did not have a say in any of this. I thought of Maria Valentini, so easily talking and laughing with Uncle Giacomo. I so looked up to her, but how could I ever talk with a boy like that? I was not even allowed to talk to boys, except the Valentinis. I said a prayer to Heaven and drifted off to sleep. Tomorrow was Sunday, and the rituals of the day would be waiting for me.

## Going on Vacation

In the springtime of that year, when I was ten years old, we received a phone call from Italy. It was my Uncle Giovanni, my mom's older brother. He wanted to talk to her about Uncle Bruno's upcoming trip home. Bruno was now a senior in high school. He and his best friend, Vince Valentini, had decided to take a trip to Italy in the upcoming summer to celebrate their graduation. The fact that Italy was on the phone caused great excitement for everyone. We knew, though, that we had to be brief because it cost a lot of money to make such a call. Even though Uncle Giovanni was paying for it this time, we knew to respect that principle.

I sat on a chair in the dining room, right next to the red chair where the phone was, trying to hear. Mom was the first on the phone. But, to my dismay, I could only hear one side of the conversation.

"Hey, Giovanni. How are you?"

"*Ehh*, we are doing good here. I miss home, though."

"Yes, Bruno is leaving at the beginning of June."

"What?"

"Marisella?"

"Oh, I don't know. She is very busy here."

There was a long pause, and I could see Mom was listening. She glanced over at me, and I could see she was thinking. She began nodding, then her lips tightened some, and a half-smile came over her face.

"Yes, it would be good for her."

I could not imagine what they were talking about, but I was beginning to get an idea.

"The whole summer?"

Again, there was quiet. Mom was listening again.

"OK. If you will pay for her ticket, she can come."

My eyes widened, and I wondered if I had just heard what I thought I heard. Butterflies began fluttering in my stomach, and a surge went up my spine. How could I possibly go to Italy? I had never been anywhere by myself except walking to school. That in itself was scary for me.

Mom handed the phone to Nonno Ernesto, then turned to me. "Uncle Giovanni wants you to come to Italy with Uncle Bruno. You are going to spend the summer at his house."

Her words washed over me like a bucket of cold water. The sound of it did nothing but scare me. At the same time, though, a little voice told me it was a great privilege and honor to go to the place I had only heard about in countless stories from Nonna.

"Would you like to go?" Mom asked.

I swallowed, gathered my courage, and said, "Yes."

## Crispino and the Car

It was the very first day of summer vacation. We were allowed to go and play at a neighbor's house, the Romalas, who lived next door to the Valentinis, one street over. This was newfound freedom for me, as I had never been allowed to leave the yard the previous summers. I was not sure why the sudden change. Perhaps it was because the Valentinis lived next door, or perhaps it was because my brother would be there. I did not understand how his being six years old and going to the same house as I changed anything. But mine was never to question why, just to do as I was told. Besides, I was not going to argue against this sudden freedom, but I could not wait.

Before we went, I had to help Nonna first to finish all of our chores. Crispino, being one of the boys and only six, had no chores. So he was allowed to go before me. We were meeting Marco Romala and his sisters Stephanie and Annamaria to play freeze tag in their yard. Mrs. Romala and my mom had arranged it the night before on the phone.

Nonna was cooking. I was finishing up with one of my last duties, which was setting the table for dinner. Papa was home, fixing the gate at the back of our property that led to the alley.

The phone rang, and Nonna shouted, "Mari, get the phone!"

I set down a handful of forks, wiped my hands on my apron, and ran to the red chair in the dining room. "Hello, who do you wish to speak to?" We had been taught to answer the phone that way.

A frantic voice on the other end shouted, "Get your mom!"

"Nonna," I shouted. "Hurry!"

Nonna ran to the phone. "Hello! Oh, no. Where? Is he OK?"

Nonna listened, hung up, threw off her apron, and grabbed Danny. She ran outside. "Cresenz, Crispino has been hit by a car! He is by the Valentinis."

Papa stood still for a minute, his furrowed brow showing he was processing what he had been told. Suddenly, he ran toward the alley and used his hands to grab the top and jump over the fence. He disappeared down the alley.

Nonna, carrying Danny and me, ran to the gate, opened it, and headed down the same alley. Papa had already turned down the side street.

We ran down the side street, then turned down Colgate Ave. Already, a crowd was gathered in the street not far from the Valentini's house.

"Oh, my God," Nonna screamed as she began crying. I could not see what she saw, but my heart seized up at her words. Suddenly, I saw Crispino lying on the street, not moving. I started to cry.

Two ladies were kneeling next to the still body. Papa was standing over them, raising his hands in the air, looking at the sky, then back down at Crispino, up and down, up and down. All the while, he was swearing his head off in Italian, screaming, "I told you! I told you to watch!"

I knew my Papa could never handle what was happening, and he would not stop. So, I prayed that my brother could not hear the abusive language. Most of the faces were familiar to us: people from the neighborhood and the Italian community. We exchanged a glance while focusing our worried faces on the asphalt, trying to ignore Papa, who was embarrassing us.

Asunta Valentini ran over to us. Nonna cried, "Asunta, what happened?"

"Crispino ran into the street and ran into an oncoming car."

We had not noticed before, but now we saw the car's driver. She was crying and shaking as some of the neighbors tried to help calm her.

Then we heard the sirens. The ambulance was on its way. I still could not see my brother's face and was beginning to get very scared. Danny started to cry.

The ambulance and a police car pulled up together. The paramedics looked at him, then rolled him onto a stretcher and whisked him away. Papa went with him in the back of the ambulance, still shouting, still cursing in Italian.

The police began taking a statement from the woman. Asunta went over to listen. We stayed where we were, afraid to go closer.

The ambulance started its sirens, alarming us, and whisked him away, and I was unable to see my brother's face. I just wanted to see my little brother's Italian-tanned face. Instead, I found his black sneaker a distance away from the accident.

My heart sank to my stomach. I had a lump in my throat and was unable to breathe. I kept saying to myself: what if I never see my brother again, and all I have left of his memory is this black sneaker of his that he left behind?

In my youthful mind, I wondered how he would walk around the hospital if he could walk again and how he would be able to walk from the car into our house after he was discharged if he was shoeless.

Asunta came back over. She said, "The police said they think Crispino is going to be OK. They said another boy named Marco who was also playing there, went out into the street first, and he missed the car by an inch, and that's when the lady put on her car brakes and hit Crispino, who was chasing him. She was going slower when she hit Crispino, so the impact was less severe than it could have been."

They decided to keep Crispino overnight. When my parents came home, Papa and Mom's arguing stopped my thoughts. Papa blamed Mom for allowing him to go out to play. He boomed, "I told you not to let them play at the neighbor's house." There was no calming him, no matter what my mom said to him. I partly blamed myself for not getting my chores done faster.

***

The next day, Crispino came home from the hospital with nothing more than a big bruise on his shoulder and leg.

It would be the end of going out to play, but it did not matter now.

I was leaving for Italy in five days.

## Summer in Italy

The day of my vacation to Italy finally arrived. I was given new clothes: three pairs of pants, three pairs of shorts, all new underwear, six shirts, a new bathing suit, and a new pair of tennis shoes. Everything was packed into a small suitcase Mom had. Many people came to the house to wish me goodbye, including Uncle Tony. He had a small tear in his eye when he said, "Padina, I am going to miss you. Now you be safe, and may God go with you."

"Thank you, Uncle Tony," I said as he drew me in and gave me a warm hug. He then put $10 dollars in my hand and told me to buy something to eat at the airport. I could not believe it. I had never had more than a dollar or two at the most. Now I had much more.

We were driven to the airport, and I labored to stay right next to Uncle Bruno and Vince as we went to the airplane waiting section. Then, finally, we boarded the plane. I sat between both young men, and soon the plane took off.

I was shaking, clutching the armrest, and digging my fingernails in. It felt like forever before the plane seemed to level off and ease into a smooth ride. I glanced out at the clouds and would not look down. I was too afraid.

~ ~ ~ ~

When we arrived in Rome, we rented a car and drove to my Nonno and Nonna's hometown in Scauri. It was just over a two-hour drive from the airport, and fortunately, I was with Uncle Bruno and not Papa, because he was willing to stop and buy us all something to eat. I felt overwhelmed at the sense of freedom I had and the opportunity to have such delicious foods.

We went to Uncle Giovanni and Aunt Vilma's house when we arrived. Vilma had two boys, who were not yet two and three years old. They immediately took to me. We had a sumptuous dinner and spent the evening talking and laughing around the table before watching TV at night. I was surprised at the TV shows they watched. They were not in English, like our TV at home. All was in Italian. The commercials, too, were in Italian, but they were much racier than commercials at home. Partial nudity occurred in many of the commercials that night, and it seemed like no big deal to them. Of course, Papa would be going through the roof if something like this was playing in our house.

That night, Uncle Bruno and Vince said they were leaving in the morning to travel. I imagined I was going with them, but we had not talked about it. Uncle Giovanni then said, "Marisella, you will be helping Aunt Vilma with the children. She goes to the beach at first light, and when you all come home, you will help her prepare lunch."

I did not mind any of this. Going to the beach sounded fun—until the following morning.

*** 

It was 5:30 a.m. and still somewhat dark outside when Aunt Vilma called into my room. "Marisella, get up. It is time to go to the beach."

I dutifully got up and made my way out of the spacious bedroom I had been given to go to the kitchen. Aunt Vilma had already packed a large bag, and both boys were dressed in a T-shirt and shorts, ready to go.

We walked for a half-mile through the quiet streets of Scauri, then turned toward the sea, traversing narrow side streets, all just waking up to the barely rising sun. I was amazed when we got to the beach and stepped onto the sand. I had never in my life seen something more beautiful and peaceful. We were not the first ones there. There were others already set up with large umbrellas.

We rented one, set up in a spot not too far from the water, then waited for the sunrise. The next four hours were spent running after the boys while Aunt Vilma read her book in her beach chair. I went into the water, but only up to my knees, and had to be careful to hold onto the boys, who were acting wild. I was exhausted. We went back to the house, and I wanted to do nothing but sleep.

But we could not sleep.

Uncle Giovanni was coming home for dinner. Dinner in Italy was served at 1:00 p.m. and was the main meal of the day. I had heard of this but never imagined living it.

After helping Aunt Vilma cook, we got the boys changed and waited.

Uncle Giovanni came home, and we ate a giant meal. Afterward, I was told to go back to my room, as everyone was going to take a nap.

And they did.

And I did.

That evening, we stayed around the house. I was to play with the boys and help with the preparation of the light evening meal. Afterward, we watched TV again. Tonight was a weeknight, and many of the shows we saw were actually American shows, like Happy Days and Charlie's Angels, but they were dubbed into Italian. It seemed funny to me, and yet

I felt closer to America. Not to home, as I was not allowed to watch TV at home that often, but I was closer to America.

\*\*\*

The next day, and the entire week, the routine was exactly the same, even on Saturday. On Sunday, we all slept in and did not go to the beach. We did not go to church either, which I thought was very strange. All over my uncle's house were crosses, pictures of the Blessed Mother, and a picture of the Pope in the center of the kitchen. This was Italy, where the Pope lived. But there was no mention of church.

After Sunday, Monday morning at 5:30 came again, and the week began anew.

Our problem with my bedroom door made my uncle very mad. Every time I left the guest bedroom, I would leave the door open. The door would slam shut and jam because the large bay windows had a strong current flowing through my bedroom. The jamming of the door cost money and time for my uncle. An appointment had to be made for the professional doorman to come and re-open the mammoth wooden door. It happened a few times until finally, I remembered to keep the window closed.

~ ~ ~ ~

At one point during my stay, I was allowed to spend a long weekend with my distant cousins. Aunt Sylvia was Nonna Rosa's sister. She and her husband, Marco, had three daughters. They were all older than I was. When I arrived for the weekend, only the middle daughter was there. Her name was Faustina. She was eighteen years old and very pretty. Since it was summer, she had no school. One of her main jobs was helping to take care of their aging grandmother, who lived with them.

Throughout the day, Faustina talked with me, asked me questions, and fixed me things to eat. She was very nice. But her dad was not. His name was Amelio, and he was very strict. Often during the weekend, he would chastise her for something that was not done right, or order her to do this, or that. In between seeing to his dictates, she would have to tend to meals for her grandmother and take care of laundry. Taking care of laundry in Italy was very different from in America. Clothes had to be washed by hand in a slop sink at the side of the house. After that, they were cranked through a ringer, then hung on large clotheslines that stretched between houses or through backyards.

I saw a lot of me in Fausta. She was like a slave to her family, and I did not understand why this was allowed. It made me fear growing up, as she was nine years older than me, and I was afraid I would never be able to be free.

~ ~ ~ ~

The following Saturday, we decided to visit Matese on the weekend, up in the mountains. Matese was a special restaurant, a favorite with people in the city. My uncle collected cars, and we used one of the old-fashioned ones. The climb in the car was supposed to have been a treat, but the trip up the steep mountain greatly disturbed me. I became sick and nauseated and as the air became thinner, I became weaker.

Finally, we arrived. I barely made it into the restaurant on top of the mountain and proceeded to order my meal. The antipasto was a white slab of cheese with tiny worms on top, squirming around all over the cheese. My uncle insisted that I eat a piece and try this rare authentic cheese. "It's a delicacy, and you must taste it!" he said forcefully.

I was on the verge of tears, and my nausea from the trip up was still in place. I did end up trying a tiny corner, but shortly afterward, when the attention was no longer on me, I ran outside and vomited on the side of my uncle's treasured antique vehicle. I could not help myself, and he was disappointed in me.

But the worst part of the summer came at the end.

Bruno and his friend Vince took me out in a little boat. I sat in the middle as they rowed into the Mediterranean, not too far from the beach. I was very nervous, as I did not know how to swim. I pleaded with them to turn back. At one point, they were horsing around. I tried to stand up to get out of their way, and I tripped over the oar and fell overboard.

My mind screamed in panic while my mouth gripped shut, tight as a vice. I was sinking, and it was dark. My feet hit the bottom and I was sure I was going to die. I looked up to see glimmers of light and held my mouth closed ever so tight. I was panicking inside, knowing I could not hold on. Then I used my legs to push myself back upward and drifted toward the surface. Suddenly, Bruno's arms grabbed me and pulled me out. My mouth exploded open as, gasping for air, I started to cry.

They took me back to the beach, but it did not stop me from crying. I thought I was going to die, and I vowed never to go on a boat again.

On one of the last nights there, my two uncles wanted me to meet all of their acquaintances at the local pub. The Italian bars allowed families and youngsters of all ages to eat ice cream and sip coffee. They had a piano there, and my Uncle Giovanni asked me to play a song by heart that I had played while he was in Cleveland. I did not want to, but felt forced. I nervously started, but halfway through, I was unable to finish. I felt very embarrassed. I played this song at home for many years, but I had a songbook in front of me.

It was a fitting end to my vacation. However, I could not wait to get back to my Nonna. She was my best friend, and I missed her terribly.

# Home

Our plane flew across the ocean and brought us back to the United States in late August, five days before my birthday. Mom was waiting just inside the airport. I ran into her arms and exclaimed, "Mom, I missed you!"

"Welcome home, Mari," she said as she kissed me warmly and hugged me tightly. "Nonna is waiting for you at home, Mari. She misses you more than anyone."

I wiped a tear from my eye. "I miss her too, Mom."

We got our luggage and headed for home. Driving from the airport, with Uncle Bruno and Mom in the front seat and me in the back, I looked out the window, thinking. I had seen a whole new world, a vast world filled with people from all walks of life. I realized that my entire life had so far been spent in a tiny little corner of the world, sheltered from everything around it.

My vision of life had expanded, yet I was returning to our tiny little city lot farm on Lorain Avenue. I felt much more mature than when I left, and this knowledge made me anxious. I did not know why, but it was as if I was suddenly saying goodbye to this wider world I had just experienced. I did not want to say goodbye, yet there was nothing else I could do. The harvest season was about to begin, and school would be starting, and I wondered what the year would hold.

# Life Resumes

Life with Nonna began in earnest. I loved seeing her again, talking with her again, and working alongside her. She was my best friend, the one person in the world that understood me more than any other. Of course, we immediately set about getting ready for harvest time. Our garden was burgeoning with ripe vegetables, and my eleventh birthday was right around the corner.

The excitement of returning home was magnified every evening, as our return from Italy had ushered in a wave of evening visitors. The Valentinis come one night. The Ramalas came another night. Uncle Joe and Aunt Maria came another night. Uncle Giacomo and his new wife, my beautiful new aunt, Maria, who was now Maria Zottola, instead of Maria Valentini, came another night. It seemed everyone wanted to visit and talk with Uncle Bruno and me, too, as we were freshly connected to Nonno Ernesto and Nonna Rosa's home in Italy.

Between visitors, summer evenings were spent by Nonno Ernesto's side, watering the garden and inspecting the vegetables. Having just returned from his home and a large farm in Italy, I had a new understanding of my grandfather. I now saw his noble countenance in a new light. He cared for acre upon acre of olives, wine, and greens in Italy. Most of it had been let go, for now, because he was here. His son, my Uncle Giovanni, hired a few people to take care of the olive trees and grapevines. But even I could tell they were not being cared for as my Nonno Ernesto would take care of them.

He was here now, in a tiny laboratory of America, performing his magic in a much smaller way, and at the same time, in a much more important way. He was here because of me.

During the days of my return, I hardly had time to sleep. Every day was filled with early rising, and quiet morning time in the kitchen with Nonno and Nonna while they readied to send Papa off to work in the factory. After this, Nonna and I began our chores around the home. We would be in the kitchen, stripping down the beds for their laundering, and working in the basement preparing tables and shelves for the coming harvest. We were outside, inspecting the long narrow alleyways of our garden in the warmth of the late summer sun.

My brothers would wake at their leisure and run out to play in our enclosed city yard. They had become close playmates during my absence. Crispino was now seven years old, and Danny was three years old. I was glad they had each other and even more glad that while I had been away, Nonna had potty trained Danny, for the most part.

Papa seemed to be increasingly nervous. Having spent the summer apart from him and been around stable adults, like Uncle Giovanni and Aunt Wilma and some of their friends, I understood Papa more. He was not well. I now had some insights into his facial expressions, his way of talking, and how he reacted when he became upset. There was something deeply wrong, something worrying him. I wished I could help him, and despite how hard it was, I would try hard not to upset him.

So much had changed during my trip to Italy.

More than anything, I had changed.

## Uncle Mario and Aunt Jean

Three days before my birthday, Uncle Mario called. They were coming to Cleveland for my birthday. Immediately, the excitement in the house erupted with the cleaning and preparations. They, of course, would be staying with us.

When they arrived, Aunt Theresa asked Mom to take us to the store so she could buy me a dress. Aunt Theresa did not drive. So, on Saturday, my mom and I drove downtown to the May Company. Aunt Theresa helped me pick out a beautiful red-flowered dress. As I came out of the dressing room, she kneeled in front of me, straightening it some, checking the waist. Finally, she said, "Marisella, you are growing up so fast. You will be a woman soon, and I want you to look beautiful."

"Thank you, Aunt Theresa."

I wanted to be a woman, but did not know what it meant. I knew it meant getting married and having a husband and children, but it all seemed a million miles away.

When we returned home, Nonna had already made the cake. Uncle Mario was sitting outside on the patio, talking with Papa, Nonno Ernesto, and Uncle Tony. We went inside. Aunt Jean was sitting at the table with

Nonna, talking with her. Uncle Tony's daughters were there too, and the cousins were already well into playing games in the house and outside together.

"Hi, Brigida. Hi, Theresa," Aunt Jean said. Her face seemed bothered. She was not herself.

Before we could settle, Uncle Mario came in from outside, announcing in his broad accent, "OK, everyone. Get ready. We are going to get ice cream."

"What! Ice cream!" Aunt Jean said, wide-eyed, her countenance immediately improving.

Moments later, almost fifteen of us walked down the long alley toward the ice cream store. When we arrived, we all crowded around the order window. Uncle Mario said loudly, "Get what you want! It's my treat!"

Uncle Tony protested, "It's OK, Mario. I will pay for my family."

"No, Tony, it's OK. I got this."

Uncle Tony acquiesced.

Uncle Mario then said, "Jean, what are you getting?"

"A fudge sundae!" Aunt Jean said

"Well, get two scoops!" he said.

"Oh, my God," Aunt Jean said. "I don't think I can handle even one."

"Well, get two. And get extra fudge!"

We all giggled. It wasn't funny, but how Uncle Mario said it made it funny. The way Uncle Mario said everything sounded funny.

That night we celebrated my birthday with a large gathering at our home. It seemed that everyone was there, including Uncle Tony's family, Uncle Joe's family, Aunt Mary's family, and the Valentinis.

It was noisier and more fun than I ever remembered. It was a resounding singing of Happy Birthday, with Uncle Tony outshining everyone with his operatic voice. I blew out my candles, wondering what the year might hold for me, and making my wish. I wished for a happy year and for Papa that he would start to enjoy life. I also wished that I could go back to Italy someday. Afterward, we all enjoyed the large cassata cake Nonna and I had baked earlier in the day, and there was none left over. Right after the company left, Nonna, Mom, and I quickly cleaned up the kitchen, went to bed, and fell asleep, completely exhausted.

# The Piano Recital

Once sixth grade began, I found myself at a new school. St. Coleman had closed the school, and I was enrolled at Gordon School, a Cleveland Public School also located on 65th Street. It was a vastly different school, with mostly new faces. Many of the children were black or Hispanic, and there were a lot more kids at the school. It was a very noisy, bustling, crowded place. It was very different from St. Coleman.

The teachers were different, too. Since I was now in what was called middle school, we went from classroom to classroom. I saw different teachers all day long. Some were nice and kind, as most of the teachers and nuns at St. Coleman had been, but some were not so nice and not so caring.

It was the same distance from my house, but now I had to go down Lorain and turn right, not left. I also had to cross Lorain, which was a very busy street at any time of the day.

I didn't like this school at all. I didn't like the teachers or children either. Yes, there were some familiar faces, including my friend Maria, but I hardly saw her. After the first week, I went home and told my Nonna, and I cried.

Nonna said, "Don't cry, Mari. You will get to know the other children. Give it time."

I trusted Nonna and dried my tears. Coming home never felt so good as it did now. Every day I longed for the last class to end, so I could go home to Nonna.

During the second week, Mom reminded me that it was Tuesday and that I would resume my piano lessons today after school. Now my walk would be longer, as Gordon School was several blocks farther away. I dreaded having to make the walk by myself. It was supposed to be simple, but all that day, I wracked my brain, trying to memorize the walk in my mind.

After school, I took the long walk to Mrs. Dembecks, relieved when I arrived. It had not been too bad. She greeted me with a warm hug and got me some cookies, then asked me about my summer.

Once the lesson started, she informed me we had a recital coming up and only six weeks to prepare.

"A recital? What is that?" I asked.

"You are going to play three songs for the church next door."

There was a non-denominational church two doors down.

"Oh, that is nice," I said, hiding my sudden apprehension at having to perform.

~ ~ ~ ~

For the next six weeks, we practiced the songs I was going to play. I relaxed when I played for my teacher because she was continuously encouraging, as teachers are meant to.

At home, it was different. We were strictly forbidden to play the piano when Papa was home. We could also not play it when the adults were asleep. So the times I got to practice were very short, and I had to deal with my brothers trying to interrupt me by running around or running past and banging on the keys. It was always nerve-wracking.

Finally, the big day was nearing. It was going to be on a Sunday afternoon, right after a church service and social at the interdenominational church on W. 65th. My grandparents could not attend because they had to go to church themselves on Sundays. Papa could not attend either, as he was working on Sundays now. Only Mom could come, and she said she would ask Uncle Tony.

I tried to hide my disappointment. I don't think anyone in my family knew how much this meant to me. It was one of the biggest days of my life, and I was very nervous. Still, at least Mom and Uncle Tony would be coming.

After dealing with my brothers all morning, I snuck into the bathroom and put on my orange flowered dress that had been bought for my trip to Italy, along with my medium-sized white sandals.

I stayed in the living room, anxiously waiting, while Mom was in the kitchen stirring the sauce and getting a few things ready for the Sunday lunch. There was a knock at the door. It was Domenic Valentini. I did not want to see him, and I stayed in the living room, hoping he would hurry up and leave. As time passed, I wondered why Mom was not getting ready.

Finally, I went into the kitchen.

Mom and Domenic were sitting at the table, drinking coffee and laughing. I did not understand why he enjoyed making her laugh so much.

"Oh, Marisella," Domenic said, surprised to see me. He looked me up and down quickly. "You look so pretty in your dress. Where are you going?"

"I have a piano recital." I glanced at Mom, who seemed to be caught up in her own world. Mom half-smiled, then looked over at the food cooking on the stove and said, "You go yourself, Mari. I cannot come."

Her words crushed me. I could not believe she had changed her mind with hardly a passing thought, but I bravely smiled and said, "Okay, Mom."

I left right then and quietly walked to the alleyway at the back of our yard and walked alone on the quiet Sunday late morning down to W. 65th and over to the church.

I felt so sad that no one was with me. I wanted to turn around, but for what, and to where? I was so sad that I didn't even want to go home.

The church inside was pleasant and seemed more like a carpeted hall than a church. There were not many people. Most of them were the parents and families of a few of Mrs. Dembeck's other students who would also be performing.

When it was my turn, I nervously sat down, sat up straight, and tried to play as best as I could. Looking out at the faces, they were smiling, but none of them were faces I knew.

At one point, I made a mistake and froze, but then, feeling the pressure, I quickly started again and finished.

Mrs. Dembeck hugged me, but it did not mean anything.

I walked home alone, feeling lonely and sad. When I arrived, the table was full of people having the traditional Sunday lunch. Mom asked, "How was your recital, Mari?"

I bravely smiled and said, "It went well."

I went into the bathroom, took off my dress, and looked into the mirror, watching a few tears come down my cheek. I wished someone had seen me. Now it was over, and now I had nothing more to look forward to.

# Apartments

We worked hard as a family during that harvest season. All the traditional foods were preserved, and our cellar was stocked again with its array of colorful jars that would sustain us in the coming year. Gordon School was hard, and I did not enjoy going anymore, but I had to. My brothers were free to do what they wanted and play a lot more than I was able to. When I had time to play with them, we played school in the basement. I would stand before the chalkboard and teach them pretend lessons. We also played hide and seek. Then, as the dark time of the year approached and when I had time, I retreated into the pantry, closed the door, and spent quiet time with my Lite Brite.

One evening, we got a call from Uncle Joe. Immediately, my parents were very excited. They left to go and meet him somewhere.

When they returned, I heard why. Uncle Joe wanted them to buy the apartment building next to his. That was where they had gone—to see it.

A week of nervous energy unfolded, with lots of talks around the kitchen table. My parents wanted to move forward, but were naturally a little afraid. They went to the bank and were approved. They bought it.

One Friday evening, we packed into the car and drove out to the suburbs. As we pulled around a corner, an enormous three-story building stood like a lone sentinel on a hillside corner. It had six apartments in it, two on each floor. Since it was built on a hillside, the back had six garages on the ground floor.

My brothers and I ran outside as Papa, Mom, Uncle Joe, and Uncle Tony stoically walked outside, talking, observing, and pointing things out they wanted to do.

When it was time to go inside, we were called over. My brothers were laughing and fooling around, chasing each other.

"Stop it!" Papa yelled.

We walked into the back hallway, where the staircase led up to the three floors where the apartments were. Immediately, my brothers took off chasing each other.

"Crispino!" Papa yelled.

"Cresenz! Be quiet!" Mom replied, nervous we were so close to the tenants' doors.

Things settled down, and we quietly walked up to the top. I could not believe that my parents now owned such a luxurious building.

*** 

The following morning, I was awakened early. Mom, Papa, and I had a piece of toast and coffee, then got in the car and headed to the apartment building. We started in the laundry room, filling two buckets with water and soap. Papa went outside and began cutting the lawn. Mom and I went to the top floor and proceeded, on our hands and knees, to wash each landing and all the steps going down. It took over an hour. When we were done, we changed the water, and we went to the front steps, which were narrower, and only three flights, and proceeded to do the same.

I was glad it was early so that the tenants would not see me. I was somewhat embarrassed doing this menial task and wanted to clean incognito. When I saw tenants coming out of their apartments or heard me cleaning by their door, I would graciously greet them, hoping to be invisible somehow. I couldn't, though, because there was no escape but to greet them and say "Hi."

Mom said, "You help us now, Marisella, and someday we will help you."

My parents had told me this before. They would say things like, 'You will be taken care of.' or 'You help us now, and we will help you whenever you need it.' I didn't know what that meant, this verbal discourse. It was a heartfelt verbal agreement of some kind. I didn't see rebellion as an option because I lived in my parent's home, and all was provided for me. I was content. I was trusting of them, and they knew they could count on me to assist in whatever the family needed. The survival of the family depended on all of us working, sweating, eating, sacrificing, and laboring together. So, I rarely had time to watch cartoons because my brothers were younger, and I was the oldest. I had more responsibility. When I was cleaning, and my brothers watched cartoons, I asked why they were allowed to watch them and not me. I was told that boys were unable to strain themselves because they would get a hernia and not be able to father children.

I knew this was ignorant thinking.

I knew at a young age that this was not common-sense thinking.

I knew this came from old wives' tales, part legend, part ignorance, and part culture.

The Italian culture favored the first or second and even third son whether they were the oldest child or not. Italian sons' well-being was favored over the daughter's well-being.

When we got home, Nonna was in the kitchen. "Come, Mari," she said. "I made you some oatmeal. We have lots to do."

I was so hungry, as we had left over two hours earlier. After we ate, I had to go to Italian class. After that was over, Nonna and I started our traditional routines we did every Saturday. Our ritual was cleaning the house, cooking the lunch, and making bread for the week. I believe the consistency in our daily schedules gave me comfort.

In the afternoon, I would do the last duty, dusting our wooden and linoleum floors with Pledge. Right after, my brothers and I would have fun sliding with our socks. I made sure that plenty of Pledge fell on the area where we could slip and slide to our heart's content. My brothers made me laugh constantly. As Saturday afternoon faded, we waited for Mom to get home with the groceries. Then we would feast.

## The Tax Man

Right after Christmastime, the tax man came to our home for the yearly visit, and we all became excited. I was in charge of baking a special coffee cake called "Tortano" before he arrived. Mom and Papa were arguing about the apartment bills. They could not find them all, and this was very important for the upcoming appointment.

Finally, the doorbell at the side door rang. Immediately, Crispino and Danny ran to the door. Papa shouted at them, "Boys, stop! Sit down!"

Mom ran to the door, and shooed them away, then glared at Papa. We all gathered near the door, next to Papa, watching. Finally, Mom opened the door, and her face changed countenance perfectly with the opening.

There stood the tax man.

He was a short man, well bundled for the cold weather, wearing a heavy gray overcoat and black business hat. He wore thick black glasses that were dotted with the falling snowflakes. In his hands was a black briefcase.

"Come in," Mom said.

"Thank you," he said, in a thick, businesslike Italian accent.

He walked past us, barely looking around him, and went right to the dining room table. He took off his overcoat and hat. They had hidden him well. Underneath, he had brown pants, a black belt, dark brown shoes, a white shirt, and a red tie. He was round in the middle, with a balding head. His name was Vinny. He did taxes for a lot of Italian families.

Mom and Papa sat across from him at the table, with two separate shoeboxes filled with papers in front of them. Papa was upset and wore a slight scowl on his face. This was normal for Papa, especially when someone had just tramped into the house with snow and ice on their feet, but Mom was nervous, and this was not her normal demeanor. I knew this was a very special appointment because the dining room table was used almost exclusively for such meetings.

The tax man went to work quietly, taking his adding machine out of his briefcase, along with several sharp pencils, printed forms, and green paper. He plugged the adding machine in and looked up at my parents, smiling.

"Let's talk about the apartments first."

Mom nervously reached into one of the shoeboxes and began taking out receipts and handing them across the table. The tax man would inspect them, sometimes ask a question, then make a notation, and reach out to be handed the next. We quietly listened while my mom and dad answered all his questions.

This went on for over an hour.

At one point, the tax man's fingers began flying over the adding machine. Every time he hit a certain button it would print something on a roll of paper that it fed out.

Crispino kept running around the dining room table and jumping over the cord that stretched behind the tax man to the plug on the wall.

All at once, the adding machine stopped, and we turned. Crispino was lying on the linoleum floor. He had tripped over it and pulled the cord out of the wall.

"Crispino!" Mom yelled.

Papa jumped up, raising his hand. "Get out of this room!" Then he turned to Mom. "I told you!"

Mom, visibly embarrassed, yelled, "Marisella, take your brothers out of here."

She turned to the tax man. "I'm so sorry."

He closed his eyes, nodded, then plugged in the machine, scooted his chair back to cover the path, and started re-adding. A long time went by.

Then, the coffee and the Tortano were brought out, and we celebrated the completion of their taxes.

# Avon Lady

Near the end of the school year, Mom left a note for my brother and me to take an envelope of money to the Avon lady after school. She lived one street over, down the alley, on a cross street that connected to Colgate.

Having been given our task after school by Nonna, we were elated. Doing this simple task meant we had freedom. Crispino and I took off running to see who would arrive first at the house. We loved the warm spring air on our faces, and the freedom to be without adults to do what we wanted, even if for a short time, was exhilarating.

The Avon lady had four kids, but I didn't see anyone around. So we entered the gate and approached the side door. It was a storm door, with the screen on the top, glass in the middle, and aluminum on the bottom. We knocked, but there was no reply. So, we waited a little bit and knocked again; still no response.

I said, "Crispino, let's leave the bag hanging from the doorknob, and let's go home."

"Wait, we can try one more time." Crispino was overly rambunctious and full of energy most of the time, and it was no different now. He gave a large thrust and jumped, turning mid-air to do a 'behind' slamming into the glass to create a loud knock. It shattered. We froze and looked at each other, wide-eyed. It mattered not that Crispino had done it. Papa would have both our hides.

We ran home.

All the way home, I kept thinking and dreading what would have to be said. Though Crispino was four years younger than me, it was my responsibility to watch him. And I was watching him, so while I knew what just happened, I could not believe it.

To my surprise, Mom was not upset and wisely said they would leave Papa out of it. No punishment was needed. When I told her Crispino did a behind slam into the glass, she looked at Nonna and started to laugh. We all started to laugh. We went over and apologized to the Avon lady, and Mom paid for the repairs.

Later that night, at dinner time, Mom made an announcement. She was having another baby near Christmas.

We were all happy. Deep down, though, I knew it would mean more work for me. I already had my hands full entertaining my brothers, who were seven and three. Soon, I would have three brothers under me.

## St. Rocco's Summer Festival

It was the end of summer, and we were at the St. Rocco Summer Festival. Nonna, Mom, Crispino, and I drove there for the opening night. It was a hot evening when everything felt muggy and sticky. Crispino and I had the time of our lives going on rides. We could only do this because my mom had bought us enough ride tickets. Had Papa been there, we would have only had a few.

As our allotted time came to an end, Crispino and I somehow had only one ticket left. I imagined that Crispino had lost one of his, but no matter. I gave the last ticket to my brother. I was tired and thought he would enjoy the last carnival ride more than I did. So, he hopped on, and Mom, Nonna, and I went to the side rail to watch him.

The ride turned around and around slowly. I decided to push the ride as it went around to make it go faster so the ride would end sooner; therefore, we could go home faster. I was tired.

I had a gold ring with a red stone on top of my middle finger I had gotten from Uncle Giovanni when I was in Italy.

As I pushed the ride around with my right hand, I suddenly felt a tug of my finger and my arm being pulled. My grandmother felt the stone of red hit her chest, and it disappeared. Then, I started screaming, for my arm was being pulled in the opposite direction to my body. I thought my arm was going to be pulled off, and I was going to die.

I screamed. The ride kept pulling me. I was trapped. I was scared. I prayed for deliverance. The ring finally snapped with great force, and my finger started bleeding, flowing freely like a river. The pain was intense.

I was saved, and in my heart, realized it was not my turn to leave this world.

I cried loudly and with lament, as I had never felt such profound pain. I felt queasy and faint at the same time, enduring the excruciating pain as my finger throbbed. Nonna wrapped it in a cloth. I was told under no circumstances to take off the cloth. I was told to keep it on; no matter what, it must be covered. I tried to remove the cloth, desperate to see my finger. Nonna shouted for me to do exactly as she said, or I could lose my finger.

Immediately, I thought of marrying one day. Who would want to marry a girl with a missing finger? I was upset with myself that I had given my ticket away to my brother. I was sad that I was too nice. I felt that I was being punished for being a good girl. I was a kind sister that didn't deserve to be in severe pain. I prayed that I could avoid the hospital visit and not have to get painful sutures.

We left the festival immediately, my hand wrapped in a cloth, hurrying out of the carnival parking lot to a nearby friend's house who lived on that street.

As we hurried down the sidewalk and the carnival noise faded, I started to feel guilty. What if I had to go to the hospital? Papa would explode at the hospital bills. I felt I deserved to get injured because I had no business sticking my hand on the ride and pushing it along.

The woman at our friend's house cleaned the blood and determined I would not need stitches. It was a long thin cut that went completely around my finger, but it had not gone deep enough. So, she wrapped it in gauze, and we went home.

I was banned from washing the dishes, which I washed by hand. I was exempt from many chores, as I had to keep my finger dry and covered. The only person to take off the homemade plaster and responsible for the care of my finger was Nonna Rosa. The process of healing took time, but eventually, it happened.

I had to get better. My twelfth birthday was in another week, and the harvest season was again around the corner. Gordon School also loomed large, as it, too, would be starting. I was not looking forward to any of it.

# Ignatius

I had a surprise the day before school was to start. Mom came home early and asked me to go somewhere with her. So, we went out to Lorain Avenue and waited for the bus. Finally, we got on, paid the fare, then sat down.

"Where are we going?" I asked.

"I am taking you to see your new school."

"Oh, really. What school?"

"St. Ignatius has openings. We are going to register."

"You mean I don't have to go to Gordon anymore?"

Mom smiled and patted me on the leg. "That's right, Marisella. I know you didn't like it. So… I called St. Ignatius, and they said you can join. But pay attention, because you will have to take the bus here every day. It is too far to walk."

My mouth dropped open a bit as I looked out the window at all the people, stores, streets, and cars we were passing. I quickly looked behind me, suddenly fearful I would get lost. I began to try to memorize all the stores we passed, but it was all coming at me too quickly.

Before long, we exited the bus. As soon as it pulled away, I gazed upon a towering church across the street. It was taller than any I had ever seen. Next to it was a large school building, much larger than St. Coleman. We crossed Lorain and went in.

The halls were tall and wide, filled with students and teachers, some in groups, some in lines, some hurrying to or fro. We walked into the office. Two secretaries were sitting behind a counter with three offices behind them. This was no small school.

After waiting, the assistant principal called us in.

When my mom told him I was in seventh grade, he seemed surprised. "How old is she?" he asked.

"Twelve years old," Mom said.

"Very well. We will call Gordon School to transfer the records."

He smiled, then stood. "Welcome, Marisa. Mrs. Hildenbrandt sitting out there will get you a couple of uniforms. You start tomorrow. Be here at 8:15 a.m., Marisa, and I will take you to your class."

I was so happy to hear all of it, especially about wearing uniforms. I missed that, and in my mind, it made life much simpler.

We took the bus home. I nervously memorized every store all the way home, especially after Mom said we were getting close. Though I lived on Lorain Avenue, I rarely remembered seeing most of these stores. I never had to memorize them. Finally, Mom pointed to a shoe store. "When you see that shoe store, it is time to go up and get off."

We quickly went to the front of the bus, and it stopped right near Joe Peep's Pizzeria. I sighed with relief as we got off and looked down the street at the nearby stores so I would remember tomorrow.

As soon as we got home, we ate dinner, then had to begin the tomatoes. They were already spread out down the basement and ripened to the point that they had to be canned.

All of us, except my brothers, went down to the basement. We worked until 9:00 p.m. cutting and cooking a good portion of the tomatoes. By the time we had to stop, we had finished nearly half. We would resume tomorrow night.

***

The next morning, I put on the uniform for St. Ignatius. It was very large on me. Mrs. Hildenbrandt had told me I fit better in a fifth-grade uniform, as I was very petite. But since the junior high uniforms had a different color scheme, I would have to wear it. Mom pinned it up before I left and promised to use her seamstress skills to alter it for me, but because we were in the middle of canning tomatoes, she would not have time until the weekend.

After eating some toast and drinking coffee, I nervously walked to the bus stop Mom and I had gone to yesterday. When the bus pulled up and the door opened, a tall black man with a cap sat looking at me. I hesitated to get on, double-checking the route number once more, not wishing to get on the wrong bus. I pulled myself up the first step and climbed in. "Sir, I have to get off at St. Ignatius. Can you help me?"

He smiled. "Sure, little girl. Sit right there in that first seat. I will help you."

I was so happy that he would help me, and I did not have to worry anymore. As I sat watching the stores go by, no longer trying to memorize them, I saw my world growing again. Finally, I had freedom, and I felt very happy.

When the principal took me to my class, I was afraid to go in. So, I trailed behind him while he went into the room, standing in his shadow as much as I could while he introduced me.

The teacher's name was Sr. Louise. She was a somewhat rounder nun with gray hair and a set jaw. She smiled at me and gently bent down, saying, "Don't be afraid, Marisa. You are welcome here." Then she stood and turned to the class. "Everyone, please stand, and let's give a hand for Marisa."

Everyone stood and began clapping. I felt like a star. Sr. Louise continued, "Darcy, Denise, come up here and help Marisa. I want her to sit at the new desk I set up in between you two."

The sister turned to me. "Go with them, Marisa."

I met the two girls as they neared the front. They looked exactly alike, and I quickly realized they must be twins. I had a feeling it was going to be the start of a long friendship.

***

That night, we worked on the tomatoes again and did not finish.

On the third night, we finished making 150 jars of sauce. I was so exhausted. The following day, I fell asleep on the bus. I heard the driver say, "Little girl! Little girl!"

I jumped up, my eyes wide, and ran the few steps to the driver, anxiously peering out the window. St. Ignatius was there. Luckily, I had not missed it. I sighed.

The driver told me, "Don't worry, young lady. What is your name?"

"Marisa," I said.

"Well, I am Mr. Jones. You don't have to worry. I will always make sure you don't miss your stop."

I smiled. I had never really talked much to a black person before. But I liked this man and was grateful he was going to help me.

# The Day Nonna went to Canada

In the middle of September, Nonna Rosa went on a bus trip to Canada for the weekend with some of her friends. It was the first time ever that she had left our home for more than a few hours. I felt so lost and abandoned. Nonna was my best friend. She was my teacher, mentor, and mom in many respects. She was my everything.

Every day, she was witty and funny, the life of our home, keeping everyone's countenance up in the midst of their days.

Her absence was sorely felt. No one, except me, was there to automatically make the meals. Nonna had asked me to make pasta for everyone while she was gone. I did my duty, cooking the pasta, making the salad, putting out the bread, and setting the table. None of it was the same, though. There was no laughter, no easy-going small talk while we worked. Now, I had just to get it done, and the joy I usually had working alongside her had vanished.

I couldn't wait for her to return. I said my evening prayers before bed, hoping she was enjoying herself and would return home safely. I was experiencing a little separation anxiety, and the house felt emptier. The house had something missing during those two days. Something big was missing. The heart of our home was missing.

When she returned home, I felt like crying. I was so happy to see her because her absence had left such a hole in me. She brought back souvenirs and described her adventure. She mentioned how she missed all of us. She was glad to be back home safe and sound. I said, "Nonna, don't go on another trip because I missed you too much."

She replied, "I won't go anywhere far because I didn't like it that much to want to go again, or for that matter, go anywhere else. I have everything I want right here."

I realized then that if anything ever happened to her, I would not be able to carry on.

# Girl Scouts

During the first month of school, a representative of the Girl Scouts came in to talk to our class. I loved hearing about everything they did, even some of their outings and camps. I just knew that I had to become a Girl Scout.

So, I decided to talk with the representative. She was a mother from the school, Mrs. Dewerth. Her son Al was in my seventh-grade class. She told me I would make a great Girl Scout.

Now, I had to go home and convince my parents.

It was a Friday evening when I had my first chance, but we were busy in the basement the entire night bottling eggplants. So, I waited for the next day. Now, I had a problem. Papa would be home Saturday and Sunday. But I realized I needed his permission anyway, so I felt I might as well get it over with.

Saturday, we all gathered for the evening meal. Uncle Bruno was out with his friends, so it was only Nonno and Nonna, Mom and Dad, and me and my brothers. As we started to pass around the food, I said to my mom, "A lady came to school to tell us about the Girl Scouts."

"What is the Girl Scouts? Is that like the Boy Scouts?"

"Yes, it is the version of the Boy Scouts for girls."

"*Hmmm*…. what do they do?"

I glanced over at Papa. He was listening, though not with his eyes. His eyes were busy watching his spaghetti as he twirled his fork and lifted it to his mouth. But he was listening. Nonna Rosa and Nonno Ernesto did not say anything. They tried not to get involved in matters that clearly belonged to my parents.

Just then, there was a knock at the door. It was Uncle Tony and Aunt Jean.

I suddenly had no idea if this was a good or bad thing. Uncle Tony could sway Papa sometimes, and perhaps now would be one of those times.

Jean started, "Oh, Brigida, did I have a week. A lady I work with was sick all week long. I think she is just using up her sick time. My boss made us all take on her work. That's not fair! My dad told me the same thing. He says we need a union down there. My brother hates unions. He argues all the time with my dad about it. I feel like calling in sick now. It's not my job—"

"Jean!" Papa shouted.

"What?" she asked, looking at him.

"Eat and stop talking!"

Jean looked over at Brigida, then said softly, "Well, between you and me, I don't think there will be any union."

Papa put his fork down and swayed back, raising his eyes for a moment. He was deeply troubled. I knew now was not a good time to talk about the Girl Scouts.

It was silent as Mom got two dishes and passed the food to Uncle Tony and Aunt Jean.

When Mom finished, she asked, "So, Marisa, what do the Girl Scouts do?"

Aunt Jean exclaimed, "The Girl Scouts! So is Marisa becoming a Girl Scout?"

Uncle Tony said, "Jean! Let Marisa talk."

All eyes turned to me. I felt so pressured. My answer would determine everything.

"Well… they sell cookies… and…. they do things for the elderly…. And they go camping sometimes…. And go places to do things…."

Papa raised his voice. "You cannot go camping, Mari. You are too young!"

"We go with some of the parents, Papa. It is fine."

Mom asked, "Why do they sell cookies?"

"To make money, I guess. I don't know what they do with it."

"Girl Scout cookies are my favorite. I remember—"

Tony jumped in, "Jean! Let Marisa talk."

"Oh, all right," Jean said.

"When do they meet?" Mom asked.

"They meet on Tuesdays and Thursdays after school. Can I join?"

Mom took a deep breath. "Mari, you don't have time for that. How are you going to get there?"

"I can take the bus," I said.

"No, it's too late then. No, you can't do that. It's better you stay here."

"But, Mom, I want to join."

"No, Mari!" Papa said, raising his hand and waving it. "You cannot go camping. We need you at home!"

Aunt Jean started in.

"I think you should let her. Marisa would enjoy being a Girl Scout. I was one until I was sixteen. Oh, boy, did we have a mess? There was a big dance. Oh never mind. You should let her join."

"No, Jean! Stay out of it!" Papa yelled.

Aunt Jean scowled at him.

Brigida asked, "What was the mess, Jean?"

"One of the girls in our troop got pregnant. That was the end of her and the Girl Scouts."

"How did she get pregnant?" Mom asked.

"How do you think!" Jean said, wide-eyed. "It didn't happen in the Girl Scouts."

"Jean!" Uncle Tony said. "Stop talking about that."

I looked over at Papa. He was fuming inside, deeply troubled by Aunt Jean.

All grew quiet.

I frowned and quietly finished eating with everyone else. The answer was no, and it would never change once the answer was no. The conversation turned to something else, and when it did, I got up and went into my room. I felt broken and discouraged. I cried, thinking about what I would tell Mrs. Dewerth.

## Haunted Basement

As Halloween neared, my brother Crispino and I decided to make a haunted basement. We were not allowed to go to real haunted houses. So right after we finished the olives, we got started. I began by cutting out Boo Berry and Count Chocula cereal box figures and taped them to the entrance of our basement steps walls. We hung sheets so we could easily walk through the frightening maze. Our plan was to have our cousins go through it when they came over. We set up stations to scare them.

When I told Nancy at the next-door masquerade shop about our plan, she gladly donated to our frightful cause. To my surprise, too, our parents encouraged us to use our imagination and creativity. We spent days and days getting ready for 'opening night.' We practiced for many hours in our basement until we perfected and timed all the scary stunts flawlessly to the Halloween music.

At first, my brother would hide behind a sheet with gloves on like a werewolf's hands. Then, as his victim walked past, he would reach out, trying to grab them. Then we filled a shoebox with peeled grapes. A sign hung on it that read ghoul's eyes. We also made life-size spider webs out of yarn from my grandmother's sewing basket and hung them around the basement pathway. Our masterpiece was a life-size mannequin that Nancy from the masquerade shop let us borrow. We put a witch robe and witch hat on it and painted glowing eyes on the face. A real broom stood next to it. Everything was topped off by setting our record player there and putting on creaky music with chains rattling to set the panic mood.

~ ~ ~ ~

The day arrived when we had our first customers. Aunt Mary and her girls came over to visit, and no one was allowed to come downstairs until we were ready.

Crispino and I went downstairs and turned on the music. Then, we took our places. I was the guide. My job was carrying a flashlight and ensuring each person went to all the stations. Crispino, of course, donned his werewolf gloves and hid behind the sheet. Then, one by one, I called my cousins down, starting with the oldest, Rosemary. She screamed loudly through the entire maze, sending frightful chills up the stairs to those still waiting.

The scariest trip was for my cousin Italia. She was only six, and once I led her through, she froze. She had gotten a glimpse of Crispino with his gloves. They were close in age, and though she knew it was Crispino, she was still scared. She decided to run past, but screamed so loud that it excited my brother Crispino. He made it difficult for her to get past.

All the remaining cousins had to contend with the newly animated person at the werewolf station, who now insisted on accosting each victim with his werewolf gloves. Each of my cousins took multiple turns through until finally, I heard Papa shouting for us to stop screaming so loud.

We stopped and went upstairs to play so as not to ruin our haunted basement. It was a great success, and over the next week, more of our cousins and friends came through.

~ ~ ~ ~

That year was my most memorable. Halloween was my favorite holiday besides Christmas and Easter. I was invited to a Halloween party at my teacher Ms. Sheehan's house. All the students in her class were invited. It was an after-school party that would last from 5:00 p.m. to 7:00 p.m. I was allowed to go, and Mom said Nancy at the shop next door would give me an outfit. Going into Nancy's shop was magical. The rented costumes had accessories and jewelry for adults attending parties. Of course, Nancy sewed a fairy godmother costume for me, and I was happy that it was not a store-bought outfit. In addition to my dress, I had a sparkling crown and lit-up wand. Though the party only lasted two hours, I received many compliments on my costume.

# Another Boy

As Christmas time neared, Mom's pregnancy progressed. She began getting migraines around this time, which meant that the Thanksgiving and Christmas holidays were more difficult. Our home had become more stressful, and now with a new baby coming, we would have to adapt.

Three days after Christmas, Papa had to take Mom to the hospital. The baby was coming.

This time, the delivery was fast. The next morning, we received the phone call. Another boy had been born.

Mom and Papa decided to name him Ernesto in honor of Nonno Ernesto. A wave of jubilation and congratulations ran through the house. When Papa came home, the visitors started to come for coffee to bring their glad tidings. Within the week, Mom came home, too.

My new brother was chubby, built like a tiny bull. He reminded me very much of Nonno Ernesto, who was also built like a bull. He had lots of hair, too. It seemed even more than me. It was thick black hair, shiny, and full of health. Seeing him gave me great joy and, at the same time, a tinge of sorrow. My duties helping take care of him started almost immediately. First, it was helping Mom, who was still recuperating, by retrieving diapers and bottles. But it would not be long before I was expected to help change him or feed him at any time if Mom was busy, resting, or at work. He was a beautiful little baby, though, and I wondered if someday I would ever get married and have my own children.

# Womanhood

During the springtime of seventh grade, I noticed that my chest was starting to grow. It scared me because I did not want to change. Nonna noticed too. One day while we were making supper, she came over to me and hugged me tightly, then held me apart from her. She smiled warmly. "You are growing, Marisella. You are becoming a woman now." She hugged me again. "You are going to be a beautiful wife and mother someday, Mari."

That Friday morning, after Papa had left for work, Mom called me into her room. "I have to talk to you, Mari. Come in and sit down."

I sat on the chair across from the bed, and Mom sat on the edge of the bed.

"Mari, you are growing into a woman now. I wanted to tell you something that Nonna told me a very long time ago. Your body is going to start changing." She smiled. "You see, your chest is growing. That is part of being a woman. You will start having a small amount of blood coming out of you, too, down here, where you go to the bathroom. But it is nothing to be afraid of. It is part of being a woman, too."

I felt so embarrassed hearing all of this. I tried not to show it as I wanted to understand. All I kept thinking about was 'why?'

Mom continued, "Once you start to have blood, that is called your cycle. It will only last a few days, and then it will be gone. It will then happen every month, only for a few days. You use a small pad to take care of the blood. It is fine. Now, the one thing I want you to know. This time that comes once a month is nothing to be sad about. It is part of being able to have babies when you get married. Nonna told me long ago to call it my friend. Because, one day, that friend will not come. It will stay inside you.

That friend will be a baby growing within you. That is how women have babies. Do you understand?"

"I think so," I said, even more embarrassed now. How could I possibly grow up and have babies? I was only twelve.

"Well, don't be afraid if you someday see blood in your underwear. Just let me or Nonna know, and we will give you what you need."

"Okay," I said, now sinking deeper into embarrassment and dreading the day I would have to tell them this.

"OK, tomorrow you and I will go to the store. You will have to start wearing a bra. I will buy you two of them."

"Do I have to?" I asked.

"Yes, but don't worry. Every woman wears one. You know."

I dreaded having to wear such a thing. I would die of embarrassment if my brothers found out, but how could I hide it from them?

Mom smiled briskly, and helped me up, then hugged me.

Nothing more was said about it.


# Faustina

Right after Easter, we got a phone call from Italy and Mom answered the phone.

"Hello?"

"Hey, Zia Silvia. How are you?"

There was quiet.

"What!" Mom said. "Why?"

Again, there was silence.

"Let me get Rosa," Mom said anxiously. Zia Sylvia was my Nonna's sister who lived in Italy. I wondered what all the sudden drama was about.

"Mom," she cried out.

Nonna Rosa had been outside and came running in. "Who is it?"

"Sylvia."

"Sylvia!" she exclaimed with narrowed eyes as she took the phone.

"Pronto."

Pronto was the Italian way of saying, go ahead.

Nonna listened, *oohing, ahhing,* and *oohing* again. "When?"

She listened again.

"Here! In America!"

She listened. Then started raising her hand in the air. "Hold on!"

"Brigida, come here."

Mom came closer. Nonna handed the phone to me. "Hold this, Mari."

Mom and Nonna walked into the kitchen. Nonna called outside into the garden for Nonno Ernesto to come inside. I thought about saying 'Hi,' but I wanted to hear what they were saying. So I held the phone and listened to them in the kitchen.

Within moments they were talking. Nonna Rosa was exclaiming, "You know how he is. He wants her out of the house. She wants to come here, but... Do we have room?"

"Mom, we can make room. What did she do!"

"She didn't do anything! You know Amelio has always been very nervous about his daughters. For some reason, he does not get along with her. Now, he is mad because she has a boyfriend. He said it will be a scandal."

Mom protested, "How can there be a scandal?"

"I don't know. Sylvia said Amelio saw them kissing, and he went ballistic."

Mom thought for a moment, then said, "Let her come. We have room. We will help her."

They both turned to Nonno Ernesto, who shrugged, then nodded, signaling his approval.

Nonna returned to the phone, and I suddenly realized our home was about to grow again. I did not mind because I liked Faustina. I had spent time with her in Italy. She was nine years older than I was, but that was OK, because I liked her.

Nonna said, "Tell Faustina she can come here and stay with us."

Just then, there was a knock at the door. It was Uncle Tony and Aunt Jean.

Nonna hung up the phone and put her finger to her lip, signaling silence.

Mom said, "Come in."

They came in and sat down. Jean started, "Oh, Brigida. Mom is all upset as my brother won't go to the doctor. He says he's fine, but I don't think he is. He's been bleeding for over a month and it's a big mess. My dad is mad too. Anyway, I am going to call him when I get home to see if I can convince him."

Mom, Nonna, and I sat still, listening, waiting for her to finish. Suddenly, Crispino burst into the room, followed by Danny. Crispino said, "Faustina is coming to live with us!"

"What!" Jean exclaimed. "Who is Faustina?"

Mom's face grew cross. "Crispino, be quiet!" Then she shook her head. "He doesn't know anything."

Uncle Tony chimed in, "That is good news. I remember Faustina. She is very nice. You will have a big sister, Mari."

I smiled. Uncle Tony always made good come out of turmoil.

"Why is she coming here?" Aunt Jean asked.

"Jean!" Uncle Tony said. "Let's change the subject."

Jean said, "I brought some bananas for Cresenzo. I know he likes them."

Mom rolled her eyes some and smiled. She held her head, and I could tell she was getting a migraine. "Mari, help get the baby fed. I have to lie down."

Uncle Tony and Aunt Jean left, and an uneasy quiet settled in. Everyone was happy, but everyone also knew that Papa had not been told yet, and we would probably have to rearrange the bedrooms again.

## Cattolica

I came home from school one day with a form from St. Ignatius. Mom asked me what it was.

I said, "The teacher said it was for free lunches."

"What, do they think we are poor?" Mom asked. She looked over the form and saw the income guidelines. "Sheesh," she said. "According to this, we are."

"Should we fill it out?"

"No, Mari. You don't want to eat that food, anyway. You like what you bring for lunch, don't you?"

"I do, Mom."

"Okay, then."

She tore up the form.

Later that night, as I lay in bed, I thought about my mom's statement. I never knew we were considered poor. We were immigrants, yes, and we wasted nothing. But poor was something that applied to other people. In my mind, poor applied to people who were downtrodden. Poor applied to people were miserable. We were none of those things. We were happy, full of life, and lifted by the ideas that America gave to us. We had plenty of blessings. We had plenty of food, clothing, and familial relationships. We had traditions and special occasions. We had worship days and milestone events within our family. We had holidays and holy days to celebrate as a family unit. We were not poor. We were rich.

I reflected on how our faith made a difference, too. We included everyone because we were Catholic. The word Catholic is from the word "Catolico." It means that "everyone is welcome." We never left anyone out when it was a birthday or a Halloween party because we never wanted to be left out or abandoned. We asked and invited everyone because we wanted to ensure everyone participated in the same joy, happiness, and fun we were experiencing. It was our immigrant way. It was our Catholic way.

## Faustina to Library

When Faustina came to live with us, we immediately had to rearrange the entire house. Since we only had three bedrooms, it was decided that Nonno Ernesto, Bruno, and Crispino would share one room. Me, Faustina, and Nonna would share another room. My parents, my little brother Danny, and the new baby Ernesto would stay in their room.

It was an enormous adjustment, but it was also an enjoyable one.

Trying to fall asleep sometimes with Nonna and Faustina talking was very fun. They seemed to be able to talk and laugh about the funniest and simple things. I loved spending this time with them. I considered it a great privilege.

Faustina took adult high school classes to learn English. She wanted to go to the community college soon and study to become a teacher. Because of this, we all had to be very quiet in the house when she was studying. She also got out of a lot of the chores because she was a student studying for a degree. To my immigrant family, this was the promise of America, and they would do all they could to ensure Faustina got her degree.

But more than anything, she was like a fun older sister to me, the sister I never had. Because she was twenty years old, I was allowed to go places with her. On Saturdays, after cleaning at the apartments, and Italian School, baking bread, and cleaning with Nonna, I would get Faustina and walk almost two miles to a store called Zayre's. We would walk in and look at all the clothing and household goods there. Sometimes Faustina would buy me a soda and french fries at the soda counter. While the windows of time were small and few, I had a lot of freedom with Faustina.

Faustina also often went to the library and I was allowed to go with her. I loved walking into such a large public place as our library. We would walk around and pick out books. Faustina even helped me to get my first library card, and I began bringing books home every Saturday.

But our house was very crowded now. We only really had one bathroom. The one down the basement was functional, but no one liked going there, maybe Nonno Ernesto or the older boys. It was not infrequent that Faustina would be in the main bathroom for too long. Papa would inevitably have to go, and he would start pounding on the door, shouting, "Faustina, get out of the bathroom!"

Of course, when one went into the bathroom to shower in our immigrant home, they did not come out wrapped in a towel. We had to come out of the bathroom fully dressed. That made everything crowded, rushed, and contributed to things taking too long.

## Uncle Joe and Aunt Mary

One evening, Uncle Joe and Aunt Mary came over. They had not been around as much as they used to in the last year. Uncle Joe was always going on business trips, and Aunt Mary would never divulge what he was doing. She always just shrugged and pretended she knew nothing of his travels. I suspected something was wrong. He had been going to California often, and his friend, Angelo DiMassi traveled with him. Uncle Joe had also been traveling to Italy twice a year, which I found strange. But tonight, upon his arrival at our house, he said he had important news to discuss. All three remaining brothers had been asked to come, and Uncle Tony was specifically instructed NOT to bring Aunt Jean.

My brothers and I were excited about the big meeting. This was different from merely having company over. Tonight, something important was to be discussed, and a heightened aura descended on the entire home. One by one, they arrived. First, Uncle Joe and Aunt Mary. They sat in the kitchen with Mom and Papa as Nonna Rosa poured them all coffee. Nonno Ernesto stayed in the living room because the meeting had to do with the DiRuggiero family business. Uncle Tony came in next. His warm smiles and fun greetings to all of us children lifted the mood, but only momentarily. Within a few minutes, he sat at the table and settled in for the important matter that would be forthcoming.

As I watched the three brothers gather around the table, I remembered the missing brother: Uncle Italo. He was once the unspoken leader of the brothers, and now he was gone. Uncle Joe was the leader now, and I did not think he was nearly as nice, or as good a leader as Uncle Italo had been.

Joe began in his broad groveling accent, made worse by his scarred cheek, "Hey… so all of you know… I have been back to see our land in Italy several times. It is in very bad shape. There are laws now that if you do not take care of your land and visit it several times a year, they can take it and give it to someone else."

A concerned look came over Papa's face, and Uncle Tony began nodding as if he agreed with everything Uncle Joe would say. I did not believe every word he said. A mean person could not be trusted to do what is best for everyone. Uncle Tony asked, "What should we do, Joe?"

"Hey," Joe said, sitting back, raising his hand in the air. "Who's got the money to be doing anything."

There was silence. I looked at Papa. He was grimacing, shaking his head. Uncle Tony was looking down, with a cross look on his face. I could see that Papa and Uncle Tony completely trusted Uncle Joe. Whatever he said was gospel. If he did not have the solution to a problem, none of them did. That was why their heads were down, because Uncle Joe had cast doubt on the entire equation by saying that no one had the money to solve it.

As if he had been led, Uncle Tony said, "Maybe we could all pitch in. We can get Theresa, Rose, Frank, Rafaluce, and Yolanda. With us three, that makes nine of us."

"That may be what we have to do," Joe said, satisfied. He continued then as if quickly moving on to the next part of what I could tell was a planned performance. "I am trying to arrange things with the local government, so we don't have to be so stringent, but it takes time, and…" he added, lowering his eyes, "it takes connections."

Papa and Uncle Tony both began nodding with pursed lips and half-smiles. They were proud their leader had come up with a solution.

Uncle Joe then said, "I will talk with the others and see who is willing to pitch in."

He then called to the living room, "Mary, let's go."

Uncle Joe and Aunt Mary made some more meaningless small talk and left shortly thereafter. I wondered why they had come in, had their say, which seemed like a rehearsed performance, and just as quickly left. I wondered about this land, too. We had not heard about it in many years, not since Uncle Italo had been murdered.

Once they left, Mom and Papa immediately began subtly arguing. Mom was upset and did not feel we had the money to support Uncle Joe and his trips to Italy. By now, Danny and Ernesto were in bed, but Crispino and I were hiding under the dining room table, listening to them. Papa nervously told her that we had to or we would lose the land. Mom's reply was very practical, as she did not know where we would get the money. Their voices grew louder, and the argument escalated until Papa began yelling. Within moments, he came out of the kitchen into the living room. Crispino and I held our breath. We were not supposed to be hiding under the table, listening to them, and now we were caught, trapped under the table.

Crispino and I looked at each other, wide-eyed, wondering how we would escape our perilous position. Of course, once the initial fear wore off, Crispino began to think it was funny. He made faces trying to get me to laugh, but I would not, knowing it would give us away. Of course, as usual, Crispino amused himself and snickered out loud. Papa immediately heard us. He jumped off the couch, folding his newspaper on the fly, and ran to the dining room, shouting, "You kids get to bed now!"

We scampered past him as he swiped at Crispino with the folded newspaper, narrowly missing him, and chased us through the living room. I barely made it to my room as Papa followed Crispino, who dashed in ahead of him. Papa stopped at the doorway, yelling, "Go to sleep!"

A little while later, as I lay in bed, waiting for Faustina to come home from evening classes and for Nonna Rosa to come to bed, I thought of all that had transpired. No good had come to our house tonight. It felt like a mini bomb had been delivered, and the delivery persons had left, leaving for our little family to deal with it. It had blown up, and I had a feeling it would keep blowing up.

## Faustina the Match

After six months passed, Faustina's green card was expiring. She still had not been able to finish her English classes and therefore was not able to enroll in college yet. She would have to go back to Italy. I remember the discussion we had at the table. As immigrants, we were all familiar with the rules and followed them. When Faustina started to cry at the table, Nonno Ernesto said, "Faustina, there is only one way you can stay here in America. You have to get married."

"How can I?" she asked, her eyes wet and her hands open.

"We would have to find someone," came the reply.

Everyone grew quiet.

Faustina began shaking her head. "I don't want to go back. There must be another way."

Nonno Ernesto stayed quiet. He had already told her the truth. It was the only way.

"How do we find someone?" she asked, exasperated.

I looked over at her. I could not believe she was going to marry someone she did not know just to stay in the country.

Mom answered, "We must put the word out to our friends and family. They will know someone who is looking for a wife."

Faustina hung her head back, sighing. "You better do it then, because I want to stay here in America."

~ ~ ~ ~

The word went out through the gossip vine. Faustina was looking for a husband. Mom and Nonna received some calls during this time, but nothing was materializing. As the day when Faustina would have to leave for Italy was nearing, our whole family was getting nervous.

Then, we got a call. A man named Ralph had thrown his hat into the ring. He owned a pizza shop. He was older than Faustina by about seven years, but that did not matter to anyone. The deadline was approaching.

It was a rainy Tuesday afternoon. Mom came home from work early, went to her room, and got dressed. So did Faustina. Something was going on. Nonno Ernesto arrived early too and went to his room, coming out with his Sunday clothes on.

"Where are you going, Mom?" I asked.

Mom paused, then said, "Get dressed, Mari. You are coming too."

"But where are we going?"

"You will see."

I quickly ran to my new room. Faustina was sitting on the bed with her head down, deep in thought. "Where are we going, Faustina?"

She looked up, her face set with no emotion. "To meet someone who wants to marry me."

My eyes widened, and I did not know how to respond.

Soon, our friend Asunta Valentini arrived carrying an umbrella. It had started to rain hard. Her jacket was soaked, as were the bottoms of her pants. She was going to watch the boys while we were gone. Nonno Ernesto, Nonna, Mom, Faustina, and I ran out to the car to avoid the rain. Mom drove us slowly down Lorain Avenue about ten blocks, then turned onto Clark Avenue. No one talked at all. We all just looked out our windows at the falling raindrops.

Soon, our car slowed, and we turned the corner next to a sign that read, "Clark Avenue Pizza." We came to a stop on the side, then got out. Mom pointed to the first house on the street behind the pizza shop, and we all hustled over to it, dodging puddles and the rain, and went up the steps onto the porch.

Nonno Ernesto looked at Faustina. "Are you ready?" he asked.

She nodded. I could see fear in her eyes; fear that said she was worried about making a mistake

Nonno knocked.

An older woman with gray, pinned back hair answered the door. She was short and slightly heavy, but wearing a kind smile. She momentarily glanced at me. Then her eyes went to Faustina. She then said, "*Ahh*, Ernesto, Rosa, Brigida, come in."

We all walked into the quaint Cleveland home. It was not much larger than ours, with a somewhat worn blue carpet and matching slightly faded blue wallpaper, though it was very clean. I could smell the scent of Pledge and noticed the shining furniture. Pictures of family, as well as numerous pictures of Jesus and of Mary, filled almost every wall. Finally, the woman turned to greet us more formally. "Hi, I am Ralph's mother, Celia." She reached out her hand to Faustina.

"I am Faustina."

"And who are you?" she asked, bending down, turning to me.

"I am Marisa."

The woman smiled, taking my hand for a moment.

Just then, a man with a slight limp came around the corner. His face was warm, with a set jawline. His dark brown hair was slicked down, parted to the side. He had on his Sunday clothes too, it seemed, with dark brown pants and a blue shirt slightly opened. Dark hair covered the top of his chest and lower neck.

Celia turned. "This is my son, Ralph."

Ralph walked up to us and stopped. He was looking at Faustina. I looked up at her. She was looking at him too, but her face showed me she was a bit frozen.

"It's nice to meet you, Faustina."

Faustina swallowed and extended her hand. "It is nice to meet you too, Ralph."

The rest of the introductions were quickly made, and Celia ushered us over to the dining room table. Mom asked me to sit in the living room. I did not mind because I was close to the dining room and could see and easily hear everyone.

Celia began the conversation. "So, we are talking about my son getting married. We wanted to get to know you, Faustina, and we wanted to give you a chance to get to know us."

Mom replied for our party. "Yes, we do too."

Nonno Ernesto nodded. I could tell he had a sadness or reluctance in his countenance. It seemed our party all had the same reluctance, and only Celia and Ralph did not. Ralph seemed handsome enough, but I could tell he was no match for Faustina. She was young, lively, with a spring in her step and, more importantly, in her heart. I could not see such light in Ralph.

The conversation continued for several hours, interrupted only by Celia bringing in Italian coffee and pastries several times. The conversations were tense, filled with moments of modest laughter and moments of Faustina trying to convey her meaning in some of her answers in her broken English. Ralph, too, talked about his business and how well it was doing.

I was beginning to fall asleep when I heard Celia say, "Then it is decided. It will be in three weeks on Saturday, at noon."

I sat up, and resolutions of congratulations went around the table. Ralph's mother stood up, as did everyone else. She took Ralph's hand and Faustina's hand and joined them together. I watched Faustina's face carefully. Her smile was forced, not genuine.

I looked at Ralph. His was like that of a miner who had stumbled upon an unexpected large nugget of gold.

Ralph and Faustina awkwardly hugged.

Then, as if leaving a school counseling appointment, we quietly donned our coats and went to the car.

It was dark outside and no longer raining. As we drove home, the streets shimmered with the reflection of the lights on the wet pavement. There was no talking. Silence, tapered with a general feeling of heaviness, was our friend. I looked over at Faustina. Her head was leaning against the glass, her sad expression staring into oblivion. I could see her thoughts as they turned through her mind. She was going to be able to stay in America, but she was about to enter a life she never wanted. It all felt so sad to me, absurd, and all I could do was feel sorry for her.

~ ~ ~ ~

Three weeks later, we stood in the pews of Our Lady of Mt. Carmel Church as Faustina made her vows.

After the wedding, she picked up her suitcase of clothing and left our home for good.

# My Summer Job

As soon as school ended at the end of May, Mom took me downtown to apply for a five-week program for Cleveland youth, working in city hall for Mayor Ralph J. Perk. Mom told me to put a different day on my application instead of my real birthday, so I could get hired. I was unsure if it was wrong, but she told me some of the other Italian women she knew had their children do it, and they got hired.

I filled out the application as instructed and was hired on the spot. Two days later, I sat in the front seat of Papa's car very early in the morning. At a very slow pace, he drove me down Lorain Avenue over the main bridge going into downtown, then dropped me off in front of city hall.

Right away, I was assigned to clean the hallway and rooms near the third floor where the mayor's office was located. In the beginning, there were lots of young students working. Many of them were black, and there was a natural tension between white and black kids. But I kept my head down and tried to do my job. I could tell most of the kids were older than I was.

One day, I remember cleaning the mayor's office, and it had a personal restroom. I recall being ushered out of the bathroom/office area quickly because he would be entering soon, and I had to leave abruptly. I remember the security guards saying that the toilet flushed silently so that the politician could still talk and go to the bathroom simultaneously. As a pre-teen, I thought that was a cool concept and the greatest invention. I figured whoever thought of that idea was intelligent indeed.

I also recall that my supervisor used to always look at me strangely, and I was scared to death that one day they would ask me my real age, and then I would be caught, maybe even arrested.

Papa would drop me off every morning. Then I would have to wait on the front steps of city hall every afternoon for him to return from work and pick me up. I usually arrived at the job almost a half hour before everyone else, and I went home over an hour after all the other kids left. It was what I had to do for our family, as we only had one car, and Papa drove it to work.

As the six-week program wore on, the ranks of the kids in the program began to thin out, with many of them tiring of it, quitting, and some even getting fired. One of the girls was rumored not to be coming in to clean because she had morning sickness. I had a hard time understanding how a sixteen-year-old kid would want to bear, raise, and bring another kid to adulthood.

So, I kept cleaning as the youth cleaning crew got thinner and thinner.

One day, though, I was called down to the office by my supervisor. Somehow, they had looked at my application, and they had questions.

It didn't take long for me to tearfully admit that I was younger than the age of sixteen. Finally, after several long and disappointing looks from my supervisor, she shook her head and told me I could continue working until the end of the program because I was a good worker, but I was not to say a word to anyone.

It was early July when the five-week summer program ended with the Cleveland youth. I had saved every penny of my earnings and chosen to buy a few pieces of a bedroom set. I was limited as to what could fit in the overcrowded bedroom that I shared with my grandmother. I picked out light yellow furniture with a flower pattern on it and I was very happy. My parents doubled the amount I had saved, giving me enough cash to buy the matching single bed headboard and dresser with a bookcase stand. I was now completely elated and felt an extreme sense of accomplishment. My summer of hard work, arriving early, staying late, and saving every penny, had truly paid off.

In my family, being early was acceptable. In my family, being late to work was incomprehensible. In my family, being late was rude, selfish, and unacceptable. At any rate, I was taught at a tender age to be respectful of my elders, those in authority over me and above me, and to follow the rules at home, work, and life in general.

# The Announcement

One night right after the 4<sup>th</sup> of July, we were seated around the dinner table on a Saturday evening. Nonno Ernesto was particularly quiet, but Nonna Rosa's silence was more noticeable. Her smiling, happy countenance was gone. She sat next to him, as usual, but just ate her food quietly.

When we had finished, Nonno Ernesto said, "I have an announcement."

It was rare that he spoke so forthrightly. His words were always sacred to us, but he rarely began conversations. Normally, we would look to him to add a final measure to a matter, whether good or bad. So when he said this, we all stopped and turned to listen.

"I am going back to Italy. Nonna and I will be leaving in two weeks."

I froze and looked at Nonna, not wanting to believe it was true. She was looking at her husband and I could see the division in her eyes. She would stay by his side, but part of her did not want to leave. I looked at Mom. Her face was distressed, as if she had been given the news of a death in the family.

Mom asked, "Are you going to visit there?"

"No, Brigida," he said resolutely, "I have to go back to my homeland and take care of my land. I have grandchildren there too, who also need me."

A tear rolled down Nonna's cheek.

Mom nodded as resolutely as Nonno had spoken. She was brave and strong like him and seemed determined to show she would be strong despite this devastating news.

I suddenly felt lost. The table was silent. Nonno got up and went to his room and Nonna followed him.

I went into my room, closed the door, and just sat on my bed, devastated. Nonna was my mom. She was the one who raised me. How could she leave me? I needed her. For a brief moment, I thought about going with them. But I would never be allowed to. And what of my brothers? They needed me. I was like their mom in many ways.

I got under the covers and started to cry.

# Sorrow

Monday morning, I rose early. I could hear Mom and my grandparents quietly talking at the kitchen table. Mom's voice held a sad tone I had never heard before. I went into the dining room and crawled under the table. I felt so alone and sad that I didn't want them to see me, and yet, my entire being yearned to be close to them. Nonno Ernesto was advising Mom, "Buy a house in the suburbs right away, Brigida. You have to get the children out of Cleveland."

"Why don't you come with us?" Mom pleaded. "We can buy a house with land, lots of land."

"*Heh*, I cannot, Brigida."

There was silence, and I heard Mom begin to sniffle. "I don't know how I am going to do it without you."

"Marisella is getting older now. She can help you."

The words fell upon me heavily. How could I possibly help? I needed my grandparents as much as anyone, especially Nonna. It was Nonna and me who did so much around the home. Nonna had taught me much, but I was her helper. Without her... I began praying earnestly as I felt tears falling down my cheeks. I moved my legs and made a noise.

"Who's up?" Nonna asked.

I wiped the tears away, scampered out from under the table, and walked into the kitchen, shielding my eyes from the bright light. Nonno Ernesto turned. "Come here, Mari."

I walked into his warm hug and held on tight. "I don't want you to leave, Nonno."

"I have to, Mari. You are going to be okay."

His rough skin against my cheek, the smell of his Old Spice aftershave, and his strong arms around me gave me a feeling of protection. I could not fathom this was going to end. I turned my head, watching Mom and Nonna gazing at us both, drawing in the tender moment, but it did not feel tender. It felt nothing more than temporary. It was coming to an end.

The sound of a crying baby erupted. Mom got up, wiped tears away, and attended to the baby.

Nonno Ernesto let me go and picked up his coffee. I sat across from him as Nonna got up to get me a small cup of coffee. Nonno Ernesto said, "I want you to take care of your brothers, Mari. They need you."

"Yes, Nonno."

"That's a good girl. Help with the garden too, Mari. You will have to water it and weed it. You know what to do."

"Yes, Nonno," I said in a sad tone, my eyes downward.

He glanced up at the clock. "*Heh*, I have to go to work."

"When is your last day at work, Nonno?"

"Tomorrow." He quietly got up, took his lunch, and left.

Nonna held her coffee cup, half-smiling at me. Her eyes held the same sadness I was feeling. They held compassion too. She was the only person I could be myself around, and my eyes began to water again. "Oh, Nonna. I am going to miss you."

She pulled her chair over, pulling me close. "Mari, I will miss you too. But I will always be with you. Every day."

"How?" I exclaimed.

"In everything I have taught you. In the old ways, you have learned from me. Keep them, Mari. Keep the old ways, and I will be right by your side."

I shook my head and nodded at the same time. It didn't make sense to me. None of that mattered, only that they were leaving mattered.

"When are you leaving, Nonna?"

"Saturday."

*Saturday? But how would we make bread? How would we clean? How would we make the meal? The familiar routines that were my anchor were suddenly no more.*

Mom came in holding the baby before I could reply, so I went to my room and got ready for school.

~ ~ ~ ~

It all happened so fast. By Monday afternoon, the news had spread, and the visitors began arriving in the late afternoons and evenings to say goodbye.

# The Retirement Party

We wore our Sunday clothes on Thursday evening and all walked to a nearby restaurant. Nonno Ernesto's work was hosting a retirement dinner for him. The dinner was bittersweet. There were over ten men who worked with him present, along with our family. A buffet was set against the back wall of the room while tables filled the rest of it. Steam circled up from each silver tray holding the chicken, beef, green beans, and mashed potatoes. There were rolls and butter and gravy and salad, too. Our family took a long table in the back row. The baby began crying, and Mom stepped out for a moment to calm him.

"When can we eat?" Crispino said. "I'm hungry."

"Be qui!" Papa said, glaring.

"I'm hungry too," Danny said. "Marisa, can you get me something?"

"No, Mari. Danny, just wait. It's not time yet," Nonno Ernesto said.

A man from the company wearing a suit stood up just as Mom came back inside with the baby, who had a pacifier in his mouth.

The man began, "May I have everyone's attention. We are here to honor Ernesto Zotolla for his ten years of service with our company." He pointed to our table. "Ernesto, please stand up."

I watched my strong, humble grandfather stand. He looked to me like a noble king. All our eyes turned to him as we sat in silence. Even my brothers were perfectly still. The man continued, "Ernesto, thank you. We have pitched in to buy you this gold watch. Please come up."

Nonno Ernesto walked up, keeping his eyes fixed on the ground. He extended his broad arm, took the watch, shook the man's hand, and then nodded, saying, "Thank you."

He glanced up at everyone for a moment, smiling, and again said, "Thank you." Finally, he lowered his glance to the floor and returned to us. The man then said, "Okay, everyone, come on up. We have lots of food."

Crispino and Danny bolted out of their chairs. "Boys!" Mom shouted quietly, but it was too late. Papa got up right away too, and I watched Mom roll her eyes. Nonno Ernesto and Nonna stayed seated, waiting, and though I was hungry, I knew to stay with them. After the line had formed, Nonno got up, signaling for us to go up. The boys passed us, eyes wide, carrying plates half full. Papa was still at the line, slowly moving, filling his plate at each silver basin. The line behind him was near a standstill.

"Cresznez! Hurry up!" Mom again shouted quietly, hoping only he would hear her, but almost at once, everyone turned to look at her, except Papa. Most of their faces held gratitude for her attempted aid. I looked down, horrified at the attention being drawn to us. Finally, Papa reached the end, and the line began moving as if someone had pulled the stopper out of a bathtub.

When we got back to the table, Papa was absorbed in his meal, oblivious to us. Crispino got up and ran to get more, and Danny followed. When they returned, they started laughing. "Be quie!" Papa said loudly this time. Again, several people looked over at us. I looked down, and Mom's face tightened. "Cresenz," she murmured fiercely in as quiet a voice as she could.

Finally, we all finished, and we went home.

They would be leaving in two days.

## Goodbye

Saturday morning, near the end of July, while it was still dark, I woke from my sleep, frightened I had missed them. I jumped up and ran to the kitchen. Everyone was standing in a circle: my grandparents, parents, and Uncle Tony, who was driving them to the airport. The mood was heavy and labored, and no one was really making eye contact. I ran to Nonna's side and hugged her around the waist. She knelt down, holding me by the upper arms. "I love you, Marisella. Make me proud of you."

I started to cry.

"Oh, don't cry," she said as she too began to cry.

"I will see you again," she said.

"When?"

She looked at Nonno Ernesto and half-smiled and nodded. "I don't know, Mari, but it will happen."

I looked at Papa. His head was down. I looked at Mom. She was holding a handkerchief, wiping away growing tears. Uncle Tony stood by the door, his gaze on me. He was worried. I could tell.

Then they all went outside. I stood by the storm door, watching them get into Uncle Tony's car. Then Papa, keeping his head down, shook Nonno Ernesto's hand once more and got into his car. He was going to work.

They pulled out and the last thing I saw was Nonna's face and a faint wave from the backseat. Then, my heart dropped within me, and I started to cry again.

I ran to the dining room and sat under the table, crying out to God. *Why God? Why? I need her!*

My brothers were still sleeping, and the house was eerily silent. Finally, I lay down, overcome with sorrow, and fell asleep on the carpet. I don't know how much time passed, but I heard the baby erupt with his morning cries. I sighed and went in. The terrible aroma of a full diaper greeted me. I picked him up, cringing, unable to hold my nose, and quickly lay him down on the floor, saying, "Ernesto. I have to change you."

I turned to reach for a diaper, and Danny walked in, rubbing his eyes. "Where is Mom?" he said in a worried voice.

"They took Nonno and Nonna to the airport. They will be back soon."

"I'm hungry."

"Wait in the kitchen, Danny. I will help you."

I took Ernesto's diaper off, rolled it up, and ran to the toilet to shake it out, gagging as I did. I ran back in with a wet rag and soap and cleaned him, then put a new diaper on him, pinning it carefully. Danny got up and ran out of the room, mumbling unintelligible words.

I sighed deeply. I was tired, but my brothers needed me. So I went to the kitchen, put Ernesto in the high chair, and put some Cheerios on his tray. I then got Danny a bowl, poured him some, and then filled it with milk.

"Are they coming back?"

"Yes, Danny. They will be back soon."

"No, are Nonno and Nonna coming back?"

His words struck me deeply. Finally, my heart could not hold it anymore. "No," I said. "They are not coming back."

He, too, started to cry.

\*\*\*

When mom returned from the airport, her eyes were reddened from excessive crying. It reminded me of when Uncle Italo died. The boys all ran up to her, trying to hug her, to get her attention, but she shook them off and went to her room. For almost the entire day, we could hear her crying in the room. She only came out for short times, perhaps to help with dinner, feeble as she was able to in her dire state. After her brief appearances, she went back into her room.

Sunday was the same.

I had to take care of my brothers and put up with Papa's yelling and emotions. What no one realized, is I had lost my mother too. Nonna was my real mother, and she was gone. My deep sadness had to be somehow buried as the needs of my brothers, especially Danny and Ernesto, meant there was no time to grieve, no time to cry. There couldn't be two of us crying.

## The New Rituals

As Monday arrived, I realized it was mid-summer, at least according to the school schedule. I was 13 ½, and my brothers were 9 ½, 5 ½, and 1 ½. Mom got up early and went to work. She started at 8:00 and would be home just after 5:00. Papa would be asleep till late in the morning, then go to work from 3:00 in the afternoon until 11:00 at night. He often worked overtime, coming home hours past his shift end. It was why he usually slept in.

As of only three days earlier, we would wake and Nonna would be there to give the peace and stability in the home that only a seasoned woman can give. It was summer, and we would play, my brothers more than I, but we would enjoy life in our tiny city yard.

Now, though, everything had changed.

My first day without Nonna was spent taking care of my brothers and keeping them quiet until Papa woke up. I quickly washed the dishes and set them out to dry, then took the boys out into the yard and allowed them to run around within our city lot. An hour later, I saw Papa standing at the storm door, in his shorts and T-shirt, watching us.

"Mari!!! Watch them!" he cried out.

"Yes, Papa," I said. I wanted my dad to be happy and was willing to work as hard as possible to make it so.

When lunchtime came, I changed Ernesto and put him on the high chair. I peered around the corner. Papa was sitting in the living room, with his feet curled up behind him, holding the newspaper and watching the news.

Crispino and Danny ran into the house, shouting.

"Stop!" Papa yelled.

I shouted in a low voice so as not to raise the already escalated tension. "Crispino, Danny, come over here. We are having lunch."

Unflinchingly, they turned their chase in the direction of the table and settled onto their chairs.

"Mari! Keep them quiet!"

"Yes, Papa."

I took down a loaf of bread Mom had bought at the store and a jar of peanut butter and jelly from the refrigerator and proceeded to make several sandwiches. I gave one to Danny and Crispino and took another, breaking it up in pieces for Ernesto. Then, I got some milk and poured everyone a glass, giving Ernesto his in a bottle.

Finally, I sat down, out of breath, and nervously picked at my sandwich and drank my milk.

We were all silent, knowing Papa was right around the corner.

Crispino made a face at Danny, and Danny spat out his milk. "Danny!" I yelled through gritted teeth.

"What's going on!" Papa yelled from the living room. It sounded like he was getting up off the couch.

Danny straightened up. Everyone braced for him to round the corner. Nothing.

Unspoken as it was, we all knew we had dodged a bullet. We finished, and Danny and Crispino went out to play. Papa came in, and his face grew anxious. "They made a mess!" he yelled, raising his voice and hand in the air simultaneously, shaking it.

"I'll clean it, Papa!"

He began muttering as I quickly wiped the table and counter and put the dishes in the sink. "Go sit down, Papa. I will clean it up."

Papa's eyes shifted nervously as he turned, muttering what sounded like swear words.

I took Ernesto to his crib, but he wouldn't go in. I sat on the bed, feeding him, singing the old Italian lullaby we had always sung:

*Nina vo, Nina vo, che pazienza, che ci vo. Ee ci vo il bimbaro.*
*Nina vo, Nina vo, che pazienza, che ci vo. Ee ci vo il bimbaro.*

Finally, he fell asleep.


In the afternoon, my brothers and I were outside playing school on the patio. I was the teacher, calling on them to recite the alphabet or math problems. Danny played along, but Crispino was only halfway in and halfway running around, trying to distract us. Suddenly, I heard the baby cry.

I ran inside. Papa was in the kitchen making some lunch meat sandwiches and packing them in a bag. Then it was time to go to work. But, before he left, our friend Asunta Valentini came walking into the yard from the alley. "Hello, Marisella. I can only stay a little while, but I wanted to help you." She turned to the boys. "Boys, come inside. We are going to watch TV and have a snack."

Papa came out and headed for his car, not saying a word. Asunta turned on the TV. "Boys, you stay in here. We are going to fix you something." She came into the kitchen. "Mari, let's make them macaroni and cheese. Put some water on the stove to boil the macaroni. After we are done, we will heat up some sauce for when your mom gets home."

I was grateful for her help. Her presence brought that seasoned stability I had taken for granted when Nonna was around. But she could not stay long, as she had a family of her own.

Finally, fifteen minutes after five o'clock, Mom came in, exhausted from her long day at work. My brothers immediately ran to her, mobbing her and clamoring for her attention. Ernesto cried the loudest as Mom picked him up, kissing him. I sat down at the table, watching them. There was no time, nor had there ever been, for me to clamor for her attention. Nonna had given that to me. Though Mom was the only one now, our relationship was not that way. We were more like sisters, even distant sisters.

During that first week, mom tried her best, but she spent most evenings in and out of her room with tears and sobs intermittently echoing through the house.

# The Weekend

My life existed on the routines and things we did day in and day out. Seasonal rituals also helped me to know what to do, what to expect, and what to look forward to. The past week had settled into new rituals, and they were hard and full of difficulty. Now the weekend was here. Weekends were very different because everyone was home.

Saturday arrived.

I lay in bed, wondering how things would change. I went into the kitchen, where Mom had her back to me. She was fully dressed, stirring a silver pot on the stove with a long wooden spoon. The familiar smell of tomato sauce filled the air. It seemed strange to me, as Nonna Rosa had always been the one to do this for the family.

Mom turned. "Good morning, Mari."

"Good morning, Mom."

"Pour us some coffee."

"Yes, Mom."

I poured two cups from the already percolating pot on the stove.

Mom sighed, tapping the spoon on the side of the pan to shake off the remaining sauce, then sat down. I could see she was stressed. She sipped her coffee. "We are going to the apartments today to clean. Asunta will watch the baby, but we must take the other boys with us."

"OK, Mom. Are we going to make bread?"

"No, we don't have time. We have to meet a real estate agent today. He wants to help us look for houses."

"We are moving?" I asked.

"Yes, but we have to find the right house first."

Neither of us said much as we sipped our coffee. Mom looked at the sauce. "I will go to the market later and buy some meat to make for dinner. Tomorrow, we can have pasta and meatballs."

I had heard Nonna announce our meal like this countless times. Her words were always filled with satisfaction and love, the same love she put into cooking and caring for each person. But, coming from Mom, it sounded tired and far away, like a necessary duty.

I could see she was struggling as much as I was.

*\*\*\**

At the apartments, we cleaned the steps and did our best to keep Crispino and Danny from driving Papa over the edge. Once again, we did the back steps first, then went around to do the front steps. I was so tired. When we went home, Papa went out to the garage to organize his hundreds of tools and boxes while Mom went to the market. I stayed inside with my brothers, watching TV.

~ ~ ~ ~

When Sunday morning came, the most glaring time of absence occurred. Nonno and Nonna would normally be waiting for me to get dressed and walk the over one-mile journey to Our Lady of Mount Carmel. Today, when I woke, Danny was awake, playing with a truck in the living room. I looked at the time and thought about Our Lady of Mount Carmel. It was too far for me to go. I would never be allowed.

I went to my parent's room. "Mom?"

She lifted her head. "What is it, Mari?"

"Can I walk to Mass at St. Coleman?" I held my breath, knowing she was going to say no, but she said, 'Yes, but come right home.'

My heart leaped within me. "I will, Mom."

As I was heading for the door, I grabbed Danny. "Come in the kitchen, Danny. I will pour you some cereal." I quickly got him a bowl, then handed it to him. "Come and watch TV quietly. And don't spill it. OK?"

"OK," he said, happy I was allowing him to have food in the front room.

I turned on the TV low and put my finger to my lip, signaling quiet. He smiled and nodded, and I left.

When I got to the massive church, hundreds of people were streaming in. It scared me for a moment, but I blended in, went up the center aisle, and sat down in the first seat I could find.

I looked up at the cross, so happy Mom had said yes. This was a place of consolation and peace for me. It was a place I could pray without being interrupted, chastised, or shouted at because of my brothers. I rested here and even drifted off for a moment until the organ began, and Mass started.

That afternoon, Papa and the boys sat around the table waiting for Mom and me to put the bowl of meatballs, a bowl of pasta, and sauce on the table. It all smelled just like any other Sunday, but everything else was different. Mom sat where Nonna usually sat. Papa sat where Nonno sat. There were several empty chairs, and no one was talking. We were all just waiting.

We ate, then Papa went to read the newspaper, and my brothers and I went out to play. Then, in the afternoon, my cousins came over, and the old feelings of Sunday returned.

As I went to bed, I thought of the coming morning. The new rituals were waiting for me again.

## House Hunting

The summer was long and lonely, filled with a myriad of duties and stress. My parents began looking for a house in the suburbs in earnest. On many long, hot Saturdays and Sundays, they would have to leave for two hours at a time to go view houses. Mom had told me that we needed to work together to find a house they could afford. My job was to watch the children. It took well over a month before finally, they found a house they liked. Now, we nervously waited for the bank to approve us.

The news arrived. We were approved. On the following Sunday, after lunch, we piled into the car and drove down Lorain Avenue for what felt like forever. We passed hundreds and hundreds of stores and houses until finally, we turned. We pulled onto a wide, quiet street with large spacious homes on each side of the street. Children were playing and riding bikes all around. We pulled up to one of the biggest homes there and got out of the car. The realtor was waiting and he showed us in. I had never seen such a mansion. We went upstairs to see the bedrooms. There were five, and Mom announced that we would each have our own room.

The living room, dining room, kitchen, and family room were all large and spacious. I felt rich all of a sudden. Crispino opened the back door and ran out. We went out after him. The yard was large, with a lot of trees. Mom and Papa immediately began talking, pointing to the sun, and identifying which ones they would cut down to make the garden. There would be lots to do. We would get the keys in the fall.

## Lipstick Now and Trip to High School

At the end of August, while we were still waiting to move, Mom told me we had to go for a ride to do something. So she arranged for Asunta to come over and watch the boys.

Mom stopped the car and put on lipstick as we pulled out of the driveway. I had never seen her put any on, except for weddings or special occasions. I asked, "Mom, why are you putting on lipstick?"

"No reason," she said, adding, "I am wearing lipstick now because your grandfather went back to Italy."

"Nonno would not let you wear lipstick?"

"That's right. Your Nonno told me not to wear make-up as long as he was around and lived in the same house as us." She continued, her voice trailing off, almost to a whisper, "I would gladly not wear lipstick if I could just have them here with us again."

I said nothing, thinking, wishing the same.

We drove to St. Joseph Academy, an all-girls high school in Cleveland. As we went inside the massive vaulted halls, we passed classroom after classroom of smart-looking girls sitting attentively at desks, with their teachers facing them, engaging them. When the bell rang, the classrooms emptied, and now hundreds of girls dressed in uniforms, all much taller and more mature than me, filled the halls, darting in and out, alone and in groups, hustling to their next classes. Elegant women dressed perfectly in neat dresses, and nuns dressed in habits all carried clipboards and notebooks. They were the teachers.

I suddenly felt afraid I would surely get lost. How would I know where to go?

We registered and were given a tour of the massive facility. The day before, Papa was supposed to take me there for orientation. But he would not wake up to take me, so I missed it.

I was given a class schedule and shown where all the classes were and, most importantly, where my homeroom was. It was here I would report to in the morning. As we left it and Mom talked with the guide, I kept turning around, trying to memorize where the room was. I was petrified of getting lost.

## First Day of High School

On my first day of high school, I nervously sat at my kitchen table, eating a piece of toast with jelly, trying very hard not to get anything on my new uniform. It was still dark outside, and soon I would venture out into a whole new chapter in my life.

Mom was up. She had made the coffee and was now in her room getting ready for work. My brothers were all still asleep. I wished Nonna was there to hold, hug, and tell me she would be waiting for me when I got home. Mom came in and sat down. "Do you know where to go, Mari?"

"I think so," I said.

"There will be other girls on the bus going to St. Joe's too. Follow them."

"OK," I said with a manufactured smile. I felt terrified and was sure I would somehow get lost or get on the wrong bus.

Mom got up and hugged me. "You will do great, Mari." Then she glanced at the clock. "I have to go. You should leave soon, too."

I nodded and watched her leave for her walk to the factory where she was a seamstress. I then grabbed my lunch, put it in my book bag, and walked out onto the bustling Lorain Avenue to wait for the bus. Once on the bus, to my great relief, I saw some girls with the same uniform as I had. I could follow them.

While we passed store after store, I nervously pulled out my class schedule and began trying to remember where each classroom was. My mind frantically went up and down the corridors and up and down flights of steps, looking for each classroom. Unfortunately, the subjects being taught would be an entirely different matter. None of the subjects sounded that familiar. The old days of simple subjects were replaced with words like: Beginners Biology, Freshman English, and Algebra. I felt my entire chest tighten with the very word Algebra. I knew it was math, and I just knew I would never understand it.

Finally, we reached the main cross street, and all the girls for St. Joe's got up and made their way off the bus. I anxiously followed.

As I stepped off the bus, almost thirty other girls were all waiting for the connecting bus. They were mostly in groups, talking giddily, laughing, and having fun. They looked older than me, if, at least, much taller.

I wanted to go up and join them, but I didn't know any of them and did not know how to simply walk into one of the groups.

There was another group too, of boys. They were on their way to St. Edward and would be boarding the same bus as we would. These boys also looked much older than me, and it frightened me that I would have to take the bus with them. I did not feel ready to engage with them. I would not know what to say.

So, I just leaned against the wall of the building and kept my head down, waiting.

The doors opened with a noise when the bus arrived, screeching to a stop with a loud hiss. The boys and girls all converged near the front and began boarding. I waited and moseyed into the back of the crowd. When I got to the steps, I stepped up and crowded my way into the little room that was left. The doors closed, and I awkwardly turned to face the front as the bus lurched forward with an obnoxious roar.

Loud laughing and conversations pummeled my ears as I nervously held tight, swaying with every slowing and bump, trying not to bump into the girls in front of and behind me.

Finally, the bus roared, then hissed to an abrupt stop, and the noisy door catapulted open. I filed out and moved quickly out of the way of the mass exodus of girls in their uniforms, hustling to the long sidewalk that wove its way across the grounds to the massive school buildings looming in the distant morning light.

I kept to myself, smiling to my left and right at the other girls, trying hard to walk as fast as they were walking. My shorter, skinny legs were not used to this pace. I followed the mass up the steps to the main entrance and made my way to the homeroom I was to report to.

One of the most beautiful women I had ever seen stood at the front of the class. She wore a short blue dress and shiny light brown shoes. She smiled at me and lifted her arm, motioning for me to sit at one of the desks that had not yet been taken.

Within moments, more girls came in, and the desks filled. The noise deafened the room until the woman stepped forward and called us all to attention. I unwrapped the paper in my pocket, studying where I would have to go for my first class. Algebra. I cringed, trying to remember where it was.

The teacher began, "As a reminder for anyone new. I am Mrs. House, and I am your homeroom teacher. I will also see you later in the English class. Now, I will take attendance."

She went through the list, calling out names. Then, finally, she got to mine. "Marisa DiRuggiero?"

I slowly raise my hand, suddenly feeling the eyes of all drawn to me. "Welcome, Marisa."

She finished the list and spoke to us for a few minutes, and then the bell rang. Everyone got up and hustled out. I went to the front. "Excuse me. Do you know where this class is?"

She looked and smiled. "Yes, see here." She walked to the door and pointed down the hall. "Go to the first hall, over there, and turn right. It is about seven classrooms down."

"Thank you," I said nervously.

She bent down. "You are going to be fine, Marisa. Don't be scared."

"OK," I said. "Thank you."

# The Move

On a windy October day, a few weeks after high school started, we moved out of Cleveland. It was Friday afternoon, right after school. Everyone gathered at our Cleveland home. My uncles and aunts all helped, piling all of our clothing, beds, dressers, dishes, and everything you could think of into a truck Papa and Uncle Tony had rented. We also had to carefully load all the hundreds of canned tomatoes, olives, and eggplants from the cellar into packed boxes. These were cautiously cushioned and placed in the back of Uncle Tony's station wagon. He would drive them out slowly so none were broken. On top of the jars, a clean tablecloth was laid out, and our dried sausages were positioned and covered. They were going with us, too.

Only the bedroom furniture, dining room, and kitchen tables were brought with us, as Mom had insisted on purchasing several new couches for her new dream home.

I will never forget how vast and large the house was. It was one of the largest homes on the street, two stories tall, with a giant basement. Upstairs were four bedrooms, each larger than our entire living room in Cleveland. My parents had the largest room on one end of the long hallway. Ernesto, at only 1 ½, would stay in their room. My other two brothers each had their own rooms. My room was at the other end of the hallway. It had two windows, one of which looked down onto the front lawns of the quiet suburban street. This was not Lorain Avenue. It was Dorothy Drive. The difference was night and day, in traffic, noise, people, and every other respect you could imagine.

On the first night, I lay awake in my bed, glancing out the window across the room at the moonlit night sky. I was exhausted from moving. The room felt too large to me. Only my small dresser stood against the wall, like a lone sentinel. Guarding what, I did not know—perhaps my bed and me. I glanced at the broad doors of the closet where only a few dresses hung and hoped there were no monsters inside. There was no need for such a large closet and I wished it were not even there.

I thought of days not so long past when Nonna would be sleeping next to Faustina in a double bed not six feet away from me. I thought of the times I would listen to them quietly talking, Faustina gathering advice and unloading her concerns about life and America as Nonna Rosa patiently listened. I thought of the light of Zsacha's Fur shop, which I would never see again. I thought of Lorain Avenue, bustling with city life. Our family farm was still there, sitting silently in the moonlight, waiting for the coming spring when it would come to life again. Would it? Would anyone ever bring it back to life, or would it go the way of most city lots and become barren and simply a placeholder between closely perched houses?

*** 

The next morning, early, I was awakened by a loud pounding on my door. "Mari! Wake up! We have to clean!"

I opened my eyes in shock and realized it was Saturday morning. Yes, we always cleaned the house and did our chores on Saturday morning, but Papa had never led the charge. The pounding started again. "Mari! Wake up, Mari!"

I lifted my head and shoulders and propped myself up on my elbows, trying to orient myself to my new surroundings. The moonlight was gone, replaced by the gray early morning clouds of what felt like a brisk fall day. "Si, Papa!" I said. "I need to get dressed."

"Hurry, Mari. We have a lot to do."

I heard him turn away, his slippers shuffling down the hall, and fell back down on my pillow, sighing deeply and whispering a prayer for strength.

I quickly dressed in my Saturday cleaning clothes and took a mopina out of my sock drawer, tying it around my head. A mopina was a bandana or other cloth the females in the family used to wear in order to make sure their hair would never fall into the cooking. Since cleaning on any given day involved cooking too, we wore it for both occasions.

I opened the door of my room and stepped into the reality of my new life. Everything was silent. I walked to my brother Crispino's room and quietly opened the door. He was sprawled on his stomach, sound asleep, his legs going every which way. I thought of opening Danny's room, but I knew he was asleep. Finally, near the top of the stairs, I peeked into my parents' room. The bed was already neatly made, and Ernesto was asleep in his crib in the corner. I could already tell his diaper would need changing, but it would wait until he woke up. It had always been drilled into me, 'Never wake a sleeping baby.'

I went down the stairs, and Papa was sweeping the kitchen floor carefully with his back to me. The chairs were all up on the table. "Where is Mom?" I asked.

He turned and raised his hand in the air as his voice ascended with it. "She's at work, Mari!"

I sighed. That meant only one thing. I had a lot to do today.

"Go get the mop, Mari," he said, his voice descending this time.

I sighed again and went into the garage to get the mop and bucket. I filled them with water and put the soap in the kitchen sink. Papa was finishing, and I watched him carefully carry the full dustpan to the garbage. He set the broom and dustpan down and said, "Let me have the mop, Mari. You go sweep the front room and hallway."

"OK, Papa," I said as I dutifully took the broom, proceeded to our new and vast front room, and began sweeping its shiny wood floors. Moments later, I heard my youngest brother, Ernesto, begin to cry.

I was so tired, but there was no time for anything. I went upstairs and into my parents' room. As soon as he saw me, his crying only got louder. "Ernesto. Don't cry!" I said softly. It did not comfort him.

"I have to change your diaper."

Just then, I heard another voice. "I'm hungry!"

I turned. Danny was standing in the doorway in his pajamas, rubbing his eyes.

"Go get dressed, Danny. I have to change the baby."

Danny frowned and turned out of the doorway.

I laid Ernesto down in his crib and carefully changed his explosion-level diaper. The entire room smelled, and I almost gagged. Finally, I got the clean diaper on him, then turned to take the dirty one to the toilet to dump the contents into it. Though they were disposable Pampers, I was still responsible for dumping them, so they did not smell out the house as much.

Ernesto began wailing as soon as I left the room.

"What's going on!" Papa yelled from the bottom of the steps.

"It's OK, Papa. I had to change the baby."

I heard him mutter something under his breath, and he went back down the hall toward the kitchen.

I felt so alone at that moment. We were in a new house, with all its new rooms and new places to keep things. Mom was gone, Papa was in a bad mood, and my brothers were suddenly all in need. I looked into the mirror in the bathroom and saw nothing but a tired young girl who had to go on. I held back my emotions and went back to get my very heavy, wailing little brother out of his crib.

I carried him downstairs, shouting as softly as was possible into my other brother's room, "Come downstairs, Danny."

"Wait!" he cried.

I paused near the top of the stairs, waited for him, then went down.

As soon as we got to the bottom of the stairs, Papa yelled, "Stay off the floor! It has to dry!"

With Danny following close behind, I took Ernesto into the family room and deposited him onto the couch. "Stay here, Ernesto. I will get you a cookie."

"I want one too!" Danny shouted.

I turned to see Papa pulling the bucket into the hallway. He was done with the kitchen.

I went over to the kitchen and peered down the hall. Papa was carefully mopping with his back to me. I tiptoed into the kitchen, went to the pantry, and searched for the cookies. "They're over there!" Danny yelled.

I turned, shouting as silently as I could, "Get back in the family room, Danny."

I grabbed the cookie package, took out a handful, and tiptoed back across the kitchen, past the hall, into the family room, where my brothers anxiously held their hands out. I turned on the TV and put the volume very low, so they could see cartoons, and we all sat nibbling on the cookies, waiting for the floor to dry so we could have breakfast.

As Papa passed by us, with his head down, silently carrying the mop and bucket back into the garage, I asked, "Papa, can we go into the kitchen now?"

His brow furrowed, and a worried look came over him. He looked back at the kitchen floor, then said, "Just a minute, Mari."

He disappeared into the garage, came back in moments later, and went to the kitchen and took the chairs down carefully. Then he said, "Make some oatmeal, Mari."

I was so excited that I could finally get breakfast for myself and my hungry brothers started. I gave them each another couple of cookies, saying, "Stay here, boys. I will make some oatmeal."

I went in and began boiling a pot of water. Within ten minutes, it was ready. I scooped out a few bowls and set them down on the table. "Don't come in yet," I said softly into the family room. "It's too hot."

Just then, my other brother Crispino came running down the stairs, his feet pounding every step as if he were three hundred pounds.

"Stop!" Papa yelled from the front room, where he was on the couch reading the newspaper.

I cringed, and watched Crispino continue his jaunt down the hall, sliding to a stop in the kitchen.

"Sit down, Crispino," I said. "I will get you some oatmeal."

Moments later, my other brothers all wandered in and sat at the table. They were laughing and giggling as quietly as they could. Papa then came in and sat down, as immediate forlorn faces and silence descended on us all. I finished filling the bowls, and we ate in silence.

When we finished, the boys watched cartoons, and Papa returned to his newspaper.

I cleaned the table and washed the dishes. When I was done, I thought about watching cartoons but glanced at the laundry basket near the open basement door and knew I had to get the laundry started.

Near lunchtime, there was a beep in the drive. We all ran to the door. It was Uncle Tony.

"Hello everyone!" he announced as he walked in, wearing his blue work pants and clean white T-shirt.

"Tonnnnn!" Papa yelled, his hand raised high. Uncle Tony hugged him while Papa looked down at the floor with a heartfelt half-smile on his face. As soon as Uncle Tony let him go, Papa exclaimed, "What are you doing, Tony!"

"I have been working at the house. I wanted to come to see my Padina!" My eyes lit up as his smiling eyes turned to me. I ran up and hugged him tightly. "Hi, Uncle Tony!"

"Hello, Padina. OK, now. Everyone line up."

We all knew what this meant. First, Uncle Tony came to me and gave me a dollar bill. "You get a dollar because you are the oldest."

He then handed Crispino and Danny each fifty cents.

I was so excited, as I now had money to buy an ice cream sandwich at St. Joe's for the next four days.

I noticed Papa staring at the floor, smiling. His countenance always improved when Uncle Tony came over. Uncle Tony hugged each of the boys, and we went to the kitchen and sat down. Uncle Tony said, "So, how is everyone?"

Papa shouted, "Fine, Tonnnnn! What happened? Did you lose Jean?"

Uncle Tony chuckled. "She is shopping, Cris."

"I told you!" Papa said, his hand and voice ascending as one, alluding to the fact that Aunt Jean was always shopping.

Just then, the door opened, and Mom walked in. The boys erupted from the table and ran to the door, screaming, "Mom! Mom!"

Mom stooped to hug them and came in. "Hey, Tony! Where is Jean?"

Uncle Tony reared his head back, not wanting to go there again, and said, "She's busy doing something."

"She's shopping!" Papa exclaimed. "Spending your money, Tonnnnn! I told you!!!"

"Be quiet!" Mom said, grimacing and nudging Papa on the shoulder. "Mari, help me make some lunch. After, we have to go to the apartments."

"Yes, Mom," I said, getting up and water onto the stove to boil pasta with.

"Tony, can you come with us? Unfortunately, there is a sink that needs fixing."

"Why sure!" Uncle Tony said. Crispino threw a crumpled napkin, hitting Danny in the head.

"Owww!" Danny yelled, not really hurt. Crispino started laughing goofily.

"Boys! Stop it!" Papa yelled.

"Crescenz!" followed Mom immediately.

Crispino's face froze, and he put his head down.

It was quiet for a moment, and then the small talk resumed.

I thought about the day so far and what was to come. I was glad Mom was home, but I also knew that my new life here in this new house was going to be hard. The house was big, my brothers were needy, Papa would be here often, and I was alone.

# Volleyball

High school represented big changes for me emotionally, physically, and spiritually. The stress of it all, and the void of my best friend, my Nonna, being gone, left me very anxious. One day, I heard an announcement over the PA from the principal. She said, "Any girls wanting to try out for the first-ever volleyball team at our school please report to the gym after school."

My heart leaped within me. I had never played any sports, but perhaps this might be a way I could begin to feel more accepted. I was not a good student, did not have many friends, and had no time to play after school, as I was busy taking care of my brothers. Before, when my Nonno and Nonna were here, my sense of identity came from my home life. My duties on our family farm in the inner city gave me purpose and direction, and I clearly saw my contribution to the hard work of running that little farm. Now, being in the suburbs, doing nothing but taking care of my brothers and cooking and cleaning, I was starting to despair about things like purpose and direction. Yes, my contribution was great, but there was no longer the joy that I had once had. But if I could make the volleyball team, it would help me to gain a sense of worth I had not felt in a long time. My picture as part of the team would be in the yearbook, and the publicity would be at a level of local notoriety. I imagined my cousins, Uncle Joe's sons, hearing that I was on the team. The boys at St. Eds, the all-boys high school, might also hear and know the girls' names of the first-ever volleyball team. I wanted to be part of a team. I wanted to be noticed as a team player. With my mind made up, I was going to get on the team, no matter what sacrifice I had to make. It meant so much to me, and after that morning's announcement, I thought of nothing else but how to get on the volleyball team.

That day at lunch, I told my friends at the lunch table that I was thinking about trying out. Not only would it get me out of the house, but I would also meet new friends and have a ball trying something new and different from my old, boring routine.

That night, after dinner, I sat down at the table with my mom. Papa and my brothers were in the family room watching wrestling on TV. I spoke quietly, not wanting Papa to hear. "Mom, I heard an announcement at school today. They are having tryouts for the first-ever St. Joe's volleyball team. I would like to join."

Mom's brows sunk some, and she held her lips tightly together, thinking. "What is volleyball?" she asked.

"You know, when the girls hit the ball in the air, back and forth over the net."

"Oh, yes, I know now," she said, but then added, "Why do you want to play volleyball when you have plenty to do at home?"

Papa heard her and immediately glanced away from the TV and toward our conversation.

"It will be good for me to be on the team, Mom," I said, in as quiet a voice as I could, trying to limit what Papa heard.

"Volleyball is just a game, Mari. It is useless in life."

She wasn't getting it. I shrugged my shoulders, not sure how to respond.

"When are the tryouts?" Mom asked.

"After school," I said, hopeful now that she had turned her questioning to logistics.

But she reversed course in the next thought, asking, "To what purpose is volleyball necessary in life, Mari? Girls do not need to play sports—only boys play sports, not girls."

"Yes, they are starting to play now, Mom." It was not a clever response, but the only one I could come up with.

Papa glanced back at the TV, and then back to us, staring, trying to hear.

Mom folded her hands, glancing out the window into the dark backyard, thinking. A slight frown settled on her face, and she asked, "What time will you be home?"

"I think by 5:30 in the evening."

"How are we going to make dinner?" she asked.

"We can make it in the morning and heat it up."

She nodded, glancing back out the window. "I suppose that will work. Okay, you can try it."

I glanced at Papa. He had not heard us. He had turned back to the TV.

I hugged Mom and went up to my room, rejoicing in my coming freedom and adventure.

*\*\**

The following morning, I woke early, dressed for school, and quietly went downstairs. The warmth of the kitchen light greeted me as I walked down the hall, along with the smell of something good. As I entered the kitchen, I saw Mom at the stove, busily stirring a large pot.

"Good morning, Mom."

"Oh, good morning, Mari. You are up early."

I smiled, walked over, and peered into the pot, which was only half full of ingredients. She was in the early stages of whatever she was preparing. "What are you making?"

"Pasta Fazule," she said as she turned and took down a jar of beans from the cupboard, pouring a fair amount into the pot.

"Oh, Papa and the boys will love that."

Mom stirred some more, then took down a box of pasta from the cupboard. "Watch it, Mari, and keep stirring it once in a while. When it boils, add the pasta."

"Okay," I said. I was happy she had gotten up early. She was trying to help me because today would be my first day of practice and my first day of coming home late. I was worried about how my brothers would fare. They would be alone with Papa. Crispino would be at school, and Danny would be in preschool for part of the day. Ernesto would be with Papa all day.

"Will the boys be OK?" I asked.

"Yes, Uncle Tony is going to stop by in the afternoon to make sure everything is OK."

I felt a wave of relief surge over me. Once again, Uncle Tony was coming to my rescue or my brothers' rescue. It felt like my rescue, though, because I loved my brothers and wanted them to always be happy. Their happiness was my happiness.

Mom and I sat at the table, drank a cup of coffee, and ate some toast and jelly. Not much was said until Mom broke the silence with some news. "The Valentinis bought a house across the street."

"They did?" I said with wide eyes. A feeling of hope surged within me. We would have neighbors who we knew, who thought as we did, and though there were no girls my age, it would still be wonderful. But my joy subsided some when I thought of Dominic Valentini. I did not like him and realized that he, too, would become a big part of our life. "When are they coming?" I asked.

"In a month. Asunta is going to help watch Ernesto for a few hours a day."

"In the afternoons?"

"No, in the mornings. I will take him there when I go to work, and she will bring him home once Papa wakes up. He needs to sleep more because he works so late."

"Oh, that is good." I knew this was important, as I myself had been left with Papa when I was little. I had spent much of my earliest childhood alone in my crib, and I did not want this to happen to Ernesto.

Mom finished her coffee, checked on the Pasta Fazule, and reminded me to stir it. She kissed me on the forehead and left for work.

I looked at the time. There was still an hour before I had to walk up to the bus stop on Lorain Avenue. It was the same Lorain Avenue that reached all the way to Cleveland, but just a wider, nicer section of it.

I stirred the pot, then put another pot of water on and got the container of Quaker Oats oatmeal from the pantry. I poured enough in for the family, then set the table. Afterward, it was cooked. I drew out a ladle full and placed it in a bowl for myself, then sat at the table alone. Everyone was asleep.

One by one, my brothers woke and came down to eat. When my time to leave was nearing, I went to my parents' room and quietly whispered in. "Papa, it is time to get up. The oatmeal is ready."

I glanced over at the crib where Ernesto was sleeping and listened for Papa's reply. A loud snore shattered the momentary silence. "Papa, it is time to get up. The oatmeal is ready."

Ernesto made a sound and stirred, turning over.

"Papa," I said once more.

Finally, he too stirred. "Where is Brigida?" he asked in a low voice.

"She went to work, Papa. I have to go to school soon. The oatmeal is ready."

He sat up and glanced over at the crib. I now knew it was safe to go in. I went to the crib and gently woke Ernesto. "Good morning, Ernesto. Are you ready to be changed?"

He rolled over, and I quickly changed his diaper. Papa had already taken his clothes into the bathroom. Then I heard the shower water turn on.

It had all gone smoothly this morning, and I was relieved. However, volleyball practice was foremost on my mind, and I needed this day to go efficiently if I was going to pull it off.

I took Ernesto downstairs and put him in the high chair. I gave him his bowl of already cooled-down oatmeal, and put milk and sugar in, then sat next to him and helped him eat.

Crispino and Danny were quietly eating. They were like this most mornings, and it gave a sense of peace to the house we only felt in the early mornings.

Papa came down and sat with us. He, too, was quiet, and he too ate peacefully. No one said anything except for Ernesto mumbling some of the few words he knew.

I finished feeding him, wiped his face and clothes, and let him down.

Then I said, "Papa, the dinner for tonight is on the stove."

He glanced over with a sad look on his face. He did not ask me why I was telling him, and I sensed by his furrowed brow that he already had been told about volleyball.

I cleared the empty bowls from in front of Crispino and Danny. "Boys, your lunches are in the refrigerator. Don't forget them. The bus will be here at 8:00 a.m."

Then, I picked up my lunch, my book bag, and the extra small bag I had put my tennis shoes, T-shirt, and red shorts in, and left for school.

Throughout the day, I could think of nothing else. Finally, my last class ended, and I went to the gym and went into the locker room to get changed. The room was filled with lots of girls from the freshman class, giddily talking with each other as they dressed. I recognized a few of them from some of my classes.

I took off my blouse and quickly slipped on my blue T-shirt. Then, I put my red shorts on, pulled them up under my skirt, and only then took off my skirt. It mattered not that we were all girls. Modesty, even extreme modesty, had been drilled into me since I was a child. I then took my tennis shoes out of my bag and slipped them on. As I was tying my shoes, I suddenly noticed the nice tennis shoes the other girls were wearing. Mine were old, black, and ragged cloth tennis shoes. I had worn them for several years. They were the opposite of the new-looking, sturdy, and clean tennis shoes everyone else had on. Many of them were admiring and talking about their colors and brands. I felt on the outside right away.

Next, I noticed that they were all wearing or carrying equipment. Knee pads were already affixed on most of their shins, waiting to be pulled up into place once practice started. Many girls carried elbow pads in their hands, ready to put them on. Some wore sweat bands around their heads, and some of them carried water bottles.

I had nothing except my blue T-shirt, red shorts, and black tennis shoes. I determined right then, though, not to let it stop me. I smiled at them all, quietly put my head down, and went quickly into the gym. I would try very hard, give my ultimate effort, and do all the little things necessary to make the team. Being on time, or even early, was the first thing I could do. It would show my sincere interest in the sport.

There were over thirty-five of us, and I was definitely the smallest and skinniest of all the girls. Some of them towered over me, more so than when I saw them in the halls, and I realized it was probably their sturdy proper shoes propping them up some, while my very flat worn ones placed me down a little further closer to earth. But I stood as straight and tall as possible, paying complete attention to the two coaches in front of us, waiting for practice to officially start.

The coach was a short, stocky woman with short brown wavy hair. She wore a black shirt, blue shorts, and shiny white tennis shoes. She held a clipboard in her hand and had a whistle hanging around her neck on a thick black string. An assistant, who looked to be much younger, stood next to her wearing basically the same color clothes and carrying a clipboard, though her whistle had a white string.

The coach blew the whistle loudly. "Attention, everyone. My name is Mrs. Vance. I am your head coach. This is Ms. Marbury. She is my assistant coach."

Her voice was strict and businesslike. I stood taller and tightened my lip in an effort to show her I would do my best to adhere to her strict approach. She continued.

"Volleyball is a team sport that requires great concentration and skill. We will work hard with you to teach, train, and evaluate you. Not all of you will make the team. We have twenty slots available. The first cut will be after the first away game at St. Augustine, which is coming up in a month. A few words of advice that may help you make the team. 1. Be on time. 2. No practices can be missed. 3. There are no excuses allowed for missing scrimmages or games. And 4. No goofing off in practice will be tolerated. Ms. Marbury and I will be watching and evaluating."

I was thrilled.

With Mom's approval and the no-nonsense attitude and effort I was sure I could muster, I would be able to fulfill all her requirements.

I was a bit worried about the unspoken part of the requirements, though; playing volleyball. My only experience with any type of sports was in the backyard with my two brothers, which was scant in every way, as I never really had time for anything besides the endless list of chores I had to do at home. Chores came before free time, and for me, playing was limited.

The whistle blew again, shocking me out of my thoughts. "Twenty laps around the gym!" Immediately, all the girls began running, and I followed suit with wide but determined eyes. It did not take long for me to pull up the rear. Again, I was shocked by the sheer number of laps. But I kept going, and though by halfway through I had been lapped by some of the girls, I kept going. I finished last, but I was proud of myself for finishing, and I knew the coaches could see my effort was A level.

Next, we lined up across from each other in two long lines and were given volleyballs and a partner to hit back and forth to. This was so new to me, and I kept missing and dropping the ball or hitting it in the wrong direction. My partner was getting frustrated.

I kept trying, though, keeping an eye on the coach and assistant coach, too, knowing they would not be pleased with my performance. At one point, the coach approached.

"Look here. You are doing it wrong. Turn your wrists upward, and hold them tightly together."

I listened intently and nervously clutched my upward-facing wrists tightly together. She tossed the ball up toward me, and I awkwardly swung at it with my arms and almost missed, hitting it sideways.

"No, no, no. Go slower, and make good contact."

I felt like melting. I wanted to learn, but did not want the spotlight on me. Now, many girls were looking over as the coach picked up the ball and readied to toss it again to me. I got into a stance, holding my hands together, waiting. Finally, the ball came, and I ran up and hit it as hard as I could. My wrists ached with the feeling of the slap the ball made. The ball went straight but not far, and the coach caught it. She nodded and half-smiled. "That's better. You need to get stronger. Keep practicing."

It was already getting dark as I exited the bus and walked down the long street to my home. Mixed emotions ran through me. The freedom and adventure I had so coveted were very hard for me. My arms and wrist ached, but the dread I felt at not performing well and knowing what that might mean for my chances was even more painful. Now, I had to go home and resume my duties.

When I walked in, the family was at the dinner table, Papa with his back to me. Mom looked up, half-smiling as if to convey without words that she was not thrilled that I was doing this. The boys were all quietly eating, and that signaled to me that Papa must be in a bad mood. I quietly set my books down and went into the kitchen. Papa looked up at me, his face covered with worry. I hurriedly fixed a plate, then sat down at the table. No one said a word other than my brothers with their eyes welcoming me.

Papa finished and went into the front room to read the paper. Mom rose and started cleaning the table. I quickly finished and got up to help her.

"How was volleyball?" she asked.

"It was hard," I said.

She nodded, choosing not to ask any more questions.

I went to bed early that night, completely exhausted, feeling guilty for abandoning my duties. The words kept going through my mind, "You've got to practice," and I was completely divided about everything.

# The Verdict

The first away game at St. Augustine was looming, and that meant only one thing: the tryout period was ending, and the cuts would be coming. The game, which was only a scrimmage, would be held on Thursday after school. We would be traveling to St. Augustine on a team bus. I felt exhilarated knowing I would be on that bus with the first-ever St. Joseph Academy team to a rival school.

Practices intensified at the start of this week, as if a new sheriff had suddenly come to town. Now, all the girls were trying even harder. The weeks of practice paid off for many, and the stars and those with real potential were starting to shine.

Mrs. Marbury and Ms. Vance were more passionate and much more active, scouring the action with intense scrutiny, blowing their whistles loudly, intervening, chiding, demonstrating, instructing, and encouraging.

I was not advancing, though, and the coaches could see that. Mrs. Marbury stood near me on the sideline, watching me. I stood as tall as I could and tried to do the natural movement and bounce step the other girls did so effortlessly, hoping the ball would not come to me, but it did.

I held my arms out and hit it up, trying to do the setup shot I had been working so hard to master. It went up, but not quite high enough for my teammates to be able to do anything with, and it fell to the ground.

Mrs. Marbury blew the whistle. She yelled, "No. No. No. You have to hit it harder." She took the ball and tossed it over the net. "Hit it back to her."

The girl on the other side effortlessly hit a perfect arching shot right to me. I positioned myself and gave it all I had. Still, it did not go as expected. The whistle blew again, and the coach shouted, "Try again."

Someone sent the ball across to the other side, and again, an effortless smooth shot came my way. I watched it descend with a tear coming from my eye. I struck with all my might, and it sailed over the net. It was not the setup they wanted, but I had hit it squarely. "Okay, that's better," Mrs. Marbury said, adding, "You have to get stronger if you are going to play volleyball."

I had no idea what she meant. Yes, I agreed with her, but how could I possibly get stronger?

I felt very emotional for the rest of the practice, trying to hold back the tears. I felt so much like an outsider. The other girls did this all effortlessly. They were smooth in their initiation of the ball in play. They practically looked like professionals, hitting with grace, leaping and spiking, volleying in perfect sync, running and jumping at the net with ease. I could never do these things, and I understood they had probably been doing them since they were very young. Still, I hoped against hope that the coaches might take pity on me and let me be on the team.

I came home night after night exhausted. My wrists were red and sore, and my arms ached from so many balls slapping against my feeble arms. The practices were like getting worn out and starting a race but never reaching the finish line. I came home, saddened and stressed by my ordeal, ready to face the volatility and uncertainty of my home environment. Papa was losing his patience with my absence. Mom's patience, too, was thinning, though she tried not to show it overtly. I could tell, though.

After dinner, I helped Danny and Ernesto take a bath, then helped them get their pajamas on. I went into the pantry to get out the cereal for their nighttime snack, and that was when my big idea hit me. I would get stronger. I would lift weights. As soon as the boys were seated at the table, I went back to the pantry and took out two cans of canned peas. I snuck upstairs to my room and closed the door. There, hidden from view, I started lifting the cans, one in each hand, curling them up to try to make my arms stronger. This would be my weightlifting, and while I only had a few days left, I felt confident it might make a difference.

After about ten minutes, I was tired. Crispino came and opened the door. He saw me and said in a mocking tone, "Why are you lifting cans of peas up and down?"

"I am trying to lift weights."

"Those aren't weights!" he exclaimed.

"Shut up, Cris. You don't know anything; I am going to make the team!"

"Papa won't let you stay on the team. He is mad."

I shouted back at the top of my lungs, "Get out of my room. I need to practice."

Danny popped his head into the doorway and came in. "I don't want you to be on the team. Who will feed me snacks after school?"

"Crispino can make your snacks."

"But it's no fun when Dad watches me." He walked over and hugged my leg tightly.

"I will try to come home earlier, Danny. Don't worry."

The boys left and I sat on my bed, frustrated. There were only a few days left for my dream of making the team to become a reality. I was determined I would see it through, so I picked up the cans of peas and kept doing the curls with them. Then, I pulled out my books and tried to do my homework.

~ ~ ~ ~

Finally, the day of the big game at St. Augustine came. The team met in the gym, and each of us was given final instructions and a final motivational talk. Then, Mrs. Marbury pulled out a large mesh bag and handed each of us a shiny uniform top with the words 'St. Joseph Academy' emblazoned on the front. On the back was a number. I was to be number 23.

We all put them on, then loaded up onto the bus. It was one of the most exciting moments of my life, and I began to hope that perhaps I could be on this esteemed team, traveling to schools all over the city as a proud member of it.

We disembarked and walked into the noisy gym filled with parents and families of the other team. On the floor, a large number of girls wearing gray and red uniforms were busily practicing, with over ten volleyballs moving through the air in all directions.

We set up on the other side of the net and began our warm-ups. I felt so nervous and did very poorly in the warm-ups. This made me even more nervous.

I started the game on the bench and was finally called in. My knees felt like jelly as I rose from the bench and walked onto the court. I took my assigned place and felt my heart flutter. The sight of the other team, determination on their faces, intimidated me. The game commenced as I hoped against hope the ball would not come my way, but it did. I pressed my fists together and frantically whacked at it, hitting it straight into the air, where one of my teammates then put it over the net, scoring a point.

I was so, so relieved. Another ball came my way not long after, and I whacked at it again. This time, though, it went out of bounds.

After the game, with the dark of night already descending upon us, the bus ride home was quieter. Mrs. Marbury and Ms. Vance sat in the front with their clipboards, talking and comparing notes. Everyone knew they were deciding our fates.

When we got back to St. Joseph, the final team members were posted on the wall in the gym. I went over and scanned the list.

I was not on it.

My heart sank with embarrassment. I held back tears as I turned and walked out of the gym alone, making my way down the hall and out the front door. It was later than I had ever been out. My tears would no longer hold at the bus stop, and yet I had to hide from the few other girls standing in the dark, waiting. After a while, I boarded the bus, which soon took me out to the suburbs, where I would have to face my family and admit to them that I had not made the team.

The walk was long and heavy and full of tears. I had given my very best, and it was not enough. It was a dark, sad, and lonely time for me. Ever since I was three years old, I'd had a comrade, a friend, and a wholesome person to talk to, but now there was no one. My Nonna was gone. No one else understood my heart and my hopes. No one would listen to what mattered to me.

I looked up at the sky through tear-stained eyes, wishing I could reach her, speak to her, or hug her tightly. But she was gone. The rock, my anchor, fled back to Italy and left me frozen on the shores of my new life, a life that was very hard and lonely.

I walked into the house and was greeted by chaos. Ernesto was crying loudly, and Papa was shouting at the other boys. Mom was up in her room, lying down, which meant she had another one of her migraines.

Papa shouted at me, "Keep them quiet, Mari!"

I frowned, set down my dreams, and went to comfort Ernesto. My life would have to wait. My brothers needed me.

# Vingio

Fall turned to winter, and my first lonely year without my best friend, my Nonna, drearily unfolded. Nonna was the joyful heart of our home, the daily light in my life, my rock, and my confidant; now, she was gone. With her was Nonno Ernesto, the quiet anchor of stability. His presence, though unspoken most times, kept the emotions and noisy strife of our Italian immigrant family life in check. But, now that Nonno and Nonna were gone, there was no more heart and no more check on unbridled emotions, especially from Papa.

Mom and Papa worked opposite shifts, and because Mom worked so much, we were suddenly alone with Papa for endless hours every day. My brother Crispino and I got the brunt of his outbursts. It seemed like he was worsening in his unhappy state. His anger and moodiness were focused on and swayed by our every little move. We had always been subject to punishment in Cleveland. The Italian way of doing this was using what was called the "vingio." The vingio was the dreaded disciplinary tool made from a small tree branch. The branch had to be long and thin at the end, leafless. Once the leaves were taken off, the spanking usually began in the basement. Our egos were more bruised than our legs, and the redness went away eventually.

The infractions were small and usually meaningless, and we were punished. Larger infractions went almost unnoticed, and this always surprised me. Most of the time, it was Crispino causing me to laugh, or run, or scaring me.

The brutality ended as fast as it began, and there were always reasons for it to be administered. Papa's name Crescenzo fit not only his speech, but his reactions. He would blow up, and we would feel it, verbally and physically, and then, his heightened state would drop, and he would return to his couch with his newspaper, and a deafening silence would descend upon all of us children. It would stay that way until we naturally got the courage to start up again.

Our minor infractions were things normal children should have been allowed to do. Talking too loudly, laughing too loud, running too fast, letting the screen door slam too loudly, or worse, having one of us fall or even the boys fighting about something were normal things. But in our family, any and all of these would set Papa's episodes of anger into motion. So, I learned early on that dark year to go in the opposite direction in the house, especially on weekends.

The dinner table was the tensest time, especially if it were just us kids and Papa. If we laughed at the dinner table, we got hit. If we spilled our milk at the breakfast table, we got smacked against the side of the head. We were expected to sit up straight and quietly eat. This would never work for my brother Crispino, who would inevitably try to get one of us to laugh, and it would not work for Danny or Ernesto either, who were always bickering with each other.

I marveled at the stark contrast of us kids having dinner with Papa, compared to perhaps an evening or Sunday afternoon people when family or friends would be over. Those times were filled with joy, laughter, and feasting. They were not fake in any way. Instead, it seemed that the presence of others, unless it was Aunt Jean, of course, would temper Papa's moodiness. Though we children would still be wary of his occasional glare should we act up beyond what was acceptable in those situations.

Through it all, I felt sorry for Papa. As the oldest child, I was closely connected to his emotional life. I was connected with Mom's, too, as all oldest children are. Mom did not display emotions. She was calm and reserved. Perhaps hidden would be a better word. Her emotions only flared up when she was trying to stop Papa from one of his tirades. But Papa was different.

As I grew older, I began to understand. He was ill mentally. He had something that prevented him from being happy. That perpetual unhappiness, peppered with frequent outbursts of anger, and salted with infrequent moments of laughter when his brothers were around, seemed to be trapped inside of him. The more I realized this, the more I felt sorry for him and tried in all the ways I could to keep things the way he wanted them.

Of course, with my brothers as they were, Crispino out of control, and Danny and Ernesto always bickering and ever needy, my pursuit of happiness bordered on the impossible.

My heart ached for my Papa's sadness, and while I hated every moment of his anger, I loved him and hoped and prayed that he might be happy someday.

One saving grace loomed before us on the days we were alone with Papa. In the early evening, Mom would be home. Her return home brought instant joy to everyone. Even Papa seemed to change from a tightly tense person, about to blow up, to someone who was suddenly free from his job of watching us. All of us kids would run to the door, my brothers being the loudest, clamoring for Mom's attention. For some reason, I would be at the back, not needing what my brothers so desperately needed. Mom and I were more like sisters, and Nonna returning to Italy had not changed that.

Though Papa was watching us during the day, in fact, I was watching over all, especially my brothers. Though I possessed no authority over them, and though we would argue during the day, I was like their mom. It was me who they turned to with all of their needs, and because I had been trained and formed in life by my Nonna, I tried to meet those needs in any way I could. My life was not for myself, it was for my brothers, and it was for trying to keep Papa from blowing up.

## School was Always Hard

As the first year since my grandparents left came to the end, I was faced with the stark reality that my freshman year of high school was also coming to a close, which meant that my report card was coming. I knew deep down that it would be a shameful moment in my family's life, as my grades would not measure up. I also held tightly to the enormous fear that I would be kicked out because of it and bring even more shame onto my family.

No one knew my struggle. It was one I had to carry privately. It was not something I could even share with my Nonna when she was living with us. I was the oldest daughter of an Italian immigrant family. I had been given all the good things that life in America afforded. It was my duty and responsibility to make the best of them for the betterment of our family. I was also to lead the way for my brothers. If I failed, the entire family might fail.

All through elementary school and high school, I received no guidance. I had a poor foundation. No one at home could assist me because my parents were Italian immigrants who only finished the fifth grade in Italy. The struggle was difficult. The struggle was defined by poor reading skills, poor math skills, poor phonics skills, and poor writing skills. Even though I was smart and had common sense, it didn't matter because I did poorly in understanding the subject matter, in doing homework, and in taking tests.

In high school, most of the girls were from American families. Many of those were well off. Whether rich or not, most of these girls had normal help within the infrastructure of their homes and families. No one knew what I was doing at home. No one knew that I was slaving away as a nanny for my brothers. The little time I had left, if any, was spent studying for hours on end, racking my head trying to memorize math problems, trying, and wishing, and hoping against hope that I might understand my subjects.

The friends I made at school were all very smart, and they were kind to me. I was always amazed at how easily they did so well. Weekly, they would compare grades. It went something like this.

"Hi, MK," said I.

"Hey, Marisa. How did you do on your test?"

Slowly and painstakingly, I replied, "Oh, I got a D+."

"Oh, I see. That's okay, Marisa."

I would immediately add, wide-eyed, "I was happy that I passed. It was a hard test. I am relieved I didn't get an F. How did you do, MK?"

Smiling from ear to ear, MK would reply, "I got an A+."

Slowly I would reply, "Oh, good job, MK. I knew you would do well on the test. I knew you could do it!" I meant it, too, as I always rooted for my friends.

MK was always gracious and never gloated, even for a moment. MK understood my struggle. The fact was that I was surrounded by geniuses who received As and Bs or all As. And none of them studied half as much as I did.

Every day after lunch, I would excuse myself from the lunch table early and go to the small chapel located inside the school. There, I would pray to St. Joseph to help me. I trusted that he would, and yet it never made things easier or less scary for me. My teachers often talked to me about my grades, and I believe they understood I was doing my best. They gave me extra credit assignments that allowed me to avoid failing, and I believe this was an answer to my prayers.

The end of the year came, and I passed all my subjects. Mostly Cs with some Ds, but I had passed. I could look forward to summer now, knowing that I would not be kicked out and would be allowed to return to school next year.

## I Become the Mom

I was fourteen at the end of my freshman year. The first full summer in our new home lay before me; it was the first full summer I would not be with Nonna. I missed her terribly, though it seemed no one else did. Everyone had moved on. My brothers had never been close to Nonno or Nonna, and Papa hadn't either. I knew Mom missed them, but she was too busy to show it or talk about it. It was our new reality and one we had to deal with.

Mom woke me early on that first day. "Mari," she said. "Give the boys cereal for breakfast. There is sauce in the refrigerator. Boil some pasta for lunch."

"OK, Mom. Where is Papa?"

"He worked late. Keep the boys quiet."

"OK, I will try."

Mom left, and I could not go back to sleep, so I went downstairs. It did not take long for one of my brothers to get up, then the others. I had them sit at the table eating their cereal. It also did not take long for them to begin arguing about something. Ernesto was only four now, and his needs were great.

Soon, we heard Papa yelling from upstairs, "Be quiet!"

I told the boys to go out and play in the yard while I cleaned up the kitchen.

Then, I joined them.

It was a marvelous morning in June, one where the sky was blue and the birds were gently chirping. I felt a sense of freedom that morning, freedom I did not possess, yet freedom I longed for and could almost reach out and touch. Crispino and Danny set about going into the back yard climbing the trees. Ernesto was too little. He had tried to follow them and was standing under one of the trees, whining loudly. I got a ball from the house and distracted him by playing catch with him. The fact that we were ten years apart in age made it very fun for him and nothing but a chore for me, but we played on.

After a while, the boys got tired of playing.

Crispino asked, "Can we go watch TV?"

I sighed. This proposition was filled with anxiety for me. Of course, they could not stay outside all morning, and there was nothing else to do except watch TV. "Papa is sleeping, Crispino. We have to be quiet."

"We will be quiet," Danny said.

Ernesto clung to me. "I'm hungry."

"All right. Let's go in and eat. Then we can watch TV."

We all went inside and quietly ate some more cereal. Afterward, we went into the family room and turned the TV on low. There was not much to watch, and we settled on the Price is Right game show. An hour later, we heard noise from upstairs. Papa was up. We all cringed and waited, keeping ever still, watching the show end and another take its place. Soon, we could hear footsteps coming down the stairs, and then the walk through the hall. Papa appeared in the doorway to the kitchen. He had on boxer shorts and a white muscle T-shirt. His thick black hair was disheveled and stuck out in all directions. He looked over, and his brow furrowed. "What are you doing?" he asked.

"We are watching TV, Papa," I replied.

He silently processed my reply, sighed visibly, and walked into the kitchen. He looked around, walked to the sink, then went back to the table and sat down. We all had one eye on him and one eye on the show. Papa said, "Mari, make some toast."

"I want some too!" Ernest said.

"Si, Papa," I said as I went into the kitchen, followed by Ernesto. I sliced some bread and put it into the toaster. "Do you want coffee, Papa?"

He nodded, and I turned on the coffee pot on the stove. Mom had made it earlier to allow it to heat up.

Once the toast popped up, I buttered it and cut a half piece for Ernesto. I put two more slices in.

Before long, Papa finished eating and went into the family room. He sat on the couch while we quietly sat around him watching TV. When lunchtime was near, I boiled the water and made a bowl of pasta. We all ate in silence. When we finished, I told the boys to go out to play. Papa made his lunch, then left for work.

Peace had come again to the house, and we all anxiously waited for Mom to come home.

# Papa is Hurt

One evening, while we were at dinner, Mom heard the phone ring. Papa was at work, and we all anxiously waited to see who was calling. She picked up the phone and began listening. Suddenly her face grew alarmed, and she asked, "What? When? Is he OK?"

She hung up and turned to us, her face showing deep concern.

"What happened?" we all asked.

"Papa hurt himself at work. We have to go get him at the hospital."

"Is he OK?" I asked.

"It sounds like it. He is allowed to come home."

Mom quickly picked back up the phone and called Uncle Tony. "Hey, Tony. Can you come over? Cris hurt himself at work. He is OK, but he is at the hospital. We have to go get his car and pick him up."

"OK, see you soon."

The excitement in the house immediately went through the roof. We were all glad Papa was OK, of course, but now there was a major mission underway. Uncle Tony arrived shortly thereafter, and he and Mom left in his car.

It was nearly 8:00 at night when we heard both cars pull into the drive. We ran to the door, anxiously waiting to see what had happened.

Mom and Uncle Tony were in the drive, helping Papa get out of the car. He winced in pain and held on to them as they helped him limp to the front door. Once he opened the door, the look on his face scared me. He was in terrible pain. He took one step inside, then shouted loudly from the pain. We all jumped back, feeling the nervousness. Mom yelled, "Cresenz!"

"Be quiet!" he replied loudly.

He took another step. *"Ahhhh!"* he yelled.

"Cresenz!" Mom shouted louder.

Uncle Tony held him tighter. "C'mon, Cresenz."

Mom shouted, "Marisella, go get a pillow and blanket. He has to sleep on the couch."

Another step. *"Ahhhh,"* he yelled.

"Boys, move out of the way!" Mom shouted.

I hurried up and down the stairs as fast as I could and ran through the dining room to beat them all to the family room, where Papa would sleep. I put the pillow in place and got the blanket ready on the back of the couch. Papa sat down on the couch, grimacing.

"Are you OK, Papa?" I asked.

He turned to me, with warm eyes that were about to cry, and nodded. We all gathered around him as he swung his feet onto the couch with a loud groan.

"What happened, Mom?" I asked frantically.

"He hurt his back."

"Is he going to be OK?"

"The doctor said we have to wait and see."

We covered him up and turned on the TV for him, then we all gathered in the family room near him and waited for the excitement to die down. Before long, we all went to bed, and Papa stayed on the couch.

I went to sleep that night worried. I had never seen him in so much pain before, and I wondered what this would mean for the family.

~ ~ ~ ~

Two weeks later, we received the news. Papa and Mom returned from a doctor's appointment, and Uncle Tony came in with them. They sat at the table talking, trying to decide what to do. Papa had hurt a disc in his back. He would be able to move around again within a month or two, but he could never work in the Ford Foundry again. He would have to go on disability for the rest of his life.

I could see Mom was visibly upset with the news. She turned her head away, trying to wipe the tears that wanted to come. However, she had learned to be strong long ago, and I saw her reach within and gather that strength again. Papa was glum, his head down. Serenity was on him I had never seen before. I wondered if the pressure of having to work at

Ford suddenly being taken away from him was somehow comforting. Still, uncertainty hung in the air.

Uncle Tony said, "I will be able to help, Brigida. I can come during the day to make sure things are OK. Once Cris gets better, we can start fixing things up around here... and at the apartments." Papa half-smiled and began nodding, but only for a moment, as his face sank back to its gloomy state.

***

The next morning, Mom woke me early again. "Mari, come down and have coffee with me."

We went into the kitchen, and the coffee was already percolating on the stove. I looked over at Papa asleep on the family room couch. He had not yet gone back to his bed upstairs. Mom raised her finger to her lips, signaling to be quiet. She asked me to sit down, then took down two coffee cups and poured us some coffee.

She said, "Mari, now that your father is going on disability, I will have to work more to support the house. I have to become the dad of this house, and you will have to be the mom. Can you do that?"

"Yes, Mom, I will do whatever is needed."

"Good. Your brothers need you."

I nodded quickly. Inside, I was falling to pieces. I was already the mom in more ways than could ever be spoken or written. What more could possibly be done? What did it all mean?

We finished our coffee, and she left for work.

~ ~ ~ ~

It was now the end of July. In less than a month, summer would be over, and we would be returning to school. The news came that Uncle Mario and Aunt Theresa were coming, and this year, they were bringing Aunt Rose and Uncle Ernie. Uncle Joe had asked them all to come because he had something important to discuss with the family.

Papa had settled into his new life on disability. It seemed he was happier now than he had been in the past. Uncle Tony came around more, and it brought joy to us all, especially Papa. He and Papa had been extremely close as brothers in Italy. Greeting each other had their own special way.

As soon as Uncle Tony beeped his car horn in our driveway, Papa would drop all he was doing and run to hide behind the front door. As soon as Uncle Tony entered the house, Papa would jump out from behind the door, grabbing Uncle Tony by the shoulders, shaking him, and shouting, "Tonnnn!" 'Tonnnn' was the shortened version of Tony.

Papa would shake him longer, shouting, "Where have you been, Tonnnn?"

"What do you mean, Cris?" Uncle Tony would say, his eyes watching us kids enjoy the fun.

Papa would raise his hand into the air, shouting, "I will fix you!"

This was the same routine every time they greeted each other. The greeting was a game of Hide-'n'-Seek, and I knew it went back to their childhood.

These episodes of seeing Papa come out of his shell, even if only momentarily, were filled with happiness for us children. It was our rare glimpse into the heart of our father, who was probably capable of being happy. Papa never spoke with us growing up unless he was scolding us. The dead air was uncomprehensible and stifling. The silence made me sad and uncomfortable. If and when my dad did speak, it was in half sentences, meaning he stopped in mid-sentence, and his voice trailed off. So, I was left confused and did not know what he was communicating. Mine and my brothers' names were truncated too: Mari, Pino, Dan, and Nesto! All said with a flare and accent on the up.

## Mario and Theresa are Coming

It was the first Friday in August, and Mom and I were in the garden early in the morning, picking the ripened vegetables before she went to work. Without looking up, Mom said, "We have a lot of tomatoes this year, Mari. It will be a good canning year."

"Yes, they are so red this year."

"Yes," she said, moving quickly to strip another plant. "We will have to can early. If it is like this here, it will be the same on the farms."

"How will we do it without Nonno and Nonna?" I asked.

Mom stopped, raising her hand in the air. "We will have to do it ourselves, Mari."

I kept picking and said, "Maybe the boys can help this year."

Mom shook her head as if it was a non-starter. She put a few more tomatoes into the small basket.

"Why can't they help?" I asked.

Mom stopped. "No, Mari. The boys will only make things worse. It will be up to us."

"OK," I said dutifully. I didn't agree, though. It was always this way in regard to the boys. I was the one who did all the chores in the house. The boys did none. It was not just this way in our family, but in other Italian families as well. The boys were treated like princes. They were not allowed to do hard work because they could strain themselves and perhaps get a hernia. That would mean they could not have children. No, the boys had to be protected, insulated from all hardship, because they would be expected to father children someday. This always mystified me. The boys had so little to do with having children. If anyone, it was the girls who needed to be protected, but that was not our culture. As the oldest girl, I knew this more than anyone.

When we went into the house, Mom looked at the time and exclaimed, "Jeez, we have to hurry up. Mari, fill the sink with water. Then I will start the coffee."

I quickly cleaned the sink out and washed the stainless-steel basin as we always did before washing vegetables. I then filled it with water and dumped both baskets in. Mom sliced some bread and made coffee and toast for us. Just when we sat down to eat, the phone rang.

I jumped up to answer it. "Pronto," I said. That was the Italian word to answer the phone. It meant, "Hello, go ahead."

The familiar friendly voice came through the line. "Padina?"

"Hi, Aunt Theresa," I said, feeling the warmth and love in her voice that always set me at ease.

"Hi, Padina. How are you today?"

"I am fine. Mom and I are having coffee."

"Oh, good, let me talk to her."

I turned, and Mom got up and came to the phone. I listened intently, knowing her call must mean some news for the family.

Mom said, "Coming to Cleveland? When? Tomorrow? OK? What? You are bringing Rose and Ernie. OK? Yes, we have room. OK. We will see you tomorrow."

Excitement and happiness descended on us all at once. This was the annual excitement we lived for, a visit from Uncle Mario and Aunt Theresa. It would make our home the center of a fun universe for the next several days. Mom hung up the phone and came back to the kitchen table. She took the last sip of her coffee and looked at the clock. "I have to go to work. Tell your father and get the house ready as best you can. I will try to come home early tonight."

"OK, Mom," I said.

The day was extra hard, as news of the coming company put the boys into a frenzy. It also put Papa into his own frenzy—a frenzy of nervousness. I had all I could handle just to keep the house from erupting. There was no getting the house ready because there was simply no time. Ernesto was particularly needy today, and that did nothing except upset Papa as well as cause me to spend almost the entire day catering to Ernesto's needs.

While doing so, I made pasta for lunch and did manage to set out the large pots that Mom would need when she returned home to begin making sauce and meatballs—enough for the next several days.

When late afternoon came, Mom came home early as promised, bringing with her bags of groceries. We both donned our aprons and immediately made over 150 meatballs. After that, we started an enormous pot of sauce and readied a large bowl of kneaded dough, which we would fashion into loaves within a few hours and bake before we went to bed.

It was all exhausting and yet fun and I was filled with the anticipation of seeing my favorite aunt and uncle. Of course, this year there was a bonus. Aunt Rose was coming.

While Aunt Theresa was the closest sister to Papa, Aunt Rose was the most like him. She was stoic, quiet, and rarely talked. Unlike Papa, though, she possessed confidence and would look you in the eye when she greeted you. Papa was not a face-to-face greeter. When he greeted someone, his eyes would avert to the floor, and he would offer possibly a faint smile. On the other hand, Aunt Rose would not say too many more words than Papa might say, but she would look you in the eye and smile widely.

There was something about them both that felt like royalty. It was hard to understand, but in both of their presences, one could not escape thinking that they had somehow descended from distant Italian Royalty. Perhaps a royal family whose rights and lands had been stolen hundreds of years earlier. Yet, there was no way to take the king, or the queen in Aunt Rose's case, out of their genes.

## The Arrival of Aunt Rose

Saturday morning, we heard the beep of the horn, and we all ran to the front door. There in our driveway was a large van we had never seen before. In the driver's seat, smiling, was Aunt Rose's American husband, Uncle Ernie. Suddenly, the passenger door opened, and out popped Uncle Mario. He looked strong and tan, with his thick athletic build and dark brown curly hair. He wore the kind of shirt you would see someone on vacation in the Caribbean wearing, short sleeves with a Hawaiian floral pattern. We all wondered whose van it was, as Mario had not been driving.

Uncle Mario smiled, waved, and then dutifully opened the van's sliding side door. A beautiful arm extended, and Mario turned to grab hold of it. The arm was slender, tan, and elegant, grasping for needed help. A moment later, my Padina, Aunt Theresa, stepped out and stepped to the side.

He reached his hand in again. Now, a long slender arm, daintily pointed downward, as if ready to receive a royal kiss on the hand, extended from the van. Mario took it, and in the next moment, out popped Aunt Rose.

Aunt Rose's face held a stoic, regal, epic performance-level look upon it. Her chin was tilted up, and her lips tightly pressed together as if not to flinch for fear she might blink. Her hair was sprinkled gray and brown and wrapped up in a cascade of upward ascending buns. When her feet hit the floor, she lifted her chin again, then chuckled.

In unison, Aunt Theresa and Aunt Rose turned to us, and we snapped out of our spectacle-watching pause and ran over to greet them. All at once, everyone began laughing and hugging and greeting. The kids piled out, and the running around and playing began.

Aunt Rose's laugh was loud and gravelly, more of a fun cackle layered perfectly onto her Italian accent. Her speech was also heavily accented as she had been in Italy the longest before they came to America. "Cresenz!" she shouted. Papa walked up to her, his head down, a hidden smile peeking out from the corners of his mouth. She took hold of him and hugged him tightly and rubbed his head, exclaiming, "Cresenz, I missed you. But, hey, what happened to all your hair?"

Papa shook his head gleefully, like a dog enjoying its long-lost master's affectionate petting. Aunt Rose laughed loudly, her gravely cackle announcing a leader was in our midst.

We all went inside and, within moments, were squeezed in around the kitchen table, looking each other over, laughing, talking, soaking in the annual reunion made more special by Aunt Rose. Mom motioned for me to assist, and we began boiling the water for pasta and putting out small trays of appetizers, bread, fruits, and drinks.

Papa sat at the head of the table, his eyes cast down, with that deep, hidden smile on his face. He was thrilled to see his sisters, and nothing was going to steal this moment of heartfelt satisfaction that I could see, until the doorbell rang. We all at once turned to the front door, and I saw Papa's smile fade to worry. The door opened, and Uncle Tony proudly announced his presence with an operatic melody. Then came Aunt Jean. She was already harried, I could see, wearing light blue baggy shorts that rested just above her burgeoning knees. They walked into the accolades of all, Uncle Tony's warm smile brightening the already bright room further, with Aunt Jean's nervousness acting like a short burst of power interruption.

I watched the melee of new rounds of greetings unfold, noticing only Papa's growing nervousness. Some kids were sent out to play, room was made at the table, and Uncle Tony and Aunt Jean sat down. "Jeanna!" Aunt Rose said loudly. "How are you, Jeanna!"

I had never heard Aunt Rose call her Jeanna, and I realized that Aunt Rose could not pronounce Jean, only Jeanna.

"I am doing OK, Rose. I guess. Oh, there is trouble at home. My dad is sick, and my mom said he won't go to the doctor. My brother's worried he is going to die without a will. Then we're all up a creek. We don't even have a lawyer! Tony won't talk to him, but my boss is getting tired of me worrying about it. He says my numbers need to go up, or he may have to put me on part-time. Can you believe that? My dad doesn't have a will, and now I have to worry about—"

"Jeanna!" Papa shouted.

We all stopped and turned.

Papa sat with his arms folded tightly, His face held deep trouble, and his breathing was labored, as if this was his last gasp.

"What!" Jean said.

Uncle Tony bobbed back and forth, adding quietly, "Jean, let the other people talk."

Aunt Jean's face grew cross, and Papa exhaled loudly, trying to calm himself. Mom, seeing her chance, jumped up, announcing, "OK, the pasta is ready! Mari, help me."

Everyone seemed to forget the moment, and the talking and laughing began, except for Papa. He kept his arms crossed, his glance down, and his breathing slow and steady, as if trying to recover from trauma.

I began putting the dishes of warmed-up meatballs, pasta, and overflow sauce onto the table, and the eating began. It was quiet, and no one said a word in anticipation of the coming meal.

Then Aunt Jean broke the silence abruptly. She said aloud, "Marisa is becoming a beautiful woman."

I almost died from embarrassment.

"Jean!" Papa exclaimed again.

Jean's eyes widened. "What! She is a woman!"

I turned away, wanting to melt in front of the filled kitchen.

Papa reared back some, his eyes vaulting to the ceiling as one would plead to the Heavens.

Suddenly Crispino started from the family room, "Marisa's a woman! Marisa's a woman! Marisa's a woman."

"Shut up, Crispino!" I shouted as I set down a plate of meatballs and ran after him. As I chased Crispino out the back door, Aunt Rose erupted in a loud cackle that resonated through the entire house. He ran too fast and was far out in the backyard in no time. I was too embarrassed to go inside, so I walked to the front door, quietly came back into the house, and went to my room to cry.

The pressure of doing so much work, being the perfect daughter, and perfect servant to my family, and being embarrassed by my brother mocking me, was overwhelming. I lay in bed with my face down, crying softly.

## Aunt Theresa Explaining

As I lay on my bed, letting the last of my cry shudder away, the sounds of the loud, fun conversations downstairs began to come into focus. I wondered why I had been born into the family. I saw the wrong-doing and the ethnic foolishness. I saw, too, the constant strain caused by Papa's illness and depressed demeanor. But nevertheless, I understood that I had to serve them. The oldest and only daughter in an Italian family could expect nothing less. It seemed to me that the family needed me more than I could need them. How could I think otherwise when my entire life was serving them? From a very young age, I was an adult thinker trapped in a child's body, who, as the oldest, felt her parent's emotions deeply, and not just theirs, but my Nonno and Nonna's as well. When the family went through a situation, it became my own; I owned their pain, hurts, lashings out, confusion, moodiness, and misunderstandings. I carried along the emotions with them on my shoulders. They probably never considered this fact; I did because I lived it. So much adult thinking had been thrust on me that now, at the ripe old age of fourteen, I was wise beyond my years.

There was a knock on the door.

"Who is it?" I said in a muffled, shaken voice.

"It's me, Padina. Aunt Theresa. Can I come in?"

"Yes," I said, as I quickly wiped my eyes and sat up.

She opened the door, and her warm, caring eyes peeked in. She came over and sat down next to me. "Are you all right, Padina?"

"Yes, I'm frustrated, Aunt Theresa."

She pulled me close, hugging me. "I understand, Padina. You were born into a difficult family."

It felt marvelous to have someone understand me. We said nothing for a few moments.

I asked, "Why is Papa so nervous? It is very hard for me. And… Aunt Jean makes me so mad."

"Jean, Jean, Jean. She makes us all crazy, Padina, but don't worry. You just have to ignore her, Padina."

Aunt Theresa hugged me tight and said, "Padina, your father was affected at a very early age. He was closest to his mother than the other children. Her death hurt him very deeply."

"What happened?"

"Well, my mother was not a strong woman in many respects. Yet, she was a loving mother, very reserved, and very shy. She did not talk much either. She had fifteen pregnancies, but only ten children were born. She had a child yearly for ten years. Those of us who did survive, were malnourished and subjected to working on the farm without shoes and proper attire at a very young age. That's what life in Italy before World War II was like. There was poverty and a lack of life's basic necessities.

"I was only five, and your father was nine when our mother passed away. It hurt him more than anyone else. He completely stopped speaking for a long time. Her death had a permanent impact on him. Like her, he was shy, to begin with, but after she died, he became even more subdued.

"Soon after the loss of his mother, the war began. It was very hard on the family. At one point, they had to leave the confines of the small family farm and hide in the caves in the mountains. There was little food and very little shelter from the elements. Being cold, hungry, and exhausted due to hiding from the Nazis became a way of life for Papa. Fortunately, the war ended, and we came to America. But it has still been hard for him, Padina. Your Papa did not have the confidence or social skills to survive in a fast-paced society in America. It was very different from the laid-back farm life in the backwoods of southern Italy. That is why he is the way he is. Do you understand more now, Padina?"

"I do, Aunt Theresa. I understand him more now. Thank you."

She hugged me tightly. "You will be a beautiful wife and mother someday, Padina."

"How?" I exclaimed, wide-eyed. "I will never meet anyone. I am not allowed out of the house."

"Oh, don't worry, Padina. When it is time, God will provide."

I rested my head against her shoulder.

"Do you think so, Aunt Theresa?"

She brushed my hair. "I know so, Padina. You will see."

# The Land Deal

After a long weekend of fun with Uncle Mario, Aunt Theresa, their children, and Aunt Rose and Uncle Ernie, Sunday afternoon arrived. I was exhausted as Uncle Mario made sure we were going morning to night. His arrival always drew the rest of the family to our home for what seemed like a summer festival.

Though it was Sunday, no one went to or even thought of attending church. Since my Nonna and Nonno left, going to church on Sunday morning left with them. Though I wanted to go, there was no way. I was needed at home. Mom and I rose early, prepared café and Panatone for everyone, and cut up fresh melons and other fruits. We started the sauce early, and after breakfast, everyone went their own way to relax while Mom and I made the meatballs. Finally, it was lunchtime, as signaled by Uncle Tony and Aunt Jean arriving. It seemed that no matter who was in town, Aunt Jean would not miss a meal, though I knew Papa always wished she would. Unfortunately, she came with the Uncle Tony package, and we all had to endure her because we all wanted to see our beloved Uncle Tony. It was not that she was unkind or even not funny at times. It was rather as if a Tasmanian devil was let loose, causing frantic thinking in every direction.

After a big lunch, Mom told me to go outside and play for a while until she called me because she needed my help. I thought my chores for the day were done, and I was very tired, so I kind of talked back. At least it was my way of talking back, by quietly asking, "What are we doing, Mom?"

"We are having an important meeting here at 4:00 this afternoon. Uncle Joe is coming over to talk to all of us about the land in Italy."

"Oh really?" I said, feeling my reluctance fade away from the excitement of the words 'important meeting' and news about the land in Italy. "What do we have to do?"

"I want to make two coffee cakes and arrange all the chairs. Go outside and play, and I will call you, Mari."

I went outside to play, but the news about the land in Italy kept going through my mind. I had not heard much about the land in Italy that belonged to my papa and his brothers and sisters in a very long time. It seemed to be an important topic of conversation long ago, right before the time Uncle Italo had been killed. It appeared that the passing of Uncle Italo seemed to quiet the topic for our family. No one had ever talked much about it.

I knew that Uncle Joe seemed to be involved with it still, as I heard on various occasions that Uncle Joe would be traveling to Italy. I recall his business partners here went with him, too. Sometimes, his wife, Aunt Mary, also went with him. But there was never any news about their visits. It was not talked about or downplayed when brought up. Instead, Uncle Joe would raise his hand as if complaining that it was a lot of work, work he did for the family, but work he did not want to do.

Before long, I went inside and helped Mom bake the coffee cakes. We arranged them on the dining room table and set up the coffee cups. This was an important meeting, as we did not use the dining room table except on holidays.

At four o'clock, Uncle Joe and Aunt Mary arrived and took their seats at the large table. Papa joined them, but I noticed he let Uncle Joe sit at the head of the table. I did not like that he always did this. It did not matter to me that Uncle Joe was the oldest brother, at least ever since Uncle Italo died. In my eyes, Papa was the greater man. Sure, he was not as smart, savvy, or business-oriented as Uncle Joe, but this was his house. He belonged at the head of the table. I went into the kitchen to help Mom start the coffee.

All the children were called inside and sent down to the basement to play. Soon after, Uncle Tony and Aunt Jean came in, followed by Uncle Frank and his wife. Mario, Theresa, Rose, and Ernie all took their seats, too. Finally, the meeting was about to start.

All grew quiet, and Uncle Joe began nodding his head slowly, as if he were thinking. Finally, he folded his hands and said, "So, I called you all here because there is a problem with the land in Italy. The government says we have to go there every year and keep it up, or it will forfeit to the government."

"Forfeit to the government!" Uncle Tony exclaimed.

Uncle Joe frowned, nodding, and raised his hand. "Hey, Tony, that is what I said, but it is true. That is the reason I have been going there so often. Yes, I have had you all contribute money at times, but I have borne most of the cost."

I watched Papa shaking his head with a look of dismay on his face. It made me angry because he trusted every word Uncle Joe said, and this bothered me very much. Somehow, and this was not a new revelation for me, I did not trust Uncle Joe. Ever since the death of Uncle Italo, I had been wary of Uncle Joe and even more wary of his friends, who he seemed to hang out with more than his brothers.

Uncle Joe continued, "Mary and I have been talking, and we would be willing to buy the land from each of you. This way, we can put it in our name, which the Italian Government would find favorable, since I travel there often. This way, too, all the cost we have been putting in would be for our own land. This way, too, it stays with the family."

Aunt Rose interrupted, "Whadda, you mean, Joe? Are you going to buy it from us?"

Uncle Joe seemed frustrated that he had to say it again. He raised his hand in the air. "Hey, Rose. I am probably going to pay more than it's worth. But hey, you are my brothers and sisters."

"How much?" Jean exclaimed.

"Jean!" Tony cried out. "Let Joe talk."

"I'm just asking how much!"

Papa raised his hand high. "Jeanna! Be quiet!"

"Tony, are you going to let him talk to me like that!"

Uncle Mario jumped in, "Jean, why don't you go see how the kids are doing?"

"Tony, stop him."

"Aya, let's all be quiet!" Aunt Rose said in her queenly voice.

All grew quiet. I looked over at Uncle Joe. He was getting very nervous. I could see beads of perspiration on his forehead. He nodded, then said, "Rose, I was willing to give each of you $2,000."

"Two thousand dollars!" Jean exclaimed.

"Jean!" Papa yelled.

"What! That's a lot of money. We'll take it!"

"Jean!" Uncle Tony said. "Just stop."

"I'm just saying."

Uncle Joe nervously said, "So what do you all say?"

He waited, then added, "It has to be everyone. It has to be unanimous."

He looked at Papa. "Cris?"

Papa said, "OK, Joe."

Then Tony, then the rest all joined in saying yes. Uncle Joe took out a briefcase with contracts and a checkbook. "Everyone sign this release, and I will give you the check tonight."

I watched as everyone blindly trusted Uncle Joe. They all signed the releases and handed them back to him. Then, they all got checks for $2,000. Something about the entire thing made me feel scared. I felt like some evil deed had just been done to the family, but what, I did not know.

## They Will Get a Hernia

Uncle Mario and the gang returned to Connecticut, signaling that summer was nearing the end for our immigrant family. The school would be starting soon, and I would return to the world of the American girls I went to school with at St. Joe's Academy.

In one way, I looked forward to it. In another, I dreaded it. Mom was working longer hours, and Papa, left at home to watch us kids, was getting worse, more anxious, and more nervous, especially when Mom was at work. Summer's end meant my allotted time for needed and required chores at home would be condensed dramatically. I would still have the same chores and responsibilities. Only now, I would have to fit in taking the bus to the faraway high school, time to take the bus back, walk from the bus stop to my home, and still find time to do the mind-bending homework assignments.

Homework for me was like having to climb a small mountain without any climbing gear daily. I could never understand how my American friends could do it so easily. For me, homework usually meant beating my head against the wall, with no one to help me or even to understand what I was going through. My brothers did not understand. My mom did not understand, and Papa certainly did not understand. His mood cast a shadow over the good I tried to do by doing my homework. My brothers did not help, as they did not understand high school homework. They were busy going wild because my mom was away, and their actions only ratcheted up the anxiety and nervousness of Papa's heavy mood. I only had God to talk to, and though I knew he somehow listened to me and gave me the strength to get through, it never made it easier or even less frightening. There was no way out. It was an ancient unwritten rule that I am certain went back to the days of ancient Rome. I had to take care of them because I was the oldest, and doubly so because I was a girl. This role required countless hours of hard work with few rewards. I had resigned myself to believe that the only possible benefit was the experience I was receiving would help me when I was a mom later in life.

My life was to be a babysitter for my brothers, and if I failed, there were dire consequences. I took on the role of secondary mom. Though entrenched in old-world thinking, Papa was not oblivious to my brother's antics toward me. He was protective of me, as shown by his constant yelling and hitting us all, especially the boys. It was not violent in an old-school way, but it was emotionally so. Papa had no other tools to control us. At least he had never learned any. He wanted the three boys to stand still, keep quiet, and, most of all, obey family rules, which mainly centered around keeping still and quiet. Family rules for the boys had nothing to do with chores or responsibility.

The boys were treated with kid gloves while I, seemingly invisible to Papa and to them, worked hard. If I did not change the diapers, clean the kitchen, cook the meals, help my brothers with homework, shield them from Papa, and play with them when I could, no one would. It was all on my shoulders while Papa read the paper, watched wrestling, or chased us around the house.

I did inquire one frustrating day. I was up early and Mom and Papa were at the table. Mom was drinking coffee and getting ready for work. Papa was eating a small bowl of cereal. I sat across from Mom and asked her, "Mom, why do the three boys have no chores to do while I have to do everything? It is hard for me to keep up, Mom."

I glanced at Papa. He was probably listening, but he was fairly focused on his cereal. I was relieved, as one hurdle had been crossed. Mom took a sip of her coffee and replied, "The boys are younger than you, Mari. They cannot do the things you do."

"I could teach them," I replied.

Papa paused, then resumed eating.

Mom uncomfortably lowered her eyes, then glanced to ensure we were not upsetting Papa. She then held her coffee cup with two hands, as if steadying her answer. Finally, she said, "Mari, your brothers are boys. Boys cannot overexert themselves. They will get a hernia."

Papa paused again, glanced at Mom, then resumed eating.

Knowing the coast was still clear, and that Mom and I were having a private conversation, even though Papa was less than two feet away from us, I replied angrily, "I don't understand. What does a hernia have to do with picking up their socks or putting their toys away?"

Mom raised her hand slightly, signaling I should lower my voice, as we could both feel the budding frown and furrowing brow on Papa's face. He was listening, just not participating. Mom said, "Be quiet, Mari. You don't understand!"

"But why is it, Mom?" I had asked this question countless times, but I never received an answer that satisfied me. So I waited.

Mom shook her head, as if stating the obvious. "If they have a hernia, they won't be able to have children. So, they have to be protected."

I rolled my eyes, falling back into my kitchen chair. I had heard it all now. It was as obvious as a clear blue day. This way of treating the boys, or how they treated me, was all planned and going along just fine. The boys received special treatment, and they always would. My brother Crispino received the most special since he was the oldest boy born after me. It did not hurt his cause that he was named after Papa's father. But the bottom line was that boys in an Italian family didn't lift a finger. Everything was up to the girls. This should have been no shock to me. It was my entire life. Somehow, I just thought my brothers would grow up one day like I was forced to grow up and begin helping. Once I understood it would never happen, I knew there was no way out.

I vowed to myself on that day that I would never marry an Italian man.

# Bowling

Returning to school held a myriad of emotions. I truly felt gratitude for my friends who saw me daily at lunch. They were so different from me, and despite my ethnic background, my strange lunches made of homemade bread and eggplant or peppers, they accepted me and tried to make me laugh. They tried to include me, and yet they all knew I was not allowed to go out on weekends with them in the car blasting music with the gals. They knew I was forbidden to go yearly to Florida with them for spring break. They knew McDonald's runs were not in my schedule or my budget. I had no money and no way of ever earning money. Yet, despite all that, they continued to be my friends. It was a different kind of friendship, though, as, despite their allegiance, I was an outsider, and somehow, I understood it would always be so.

At the start of junior year, I heard about a bowling club. It was going to take place on Fridays after school. I begged my mom and bargained with my brothers. If they behaved for Papa so they would avoid getting hit, I would make them their favorite meal, snack, or treat when I got home.

At first, they did not agree, saying they would miss me. Then, the youngest whined the most, suddenly inspired by the idea that he wanted to go with me, though he was only five.

The whole thing threatened to blow up that night at the dinner table when Mom brought it up.

"Cresenz, Marisa will not be home until 5:30 tonight."

He looked up from his dish, pausing for a moment, then looked down again, asking, "Why?"

"She has to go to a club after school."

I watched him carefully. All was unfolding as I had hoped. Then suddenly, Crispino said, "Can we go?"

I glared at him. He was just causing trouble.

"No, this is for Marisa," Mom scolded.

Ernesto whined, "I want to go bowling."

Papa was bothered now, not by the idea, but by the boys' sudden uprising. The noise had invaded our quiet dinner table, and Papa was getting nervous. Finally, he asked, "Why does she need to bowl?"

Mom put an end to it mercifully. "Boys, you will behave until Marisa gets home. No more talk about this."

I held my breath, and Papa resumed eating.

It was set.

I was going bowling.

After school that day, I followed Jen, one of the girls on the team. We took the bus to Kamms Corner, as I usually did. But, instead of transferring to the bus on Lorain, I walked with her about two blocks to the Olympic Bowling Lane on Lorain Road.

As soon as I walked inside, I felt the whole world open up to me. Loud intermittent noises of pins crashing, the sound of laughter, and bowling balls rolling down the lane filled my ears. At the far end of the facility was a group of almost twenty girls from St. Joe's.

I followed Jen to the counter, where we paid for shoes. I only had three dollars, so I was sad to see fifty cents of it suddenly consumed. Then we picked out a ball. I tried to find a light one, but they were all so heavy — far too heavy for me. Jen pointed to a rack with smaller balls normally reserved for children, and I gladly took one.

We joined the other girls.

One of our teachers was there, and she welcomed a few of the other new girls and me. She gave us some lessons on how to walk down the lane. I don't know why, but it was very hard for me. Probably because of the pressure of other girls watching. Probably too, because I was not the most coordinated girl in school. Sports were something I never did, and even bowling, though not a sport, was hard.

My first several shots ended up in the gutter, though one made it almost to the pins.

It didn't matter, though, because the other new girls were not doing much better.

I played two games and had enough money left to buy a small pack of french fries.

It all felt like a wonderful dream.

When I saw the time was near, I told the teacher I had to leave and took the bus home.

When I arrived, threats of impending chaos were present, but I quickly corralled my brothers and began cooking, keeping my promise to do something special for them. My presence seemed to ease Papa's nervousness, and before too long, Mom came home, which signaled the end of the entire event.

~ ~ ~ ~

That fall also allowed me to join the St. Richard's Youth Group I had seen it in the bulletin when I went to church. I called and asked the lady in charge if she would talk to my mom. She did, and Mom said OK. It was another small freedom for me.

The group met a few times a month, usually on Sunday evenings. This was a perfect time, as family visits were over, and lunch and dinner had been prepared and eaten. Papa was usually settled down by now in front of the TV with my brothers to watch Mutual of Omaha's Wild Kingdom, followed by Walt Disney. I never wanted to miss these shows myself, but the freedom of being with other kids my age was too great to pass up.

Being there helped me to realize that my faith, which I held dearer than anyone else in my family, was real. I was not some dreamer or oddball with strange ideas. My faith was real, and here were people with similar beliefs. I realized there were others like me who held faith dear.

## First Crush

On a daily basis, the girls who took the bus to Kamms Corner had to transfer to the 86 bus that took them to St. Joe's. We were not the only ones on the bus, though. The boys from St. Eds, one of the big Catholic high schools for boys, also transferred onto that bus. So we all got to ride together for about a total of five minutes each day, as St. Joe was not too far from Kamms Corner. But, though only five minutes, you would think it was a lot longer, indeed, a major milestone in the day. The girls acted like it was their life's most important five minutes. They would be jockeying for seats, laughing with each other, arranging their hair, skirts, posture, flirting as best they could, and all that took place in less than a five-minute bus ride.

I was not part of it, as I was not even allowed to talk to boys, nor would I know how. Sure, I talked to my cousins, who were boys, but this was entirely different. These boys were not Italian, and these boys were not my cousins. Besides, how would I ever compete with all the outgoing American girls, who seemed to know just what to say, when to laugh, or when to be noticed? I kept my head down and just observed.

In the late fall, just before Halloween, I noticed one of the boys from St. Eds. We made eye contact for a moment, and he smiled at me. The effect on me was instantaneous. I had a crush on him immediately, and for the next several weeks, I looked for him every day. I said hi to him a few times, and he returned the greeting. Nothing more than that happened, as I was not confident about what I should do next.

I told one of my friends about him, and she found out his name. It was Mark.

For the next few days, I tried to figure out a way to talk with him, but I had none. Finally, my friend agreed to introduce me. She went right up to him, with me in tow, and introduced us. I stuck out my hand and shook his, smiling. He asked me where I was from, and I told him. Suddenly it was time to get off the bus, but I had done it—I had met him.

For the next few weeks, I tried to talk with him, but we never seemed to be near each other on the bus. Finally, I asked my friend to see if he would want to go out with me. Going out was something I was not allowed to do, and I didn't even know what to do, but I figured like so much, I would work it out later.

She asked him as I watched from across the bus. He smiled, looked over, and said something to her. When she returned, she told me that he did not think he would be able to go out with me, but he would think it over.

I felt dumb, and yet, I felt a little bit of hope. Perhaps he just needed to get to know me. After all, we had never spoken more than a sentence or two.

I decided to make him a small gift. I used the only things I had at my disposal. That night, after my brothers were taken care of, I used some brown rope and a couple of small wooden rings to fashion a small monkey. The two rings formed the monkey's body with a macramé stitch, a fancy word for rope tying. The floppy ears, glued-on eyes, and long curly tail were a nice gift. I was proud of it because a lot of love went into making it. I was hoping he might see that.

The next day he was not on the bus, but I gave it to him the following day. He smiled and thanked me, asking what it was. When I told him, quietly, so others would not hear, his eyes widened, and he said thanks.

I never got any closer to him than on that day. It seemed he was always on the other side of the bus, and he would not make any effort to talk with me, so sadly, my first crush came to a close.

## Winter Formal with Tom

By the second semester of my junior year, all the talk at school was about the upcoming Winter Formal. It seemed everyone was going, and I wanted to go too. Who to ask, though. I decided that at my upcoming Youth Group meeting, I would ask a boy named Tom. I got there early, hoping he would be there early too, and I was rewarded. He was. I asked him if I could speak to him for a moment. We stepped into the hall, and I popped the question.

"Hi, Tom. Hey, you know the *ummm*…. Winter Formal Dance at St. Joe's is coming up. I… well… I was wondering if you would go with me?"

His eyes widened for a moment.

I watched his eyes narrow back to normal, and his lips move, signaling he was thinking, until he smiled and said, "Yes, sure. I will go with you."

"OK, great. Thanks. I… I will *um*… well. I will call you. Write down your phone number before you leave, and we can talk about the details."

"Sure, Marisa. That sounds nice."

I couldn't believe it.

I was going to the Winter Formal.

Things like how I would get there, or who else would be in our group, hadn't even crossed my mind. But I was going, and I trusted the rest would be figured out.

The dance was in two weeks.

That night, as the Youth Group was ending, I was waiting for my mom to pick me up and talking with Karen, one of the other girls. I told her that I had asked Tom to the Winter Formal. Karen raised her eyebrows.

"You better be careful with him. He's gone out with a few girls in our group and more besides. I heard he is a sex machine."

I turned, stunned. "What are you talking about?"

"I'm just telling you what I heard. Margie told me."

"How does Margie know?"

"She went out with him!"

My Cinderella story crashed to the floor, and within moments, my mom pulled up.

"Karen, I have to go. Can I call you?"

"Yeah, sure. Hey, don't worry, Marisa. He can try what he wants. The rest is up to you."

I frowned and jumped into my mom's car. I felt so low hearing what I had been told. No way... I mean... Yes, way... Yes, up to me. No way would I let him touch me... but still, the entire idea of others knowing about him, rumor or not, made me feel so confused. It tarnished the whole thing. Should I call it off? Should I find out more? I decided to sleep on it.

*** 

The next day, I woke up with a clear sense of what to do. I would be professional and cordial about this date. I would not back out, as I felt it would be wrong to cancel based on rumors. My gut told me the rumors were truer than not, but I would go and expect him to be a perfect gentleman, for I would not have it any other way.

Yes, he had the looks, and most of the other girls were already intimate with their partners in high school, but that would not change me.

I had already promised to reserve intimacy for the one I would choose to live with for the rest of my life.

~ ~ ~ ~

The day finally came after a few weeks of preparation and attention to all the details of "the perfect evening."

I wore a light blue dress Mom purchased at a discount store at the mall. I had on matching accessories. At about 5:30 in the evening on a Friday, Tom arrived at my house, and shortly after, the two other couples arrived. The other two ladies and I received wrist corsages, and we pinned the smaller corsages on our respective date's suit jackets.

Next, we took photos.

The only reason any of this was possible was that my Uncle Tony made plans in advance to take Papa out of the house hours earlier. He made an excuse that he needed help at one of his rental properties. Had Papa been there, none of it would have happened because everyone would have been kicked out. In Papa's view, anyone who went out on a date was considered a loose woman, to put it mildly. He used an Italian word to describe such a woman, which does not sound pleasant even in Italian.

My brothers were all strangely silent, and I only imagined it was because they had never really seen me going out on a date. The other couples, too, probably stole some of their normal nerve to interject or interrupt.

All was going well.

The other girls and their dates got in the car. Tom and I lingered to say goodbye to my mom.

Then, Mom said it. I do not know what possessed her to say it, but she said it. Surrounded by my brothers, two of whom were clinging to her, she said, "Don't do anything that Jesus wouldn't do."

I froze in my footsteps, and I glanced from the corner of my eye at Tom's stunned face.

Then she went further, half stepping onto the porch, my brothers all stepping down with her. She added, "Jesus is watching both of you, even if I am not."

I lowered my gaze to the ground, unable to even glance at my date. I got in the car and tried to enjoy my evening. Strangely though, Mom's words must have had an effect on Tom. He was no sex maniac. He was not even very friendly toward me. He stayed miles away and seemed to have more fun and concern for his friends at the dance than making sure his date had a good time.

It was one of the worst nights of my life, and I don't know if Mom was to blame or Jesus was to blame, but it clearly did not go well. Or did it? Perhaps the embarrassment was the thing that hurt me the most. Up until now, because of Papa's moods and actions in public, it felt like I would die of embarrassment. And this time, having the other couples at my house, having my date at my house, and Papa not being home, I thought we were in the clear.

But it came anyway. Embarrassment unexpectedly came crashing in, and that crushed me.

I was unable to cope in my nice, comfortable dress. I felt like a lost child.

## Bachelorette Party

It was the summer before my Senior Year, and my cousin Rosemary was getting married. Since I was turning seventeen at the end of summer and going to her wedding, it was decided that I would be allowed to attend her bachelorette party. I was so excited, as I had never been to a party like that. I was reluctant at first because I didn't know what to expect. But some of my other cousins, one to two years younger than me, sisters of the bride-to-be, were going, so I never gave it another thought.

There was no discussion of the moment-by-moment events, only that it was at Rosemary's friend's house, who lived a block or so from their house in Cleveland.

Mom dropped me off, and after a few minutes of talking with my aunt, my cousins and I walked down a few streets to the party. There were about fifteen other girls there, most of whom I did not know, and all of them except my cousin, older than me. It was a warm evening, and immediately they began drinking. I remember looking around, wondering why everyone thought drinking was fun. It seemed senseless to me, but I had to endure it. To leave would embarrass my cousin and possibly even anger my parents, who were not supposed to pick me up until ten o'clock at my aunt's house. Eventually, the evening turned to night, and the streetlights came on. I thought it was the end; I was wrong. It was the beginning.

Everyone was about to go outside when someone announced that a cake had arrived, and he all had to go down to the basement. One by one, we all filed downstairs. In the back corner was an enormous cake, with one of the girls standing guard by it. No one was allowed to go near. We all stood, watching, and suddenly, burlesque-style swanky music came on. The next moment, a guy popped out of the cake. He was barely dressed, but as he rose, he began undressing even more.

I was stunned. I wanted to go outside, but I was not near the door. Almost everyone seemed in my way, so I stayed and did not move.

The women were wildly laughing, whistling, and clapping out of control. I looked at them all, most drunk to some degree, and felt sad. How was this a way to prepare for a wedding? My younger cousin Italia was near me, and I asked her, "Have you ever seen anything like this before?" She said, "No, I am only fourteen."

I kept my gaze glued to his eyes, afraid to look at the rest of him, and I noticed he was not smiling much. It was as if he knew what he was doing was wrong.

Finally, the music stopped, and he ran upstairs and left. The young women all dashed outside in an uproar, and all of them had a can of shaving cream. I wondered what would happen next. Suddenly, they all took off their tops and covered their breasts with shaving cream and ran topless up and down the street.

I went from sadness to anger to feeling appalled. I watched shamefully, and I sat at the picnic table nearest to the street closest to the fence and waited. I had no money with me and no way of calling to get a ride home. I felt myself being out of my body, wishing to be at a beach or a serene setting. I'm surprised the loud wailing and partying didn't bother the neighbors. Also, I was surprised that no one called the police. Finally, at 10:00 p.m., I went home to my aunt's house and waited for my mom to come. I never told her what happened, only that it was not very fun, and I went to confession the next week.

# Senior Year

Senior Year came too fast for me, and it went too fast for me. My brothers were still much younger than I, at this point, in eighth grade, fourth grade, and second grade. They had great needs, and I was still the one to meet them. The talk of all the girls at school was college. Who was going to which college? Applications were being sent, and entrance exams were being taken. I was struggling to get Cs and Ds in my classes, banging my head against the wall and surviving by doing tons of extra credit generously offered by my teachers.

The idea of college scared me, but I reasoned it out. It was not much different from the fear I felt leaving the comfort of the local Catholic Grade School and boarding the bus for far away St. Joe's. I trusted God would help me, as he had always helped me.

By the middle of the final semester, most people had decided where they were going to college. A few girls, who were the topic of fascinating conversation, had become pregnant and were quietly 'not' going to college. A few were even getting married. It surprised me how others reacted to such news, mocking them. It was as if these girls who had love and life interrupt their education were somehow losers. I didn't feel that way. I realized that my own mother was only eighteen when she married. Most of my aunts were that age, too. It would be very normal in the world I grew up in.

As spring came and the countdown to the end of the school year began, the announcements about prom were posted on the wall.

St. Joseph Academy
Class of 1981
Prom Night
7:00–12:00
Auditorium
Sign Up at Mrs. Ibo's classroom

The whole school went bonkers; at least it seemed that way to me. I had enough of dances after my disastrous Winter Formal with Tom Hopkins. I had already decided that there would be no more dances for me if I had anything to say about it. Still… a girl can dream of a real prince charming coming along.

On the announcement day, fourth period ended, the bell rang, and everyone headed for the cafeteria. There was extra energy in the air, which was a good one. I marveled at how the mood of an entire school could change with one bit of news. As was my custom after fourth period, I went to the chapel to pray to St. Joseph. It was not on the direct path to the cafeteria and not far from my locker, so I got to go there usually unobserved on most days. I wasn't hiding my faith. It was just something most girls didn't do, especially when the cafeteria was beckoning. Of course, it was beckoning for me too, but I only needed a short time in the chapel.

There was usually a nun or a teacher inside, and occasionally a student. It was a beautiful chapel with blue walls that a sliver of sunlight lit up, and seated probably fifty people. There was a statue of Mary on the left and the cross of Jesus over the altar. On the right side was a statue of St. Joseph. That was where I spent most of my time, kneeling in front of it. I had spent all my high school years visiting here almost daily, asking St. Joseph to help me pass my classes. He probably had a bigger job than I realized because even though I passed my classes, in most of them it was barely passing and a struggle to do that. But I realized that Jesus, Mary, and Joseph never had it easy, so why should I?

When I arrived at the cafeteria, the tables were buzzing. I quietly sat down and said hi to my friends. Marykay said, "Hey, Marisa, what do you have today?"

"Melanzane."

"Oh… what's that again?"

"Eggplant. Want some?"

"Nooooo, thanks."

Everyone laughed.

Maureen "Mo" Higgins started, "OK, who's going to prom?"

Peggy, Mo, and Sheila all raised their hand. Only Marykay and I did not.

Mo said, "Why aren't you two going?"

"It's called a date, Mo," Marykay said, laughing.

I looked at Marykay, shook my head, then took another bite of my dried eggplant on homemade Italian bread, hoping I would not be put on the spot.

Marykay added, "I may tag along and bring my sister, though."

I swallowed my food and chimed in, "That's the way, Marykay. Who needs a date!" I was always Marykay's cheerleader. Marykay was also a member of the St. Richards Youth group, but it was more. She was off-the-charts smart, and she was off-the-charts kind. When I got Ds and Fs on my papers, Marykay would encourage me and not brag about her straight As. She was kind of a tomboy who never had a boyfriend, and I could relate to her.

"How about you, Marisa?" asked Mo.

My eyes widened as I thought I had dodged the bullet. I did not want to be put on the spot, but I was.

"Oh, it's the same problem. I don't have a date."

"What about that Tom you took to Winter Formal last year?"

"Yea," Marykay added. "Why don't you ask him, Marisa?"

"I don't think he likes me," I said, shrugging.

"I heard he had a really good time at the dance."

"Well, yes, but with his friends. He hardly danced and didn't even kiss me goodnight."

"No kiss, goodnight!" Mo exclaimed. "I wouldn't go with him either! I want to be doing way more than that on Prom Night."

Everyone laughed, and I tried to smile, but I didn't think it was funny.

"Me… too," Peggy added, high-fiving Mo. Peggy and Mo were both very serious with their boyfriends, and this was no surprise or revelation to anyone.

"Oh boy…. You two…. I am going to get my ice cream bar. I'll be right back."

"Hey, Marisa," Mo said, laughing. "Don't be upset. Some guys are like that. Why don't you come along with Marykay and her sister?"

"Well, maybe I will. Thanks, Mo." I knew it would be impossible, or rather, at least improbable. My parents would probably not let me go, with or without a date.

~ ~ ~ ~

For the rest of the week, thoughts of prom filled the school. The hallways in between classes and lunch tables were alive with talk of who was going with who and who had hopes that such and such a boy would go with her, but she only needed the nerve to ask. My disaster at Winter Formal kept me slightly at bay in these conversations. I would, of course, encourage all my friends, who had hopes, but when the question came to me, I held little hope.

# The Dance

The following Wednesday evening, my brothers and I sat on the floor and couch near my papa, watching wrestling. I did not enjoy wrestling, but my brothers did. Regardless, it was the only TV in the house, so that was what we did most evenings while we waited for Mom to come home; watch what Papa wanted to watch.

Suddenly, the phone rang, and my brothers ran from the TV room, racing to answer it. Papa yelled, "Stop!" but they ignored him.

Crispino was the first one there. "Hello!" he yelled as his other arm fought off my younger brothers, Danny and Ernest, grasping for the phone. "Marisella?" he said aloud, surprised.

My eyes drifted immediately to Papa. His face showed sudden alarm as he glared into the kitchen. I scampered up and ran to the phone.

Crispino raised his eyes, smiling. I glared at him and grabbed the phone, quickly turning back to see what Papa was doing. He had started to get off the couch, but only halfway. Again, he was glaring at me.

"Hello?" I said excitedly, trying not to show it, keeping one eye on Papa.

"Hi, Marisa. This is Joe… Joe Mason. I… I am a friend of Carlo's. He said I could call you and ask if you wanted to go to prom with me."

"Oh, prom?"

Papa had stood up now and had walked a few steps toward the kitchen.

"Well, I have to ask my parents."

"Well, do you want to ask them now?"

Papa had now set down the TV guide and stepped a few steps closer. My brothers were all standing around me, wanting to hear what I was saying.

"No, I will call you back."

"When?" he asked.

"*Ummm*…. In a few days."

"Do you need my number?"

I glanced over at Papa and realized I was pushing my luck. "No, I will get it from Carlo. I have to go. I will let you know."

He replied, "OK, bye."

I smiled, relieved I had gotten through the call uninterrupted. "Bye."

"Who was that?" asked Papa.

I shook my head. "One of Carlo's friends named Joe."

"What did he want?" Papa asked in an ascending, excited, and concerned tone.

"He asked me to go to a dance."

Papa swore under his breath and began shaking his head.

"What dance?" my brother Crispino shouted.

"Shut up, Crispino. I am not going to a dance."

I saw Papa sigh and exhale loudly, glad for my response. He turned back to the couch, and we all joined him. I glanced at the clock. Mom would be home soon.

Dinner was unusually quiet that night. I kept glaring across the table at Crispino. He had that devious look on his face. Then, finally, the moment I dreaded came.

Crispino said, "Carlo's friend named Joe called and wants to take Marisella to a dance."

Papa set down his fork with a grim look on his face. Mom stopped eating. She looked at me and asked, "Who is this?"

"I don't know him."

"Well, why does he want to take you to a dance?"

"I don't want her going to a dance!" Papa shouted. "I will fix Carlo!"

Crispino's eyes widened, and he made a face. Just then, Danny punched him in the arm.

"Stop it!" Papa shouted. "Eat!"

It grew quiet. We all started to eat again.

Mom asked again, "Who is this boy, Marisella?"

Papa nervously put his fork down, and we all stopped eating.

I swallowed hard. I felt like I was suddenly on trial. "I don't know. He is a friend of Carlo. He asked if I would go to prom with him."

Papa looked down at his plate, his face full of dismay. He swore under his breath in Italian.

All eyes turned from him to Mom. She now set her fork down. "When is this dance?"

"In two weeks."

"Can I go?" Danny shouted.

"Be quiet!" Papa yelled as his face furrowed.

We all looked down at our plates and resumed eating; Mom too.

Then Mom said, "Hold on."

We all stopped again.

Mom got up and went to the phone and dialed. "Eh, Mary. Let me speak to Carlo."

There was silence as we all stopped eating. I glanced at Papa. His head was turned toward the phone as if he were a Roman statue.

"Carlo. It's Aunt Brigida. Who is this Joe that wants to take Marisella to the dance?"

There was silence.

"Are you going to be there?"

Mom nodded. "OK."

There was silence.

"What time is it at?" She was quiet, listening. "Eight to twelve. You mean to midnight?"

Again, silence, and Mom was thinking.

"She can go, but she has to be home at 10:00."

"No. 10:00, or she can't go."

Silence. Mom began nodding.

"So, you will talk to him. Make sure."

She hung up. I glanced at Papa. He had not moved, but that was a good sign.

Mom sat down. "OK, you can go. But you have to be home at 10:00."

I thought for a moment of asking for more time, but I knew that could sabotage the whole thing.

~ ~ ~ ~

There was a strange silence in the house for the next two weeks. Then, the Sunday before the prom, our wider family was over. Uncle Tony and Aunt Jean arrived first. When no one was listening, I asked Uncle Tony if I could speak to him outside. He nodded and went out back. I went out the front and ran around to meet him. "What is it, Marisella?"

"Uncle Tony. I am going to a prom, and I am worried Papa will embarrass me."

"I heard all about it," Uncle Tony replied.

"Can you come and take him somewhere Friday? It would be better if he is not here when I get picked up."

Uncle Tony nodded. "Sure, I will do that."

"Thank you, Uncle Tony."

He hugged me tightly. "Anything for you, Marisella. You have a nice time with this young man."

I felt so good talking to my savior, Uncle Tony. He was always the one to help me when dealing with Papa.

A while later, Uncle Joe and his family arrived. Carlo saw me and waved for me to follow him. We went out back.

"Marisella. You don't have to worry about anything. I talked to Joe Mason. Everything is set."

"What are you talking about? What did you tell him?"

Carlo smiled. "Don't worry, cousin. He will treat you like a perfect lady. I warned him."

"Warned him for what?" I demanded.

"You just relax. He is going to be a perfect gentleman."

"Carlo!" I said with my teeth gritted, worried he had spoiled my first big date right from the start.

"It's OK. I got you covered."

~ ~ ~ ~

The big day came, and as evening approached, I went to my room to stay out of Papa's way. Around 6:00 p.m., Uncle Tony came and picked up Papa. After that, I took a bath and got dressed. When I put on my dress and came downstairs, my brothers stared at me as if they had never seen me dressed up. Mom came over and looked over my dress, straightening it.

It seemed like no time at all when suddenly Joe knocked on the door. Mom opened it and greeted him with a look of suspicion. My brothers stood behind me, staring. Joe was tall and wore a blue suit with a plain brown tie. His brown hair was parted to the side. On his face was a smile, though I could tell he was nervous.

We greeted each other for the first time, then walked to the door. As we were leaving, Mom called out, "Don't do anything Jesus wouldn't do."

I froze in my tracks, embarrassed, unsure if I should go out or go back in. I decided to go. I said, "Don't worry, Mom."

When we arrived, we sat by his friends. Carlo was there with his girlfriend. He kept coming over and smiling at me. He would then go over to Joe and put his hands on his shoulders, saying, "You having a good time, Joe?"

"Yes."

"Well, take my cousin out to dance."

When it was nine o'clock, it seemed the party was getting going. I loved being there and seeing all the young women dressed so beautifully. For the first time in my life, I felt like a woman, and a woman from America, just like all my American friends.

I glanced at the clock. My dream night would have to come to an end soon. Joe asked me to dance, and I proudly followed him onto the dance floor and began moving to music I had only moved to in my room and in my dreams. We danced for several songs before going to the bar and getting two soft drinks.

I looked at the clock again. It was 9:20. Joe said, "Let's go back to the table."

I smiled and followed him. We sat down by his friends and their dates. I glanced across the room and saw Carlo and his girlfriend. She was sitting on his lap with her arms around his neck. Carlo was talking to her, with his face close to hers. I could see that they were intimate with each other. Joe got up, saying, "I'll be right back."

I saw him walk across the room and talk to some other people. Then he went to the restroom. I nervously looked at the clock. It was 9:30. I quietly got up, picked up my small purse, walked alone across the edge of the dance floor toward the restrooms, and then waited a little ways away. When Joe came out, I intercepted him. "Joe, I have to go home now."

His face looked surprised, and he glanced across the room at the large clock. "Oh, yeah. Can't you stay a little longer?"

I half-smiled and shook my head.

"All right. I have to get my keys. We can say goodbye and go."

"I'll wait by the door." I could not imagine any more embarrassment than I already felt.

As Joe walked across the room to our table, I looked at the couples having so much fun. The girls laughed, danced, talked, sat close to their dates, and some kissed their boyfriends. Then, the music changed, and a slow dance began.

I watched as the dance floor suddenly filled with young men and women clutching each other, swaying back and forth, talking, staring into each other's eyes. I felt like crying. I wanted this too, but with who? Joe had stayed a mile away from me.

Then I saw Joe across the edge of the dance floor, with his keys in his hand. I turned to face the door and wiped a tear from my eye, waiting for him to lead the way.

We went to the car and silently drove down Lorain Avenue to North Olmsted. When we pulled in, the porch light was on, and the front door was open, allowing us to see into the hallway. Joe smiled, turned to me, and said, "Thanks for coming."

I wasn't sure what to do. I thought he was supposed to open my door for me. Even imagined he would walk me to the door and kiss me goodnight. He was then going to ask me to go on another date with him. I was sure. So, I smiled, waiting, until I realized I was supposed to get out myself. I got out and waved as he waved back, then turned to back out and left.

I watched for a moment, then went inside.

Mom and Papa were sitting at the kitchen table. Mom looking at me, Papa with his back to me. I walked into the kitchen, embarrassed that I had been out with a man. "How was the dance?" Mom asked. I half-smiled and started to sit. I could see the look on Papa's face. He was nervous and anxious. His brows were deeply furrowed. Finally, I decided not to sit and said, "It was fine. I saw Carlo."

"Oh, good. Did you sit with him?"

"Some of the time. I am tired. I am going to bed."

Papa glared at me. I could tell he was very angry, yet deep within his glare, I saw he was worried about me, worried I would do something wrong.

"Goodnight," I said, and I went upstairs.

In my room, I carefully hung up my dress. I wondered if I would ever wear it again. What was the point of going to dances? There was no fun in them. Being picked up, going in, sitting with Joe and his friends, even leaving and driving home: None of it felt like I belonged. I would never be allowed to be like my American friends. I would never be free to do what they were doing.

I put on my pajamas and glanced at the clock. It was 10:15. I turned off the light and tried to sleep, but a growing and desperate feeling of loneliness kept me awake. I prayed, talking to the only one I knew could understand me. After some tears, I finally fell asleep.

## Graduation and Plea for College

Most of my friends had decided to go to Bowling Green College. For over a month, I had spoken to my mom about it. She didn't understand why I needed to go to college. She said it would be fine for me to just get married someday and have a family. I pleaded with her, telling her that there was no way I would ever meet anyone unless I went away.

The answer was no, but she would talk to my father. I knew that would be fruitless. I did not give up speaking with Mom at every opportune moment. I left talking with Papa up to her because if he said no, which he might if I asked, the answer would be more definitive. Mom provided the buffer. I was careful in my conversation and knew I had to be an adult, as I had been trained to do my whole life. I reasoned with my mom that education was something no one could take from me.

She wanted me to go to school locally, but I told her it would never work. I had to go away so I would be able to study. Deep down, I could see Mom struggling to let me go, but I could also see her agreement with my reasoning on her face. My leaving would be difficult for her more than anyone. I had been the mom in our home for over ten years since my Nonna and Nonno left for Italy.

None of my cousins, who were older than me, went to college. In the Italian culture, girls did not need to go to college. They only needed to marry and have a family. Something deep within me said that I had to do this for myself. I had to be strong and make something of my life.

The answer was still 'no,' and with this long of a time pleading my case, it became more like a drawn-out siege. I began to realize that it may never be anything but 'no.'

Finally, the day of graduation came. It would all be over this afternoon. Four years of very hard work would come to an end. We would march down the aisle of the church, expected to carry the values and education we had learned into the world.

In one way, I understood this and was proud of my faith and the values instilled in me at an all-girls Catholic School. But, in another way, I was still largely misunderstood and ill-equipped to do anything other than return home and continue caring for my needy brothers. It was an emotional time when I felt life calling me, but there was no way to answer that call.

We were scheduled to meet at Our Lady of Angels Church, down the street from St. Joe's, where our graduation Mass and our procession would be held. It was set for Sunday afternoon at 2:00 p.m.

The day began with everyone in the house being extremely nervous. My brothers, who seemed to instinctively know when some major event involving me was unfolding, were wild all morning, driving Papa into a nervous fit. I helped Mom make lunch. We planned to eat at noon and then leave by 1:00 p.m., so we arrived early. We never went anywhere late and always instead arrived early… very early. All morning, Papa sat on the couch, reading the Sunday newspaper, occasionally glaring at or yelling at the boys to stop and be quiet.

Just before noon, the doorbell rang.

The boys ran to the door, followed by Papa.

"Cresenz!" came the welcome cry. It was Uncle Tony.

"Tonnnn!" Papa exclaimed back, his mood instantly changing. Uncle Tony walked in, bringing a wave of needed joy for today's event with him. I ran to hug him.

He hugged me tightly, saying, "*Ahhh*, hello, Padina. So… I heard someone is graduating today?"

"Thank you, Uncle Tony."

"You are a beautiful young woman, Mari. I am so proud of you. Not many in our family have graduated from a school like you. We are proud."

"Thank you, Uncle Tony." My mood was lifted, and I knew the day was going to be OK now.

Moments later, Aunt Jean walked in. Her face held a smile, but only for a moment, as by the time she finished crossing the threshold, it had turned to a fret, and I knew the mood, just lifted, was suddenly teetering on the fence.

"Hi, everybody," Aunt Jean said, adding, "Congratulations, Marisa. Oh, what a nice dress."

Mom called from the kitchen, "Come and sit down. It is time to eat."

"Oh, that sounds nice," Uncle Tony said.

"What are we having?" Aunt Jean exclaimed.

Mom half ignored her and ushered us all in, saying, "Sit down, and you will see."

Moments later, we were all seated. Mom handed out kitchen towels and told us kids to tuck it into our necks so our clothes would not get dirty. Then, she began putting the bowls of food she and I had prepared earlier onto the table. Meatballs, pasta, pork chops, salad, bread, and more were all put down. It was a feast, a feast in my honor.

As soon as we started passing around the food, Aunt Jean started. "Oh, we've got trouble. Annette wants to go on a date with a boy from down the street. Uncle Tony hit the roof this morning."

Uncle Tony bobbed back and forth slightly, adjusting his glasses, looking at his food, and murmured, "Jeanna, be quiet."

Aunt Jean went right on. "I think it is fine. My dad says kids are getting involved too young nowadays. The girls at work said she should go. I don't know… I think she's too young, but who am I. My boss is upset too because we spent the whole morning talking about it. My brother thinks I'm nuts. I don't know where he comes off talking like—"

"Jean!" Papa yelled. "We have to eat!!!"

"What!"

Mom interjected, "No talk about anything today, except about Marisa."

Jean's eyes widened. "Well, did you let Marisa go out on dates when she was fifteen?"

"Jean! Stop!" Papa said pleadingly.

Aunt Jean sighed and took the meatballs from Uncle Tony.

No one said a word for a long time as the food was passed and everyone began eating, until Aunt Jean broke the silence. "Are you excited, Marisa?"

"Yes, I am," I replied, grateful that was her only question.

It was quiet again for a few moments.

"Marisa, are you going to college?"

"I am not sure," I replied calmly, but I wanted to scream. I had been working on my mom about this subject with no real success. My plan was to get through graduation and then keep talking with her until I could hopefully convince her. Then we would go about convincing my dad. Today was not the day to discuss this.

"My dad says girls don't need to go to college. I think he's crazy. He and my brother both think alike. Marisa will meet a nice boy in college."

Uncle Tony looked up from his plate. "Jeanna, let Marisa decide."

Ernesto whined, "I don't want Marisa to go to college!"

"Be quiet, Ernesto," Papa said, putting his fork down, leaning back exasperated.

"*Bice!*" Jean said. "I heard most of the girls from St. Joe's are going. I don't care if my brother thinks I'm crazy. His wife went to college, and look at her! The ladies at the office think it's a waste of money. They said the girls are only going to meet husbands, anyway. *Patz!*" Patz was Italian slang for "Crazy."

Papa's chest rose. He was about to end it all, and I knew my chances for college just went out the window with the words that were about to be spoken.

Suddenly, Mom put her fork down and interrupted everyone. "Marisa and I have talked about this, and she is going to college."

"What?" Aunt Jean said, wide-eyed, as the entire table grew silent.

I felt a tear forming in my eye. My months of praying, asking, and pleading had just been answered, and now my future was set. Finally, I was going to college.

As I looked around the table, I could see everything in our family had suddenly changed. My brothers were eating more quietly, slowly, occasionally looking up at me as if they knew they were losing me.

An hour later, I and two hundred others were marching down the aisle of the nearby church in our graduation gowns. We were young women who were to go out and change the world with the values we had learned at St. Joseph Academy.

## Bowling Green

One of the girls who lived on the next street was also going to Bowling Green. She had gone in the summer and gotten a job in preparation. I called her, and she said there were openings, so I made arrangements to get into my dorm room early.

There was very little talk when I told my parents I would be leaving sooner than planned. A sadness hung over the house, and I was unsure if they were mad at me for going or if they were just sad at a major change in our family's life.

Early in the morning, when I was to leave, Uncle Tony came over, mercifully leaving Aunt Jean at home. When I came downstairs with my bag packed, Uncle Tony, Mom, and Papa were all sitting at the kitchen table, quietly drinking coffee. Uncle Tony had a tear in his eye. He said, "Padina, I will miss you very much. I wish you did not have to go."

I ran and hugged him tightly. "I will miss you too, Uncle Tony. But don't worry, I will be back."

I turned to Mom and hugged her. "Bye, Mom."

"Goodbye, Mari. Here is twenty dollars for your laundry and other things."

Uncle Tony stood up. "Here, Mari. This is from Aunt Jean and me." He proceeded to hand me another twenty dollars. I felt so rich at that moment. It was probably more money than I had in my pocket in my life.

It was a lot, as tuition, room, and board were all paid for, including meals in the cafeteria in the dorm, a cafeteria I would be working at.

I turned to Papa. He was sitting at the head of the table, with his arms folded, looking in the general direction of the floor. I knew he wanted to say something, but he was too emotional, and for Papa, that meant he could say nothing. So I walked over and hugged him. He half-smiled and said, "Goodbye, Mari."

"I love you, Papa," I said, wiping a tear from my eye. Papa kept looking at the floor and nodded.

Mom got up and went to the steps. "Boys, wake up and come say goodbye to Marisa."

My brothers came down the stairs one by one, all just waking up. First, Crispino came over and hugged me half-heartedly. That was OK. That was the way he always hugged me. Then, nine-year-old Danny barreled into me and held me tight, saying, "Please come home soon, Marisa."

Ernesto was the last one down. He started to cry and hugged my waist, crying in my shirt. "Ernest!" Mom said. "Marisa will be back home."

"I don't want her to leave. Who is going to make me dinner?"

"Ernest. I will make you dinner. Now stop and kiss Marisa goodbye."

I knelt and took my fragile brother in my arms. "I am going to send you letters and call you, Ernesto. That goes for all of you. I will be back every couple of weeks, too."

There was a beep in the drive. My ride with the girl who got me the job was waiting.

As I got into the car, I watched my family and Uncle Tony stand on the lawn next to the porch, waving sadly. Their faces were sad. I know they had relied on me for so much, and now I would no longer be there. I loved them, and yet I had to go. I knew they loved me too, though my leaving was more, it was like my Nonna leaving ten years earlier. It was a pillar of the home, being suddenly removed.

I cried inside, knowing my brothers would suffer the most, not through any wanton neglect by my parents, but rather because there was no one else. Mom had to work. She had to be the dad. Now, who would be the mom? The answer… was no one.

# Campus Life

## Bowling Green University

When I arrived at Bowling Green, it reminded me of the St. Joe's campus, only ten times bigger. I was given a temporary dorm where some early student arrivals lived until the incoming freshman class arrived. This was done so no one would be alone until the school year started. My life consisted of reporting for duty at the cafeteria in the center of campus. Here, I was trained to work in the kitchen. I worked every day in six-hour shifts. Afterward, I would go back to my dorm room to read, or if it was still light, I would take a walk around campus.

After working for two straight weeks, I received my first paycheck for almost $86. I could not believe I had earned so much money. The day after receiving my check, on a Saturday morning, I walked to the center of the tiny town named after the university and opened a bank account.

While $86 seemed like a lot of money to me, I had already been told by my parents that they could only afford the tuition, room, and board. That meant that everything else was up to me.

~ ~ ~ ~

There was not much to do during that first month, but I had arrived. I called my family almost every other day and often talked to my brothers. They sounded excited to talk with me, but I could also hear the sadness in their voice.

Near the end of August, Orientation Day came. Parents were supposed to be there with their children, so they could all get acclimated to the campus. Mom told me she would not be able to make it, so, feeling foolish at not having a parent with me, I did not go. The next day was move-in day.

Move-in day at Bowling Green was like the movie The Ten Commandments scene when the Israelites left Egypt during the Exodus. For the students of Bowling Green, instead of leaving en masse, they were moving in en masse. Thousands of students carrying boxes, wheeling carts, leaning back dollies, talking, laughing, cursing, all at once. Somehow, by nightfall, everything was in the dorm rooms, and students were busy getting to know each other and organizing their things.

I had little to bring on that day, so I went up the stairs of my new dorm building, onto the fifth floor, and reported to dorm room 7. It was a large spacious room when I arrived, with five beds nestled around the perimeter, each with a dresser and shared closet in between two beds, except for bed five, which had its own half-sized closet. There was a small thin privacy wall at the head of each bed, by the dresser, where we could change with some privacy. From a furniture standpoint, there were a couple of used light brown couches, two dark blue armchairs, and five worn-out end tables with lamps set to one side of the place. Two windows looked down over the campus. There was no bathroom or kitchen. Meals were to be taken exclusively in the cafeteria for our dorm, located on the first floor. I would start work there the following evening, as my work at the temporary dorm cafeteria was over. All showers and toilets were down the hall on each dorm floor.

As I was already on campus and used to doing things early, I was the first to arrive at the dorm. My assigned bed was number two. I excitedly put my clothing into the dresser, hung up the few blouses I had, and waited. Finally, Lee Ann was the next to arrive. She walked in, smiling, with her purse on her shoulder. "Oh, hi."

"Hi, I'm Marisa."

"Hi, Marisa. I'm Lee Ann."

The next moment, an older man pushing a cart came to the door. "Thanks, Dad," Lee Ann said. "Over there, on bed one."

Her dad pushed it into the room over to bed one. Within minutes, he hung up all her clothes in the closet we were now sharing. She helped him unpack boxes of clothes and put them on her bed. Next, another box with make-up, perfumes, and jewelry was put onto the bed. Finally, another box with about six pairs of shoes was placed on the bed. By the time the cart was emptied, her bed was filled, and I could only wonder where it was all going to fit.

"I've got it from here, Dad," she said as she smiled at me again. Her dad hugged her, then opened his wallet and handed her a credit card. "Here, honey. In case you need anything."

"Thanks, Dad. I love you."

They hugged again, and her dad left, wheeling the cart away. Before he could get out the door, another cart bumped into him in the hall. "I'm sorry," came the voice of a young man. They maneuvered past each other, and another cart full of clothing was pushed in. A very handsome-looking young man followed it. Behind him was a blonde-haired girl who looked like a model. "Hi," she said. "Tony, put it all over there by bed four."

"You got it, babe," he said with a dutiful smile.

Like Lee Ann's father, Tony began hanging up clothes and putting baskets of clothing, much of it still with tags from the store, onto the bed.

The girl sat on the bed and put her purse down on the floor. "Hey, ladies. I am Sandy. This is my boyfriend, Tony."

Tony stopped, and we all said hi to each other. Lee Ann resumed putting her clothing, shoes, and other things away. Sandy began doing the same.

I looked around. The spacious room was starting to feel cramped, and we still had two more girls to go. But it didn't bother me because Mo and Peggy were coming in next, and I could not wait to see them. After Tony and Sandy finished unpacking and putting all her things away, they went into the hallway. Lee Ann and I listened to their kissing, I love you's, and difficult goodbyes. They were really in love, and I found that fascinating. I wished I had someone who loved me, but I was not sure how it would ever happen.

Finally, Sandy returned to the room, wiping a few tears from her eyes. She said nothing but went to her bed and plopped down face first, mostly hidden from our view by the privacy wall. I looked at Lee Ann, who frowned and rolled her eyes. I didn't feel that way, and I was sad for her. She clearly loved this young man, and it was a sad moment that I had just witnessed.

I got a book I had brought and went to sit on the couch. Lee Ann was busy unpacking, not talking much. I got the feeling she was not interested in being friends. Then, at 4:00 in the afternoon, I heard Peggy's laughter coming down the hallway. Peggy and Mo had arrived.

They popped through the doorway and wheeled in one cart. "Hi everybody," they exclaimed until they saw me. Mo yelled, "Marisa!" and came running over to hug me, with Peggy in hot pursuit. After two hours with Lee Ann hardly talking and Sandy in her bed, reading and half-sleeping, it was a welcome moment.

We hugged. "Hey everyone," Mo declared. "College has officially begun! Woohoo!"

"Woohoo! Yeah!" Peggy exclaimed.

I laughed and felt a joy I had never felt before. Freedom was upon me and upon us all.

In the next moment, Mo quickly took charge. She wheeled to Lee Ann, extending her hand. "Hi, I am Maureen, and my friends call me Mo. Since we are living together, you can call me Mo. This here, is my trusty sidekick, Peggy. She laughs a lot." Mo paused, looked over at her, and added, "A lot!"

Peggy started laughing, and so did I.

"Hi, Mo and Peggy, I am Lee Ann. I am from Arlington Heights."

"*Oooh,*" Mo replied tepidly. "Sounds like a nice place."

Lee Ann smiled smugly. "It is."

"OK, then," Mo said, walking back across the room until she peered around the privacy wall into Sandy's room. "And who do we have here?"

"I'm Sandy," came the voice from behind the half wall.

"Well, hello, Sandy."

"OK, girls, dinner is at 5:00. I hope the food is good around here."

"It's pretty good, Mo. I work in the cafeteria, you know."

"Good, an inside person. That is just what we need."

Mo, Peggy, and I went to the cafeteria. It was a marvelous time together, and I could not believe I was with them, two of the most popular girls, indeed the leaders, of our high school group. After dinner, we walked around campus.

As evening turned to night. Mo announced, "I am going for a McDonald's run. Who is in?"

Everyone immediately chimed in. I did not really like McDonald's, nor have the money for it. It was something I never did. But the orders started flying, Mo repeating them as Peggy wrote them down. Five- and ten-dollar bills were pulled out.

"What do you want, Marisa?"

"Umm…. I will have a small chicken McNuggets."

"That's it?" Peggy asked, pausing her pen for a moment.

"Yep, that's all I want." I pulled out a dollar from my pocket. I almost felt guilty spending money on McDonald's since I'd been taught for my entire life that it was wrong to waste money at restaurants, especially for fast food. But I wanted to fit in, and even though I had to be cautious with my money, I was sure I could afford it.

The night ended with all of us getting to know each other and Lee Ann and Sandy understanding Peggy's penchant for laughter. We all laughed that night, and it was probably, at least for me, nervous laughter. Tomorrow, classes would start, and this was the thing that I feared the most.

# Classes

On the first day of classes, the campus came alive in an orderly, quiet way. Thousands of students from dorms and off-campus houses flocked to the wide walkways that weaved their way through campus to the hundreds of college classrooms and labs.

I woke early and nervously went to the showers down the hall for the first time. There were a few other girls there, all clad in towels. I was neither comfortable nor trained to parade around in front of others in a towel, so I had gone there fully dressed. I undressed in a stall and then used a towel to get into the nearby shower. Afterward, I peeked out, tied my towel tight, then picked up my pile of clothes and got dressed again in the stall. It seemed like a lot of work in one sense, but it was no different from what I'd been doing my entire life. I was never allowed to be in my home with only a towel. I always had to go into the bathroom fully dressed and come out fully dressed. So it was the same.

After dressing, I went back to my room. No one was up yet. I gathered my ID, class schedule, map of the campus, and a few dollars and left out the door.

My first class was English 098, Basic Writing. The mere notion of English struck fear into me. All throughout high school, I got Ds in English, only passing because of instructors willing to use extra credit assignments to help me through. I had never been taught to write.

In high school, all of the other students had help with their papers. Their parents were doctors, lawyers, accountants, and engineers. Their moms were educated and often stay-at-home moms, able to spend time with their children to guide them. Many of the students had older siblings or cousins who helped out. I had no one. Absolutely no one, and because of this, I was always lost. The basic building blocks of organizing sentences into paragraphs, with the paragraphs building into the structure of a paper meant to elaborate or draw a conclusion on a particular topic, eluded me completely.

My foundation simply did not exist.

I entered the large classroom with over forty desks, already half-filled with eager students, and carefully looked for a seat. A white tabletop lectern was at the front in the center. I took my seat in the middle, about halfway down the aisle. Within five minutes, the classroom was filled.

A middle-aged woman, holding a file folder, walked to the podium and smiled. She began, "My name is Ms. Spencer. Welcome to English 098. We will have six papers due this quarter. That amounts to about one every two weeks." She held up the file folder, then handed a stack of papers to each person in the front row. "Pass these syllabuses back. Our first assignment will be a Compare and Contrast Essay. It is due a week from Friday. If anyone needs help, the hours and location for the tutoring center are on page two. Now, let us begin."

My head was spinning. Six papers. I had not written six papers in my entire life. How was I possibly going to do that? As the person ahead of me handed me the pile of papers, I took one and passed it back. I quickly looked at page two for the tutoring center. It was in the Barrett Center. I froze. I had no idea where the Barret Center was. The hours were Monday through Friday from 10:30 a.m. to 4:30 p.m. I froze again. How would I possibly have time to go there when I worked at 3:00 in the afternoon? I began to panic.

The rest of the class was a blur, with Ms. Spencer using the board to show examples of Compare and Contrast topics. I tried to memorize everything she said and wrote it down. It was not sinking in, though. Coke vs. Pepsi? What? They were the same. Ford vs. Chevy. What difference did that make? They were both cars.

After class, I walked outside the classroom building and sat on a bench by myself. I felt so alone, so lost. I watched groups of students walking by, laughing, talking, and excited about their classes. I felt so numb and scared that I had three more classes to attend. One, Art History, before lunch, and two more tomorrow. The one I feared more than the rest, Math, would come then.

After Art History, I went to the campus bookstore and bought my English book and Art History book. I could not believe how large and heavy they were. Was I really supposed to learn all this? I walked back to my dorm. No one was there, and I was glad. My head was pounding, and I needed to lie down. I closed my eyes. My mind was reeling inside, furiously trying to figure out how I was going to write six papers. The Barrett Center kept surfacing, and I feared I would not have time to go there and get the help I needed. Fear held me in my bed for the longest time until I finally fell asleep.

I was awakened by Sandy coming back to the dorm. I looked up. It was 3:15 p.m. I jumped up. "Hi, Sandy."

"Hi, Marisa. How was your day?"

"Oh, it was OK. Unfortunately, I have to go to work now."

"Oh, what time do you work?"

"From 4:00 to 6:30," I said. I quickly put on my work clothes, hustled downstairs to the cafeteria, and reported for duty.

As soon as I got off, I went to the common area of our first-floor dorm building. It was filled with students sitting quietly at tables, studying. At the far end of the large open area were pay phones.

I inserted the phone card my mom had given me to be used sparingly. Finally, my brother Danny answered in a hurried voice, "Hello!"

"Danny, this is Marisa."

"Marisa!"

In the background, I heard the chaos. "Give me the phone! I want to talk to her."

"Ernesto, wait!" Papa was yelling in the background. "Hang up the phone!"

Ernesto whined, and then the phone dropped. Crispino picked it up. "Marisa?"

"Crispino. Where is Mom?"

"Wait! Danny, let go!" Papa yelled. "Hang up!"

"It's Marisa! Danny, wait."

"Marisa. Mom's at work."

I sighed. Papa had calmed down, but my heart broke for my brothers. They were alone, and I knew they were not being taken care of.

"When is she coming home?" I asked.

"Soon I think."

"Did you guys eat?"

"Yes. I made some pasta," Crispino said. "How is college? Ernesto! Wait. Marisa, here. Talk to Ernesto."

"Marisa!" came Ernesto's sad voice. "Marisa, when are you coming home?"

My heart dropped. These were not my brothers. These were my children; I was here, and they were home suffering. Ernesto had an enormous need for attention and love. He just wanted to be listened to, understood, and have his questions answered. He needed encouragement and love. He could not get that from Papa or my other brothers. It wasn't their fault. They had no idea.

"Hi, Ernesto. I love you. I will come home soon to visit."

"How is college?"

"It's hard, Ernesto. But I want you to be strong for me. Can you?"

"I don't know. Maybe…"

"I will see you soon, Ernesto. Now you be good, OK?"

"OK, Marisa."

"Let me talk to—"

"Hello!" Papa said in his quiet voice.

"Papa, how are you?"

"Okay…" he said, as his voice trailed downward.

"Papa, I need to talk to Mom. I will call back later."

"OK, Mari."

"Papa, I miss you."

He said nothing, but I knew his silence meant he heard me and missed me, too.

"OK, bye, Papa."

"Bye."

He hung up, and I clutched the phone and turned to look at all the students quietly studying. Did I belong here? Could I ever be free to just study, like all the other students? I was needed at home more than I needed to be here, wasn't I? I set the phone down and walked back to the table where I had been studying. I felt frozen, guilty for trying to study, guilty for closing my book and ignoring my dreams. I was deeply frustrated and divided in almost every way.

An hour and a half later, after mindless drifting and flipping through my books, I went back to the phone to call my mom. Fortunately, this time, Mom answered.

"Mom, it's Marisa."

"Hey, Mari. How are you?"

"I'm OK. It is hard, but I am doing my best."

"How is the job?" she asked.

"It's OK. I got my first check. I used it to buy my books."

"OK. Good."

There was quiet for a moment. "The tuition is due next Monday," I said, feeling like a burden.

"OK. I will have it Friday. Can you come home this weekend?"

"I don't know. I have to see if there is a bus."

"OK, check for the bus, and call me. I will have the money when you come home. You can go back Sunday and pay it on time."

"Thanks, Mom."

"Alright. Have a good night."

"Bye."

I hung up, deeply frustrated. I wished I had not had to ask. I was told they would help me with my tuition. Where else could I get the money? I felt like a beggar and was taking money away from my family for what everyone felt was unnecessary. It had been a long, frustrating day and an equally difficult, emotionally charged evening.

# The Days Begin

On day two of my first week, I attended Economics 101 and Math 098. As I had expected, but desperately hoped against, they overwhelmed me from the very start. The math tutors were located in the McHenry Center, and so began my long slog through my first year of college.

Countless hours in the library. Countless trips to the Barrett Center and the McHenry Center to see the Math and English tutors. Countless hours spent standing in line, then waiting for them to try to explain to me what was happening. Countless hours spent trying to write papers in the common area downstairs. Poor grades on papers, quizzes, and tests were my weekly reminders that I was not able to perform like the other students. In between all of this, I was busy working at the cafeteria and putting in 'more time' at the library that I thought would somehow magically help me.

From Thursday after class until Sunday afternoon, the entire campus became a party center. All of my roommates participated. Bars and happy hours dominated these days for almost everyone. I would not and could not participate in this. At the very core, the idea of being in bars and becoming inebriated felt revolting to me. I simply could not understand how people could do this to themselves. Working at the cafeteria was my way out. I signed up for shifts other students did not want, working Thursday, Friday, and Saturday nights.

After work, I would often go to the library to kill more time. Even then, I still had a large problem. On any given extended weekend night, our dorm room was being used by at least one of my roommates as their place to be in bed with their boyfriend or with whoever they had dragged home from the bars. Many a night found me arriving home to hear the commotion inside, or waking from sleep to hear the commotion entering the room. In either case, I had to leave. I spent a lot of time down in the common area of the dorm with a pillow and blanket, trying to get some sleep in until I could safely return.

After a few weeks, I learned about movies being shown in the student center on Saturday nights. They cost $1 and it became my Friday and Saturday night ritual. There, I saw movies I had never been allowed to watch at home, simply because we did not go to movies or watch movies.

Our TV at home was dedicated to watching wrestling or Disney on Sunday nights, or perhaps the ABC movie of the week. But here in Bowling Green, my life was open to the big cinema, and I relished movies like *Somewhere in Time* with Christopher Reeve or *An Officer and a Gentleman* with Richard Gere. I fell in love with these big-screen actors and secretly wished I would someday meet someone just like them, who would come along and sweep me off my feet. But how could I ever meet someone? I had no social life outside of the few people I saw in my classes or the few people I worked with. There was no way I was going to meet someone at a bar, nor would being home at family gatherings ever lead to meeting someone new. I felt very stuck and frustrated. Yet, deep down, I relied on my faith and prayed to God to help me.

Somehow, deep down, I trusted that he would.

## The Days Wear On

It was a long year for me. Surrounded by twenty thousand students, yet I had never felt more alone. My roommates were kind to me, but they were not my tribe. They were not part of the same world I was part of. They knew where they were going, and somehow, they knew how to pull it all together. Yes, they, too, had their moments of struggle, but not as I did. My struggles were very private, as I was embarrassed to tell them about my grades or my deep frustration at simply not getting it.

Life at home hung over my head almost daily. Had I abandoned my brothers? Calls home were mingled with deeply mixed emotions. I could tell that Crispino, Danny, and Ernesto were not being taken care of. They missed me profoundly, and I missed them just as much. I missed Papa, too. Even though he had always been so hard on me and so tormented in his mental illness, I loved him. I understood Papa and that his illness came from long ago and was buried deep within. He didn't want to be cruel, distant, and unreasonable. I somehow understood that it was all that he could muster being stuck with us kids; kids he did not have the emotional or fatherly tools to deal with.

Mom was in her own world, trying to be the dad by earning enough money to pay for our life in the suburbs of Cleveland. But, as per our agreement long ago, when she told me she had to be the dad, and I had to be the mom, I still felt a deep obligation to my brothers. They indeed were more like my sons. Only I had abandoned them.

The end of the first year arrived with my final grades. I had managed to fail math again, and I had mercifully received a D in English. Almost everyone was going home for the summer, but I had heard that summer classes were easier. What awaited me at home was nothing more than the old slavery and a chance I might decide not to return. So, I arranged to get a job at the main cafeteria, which would remain open all summer, and I signed up for summer classes.

When fall classes resumed, I, too, resumed life with my roommates. I was starting to enjoy being a student, and I had settled into routines and discovered the means to pass my classes.

My second year went very fast. I had no idea what the end of it would bring.

As the final weeks of my second year unfolded, the girls all over the dorms discussed next year's housing. It seemed that students had to leave the dorms after the second year. Though I knew this, I was kind of caught off guard. I assumed that my friends and I would move out together. Everyone was excited to get out of the dorms and begin living with a degree of autonomy.

But no one did not ask me. Mo and Peggy made plans. Lee made plans with some other girls. Everyone was making plans, but no one was asking me. I understood that I had done nothing to warrant this. I was always kind to everyone. Somehow, they must not have liked me enough to make room for me.

I had nowhere to go in the fall. I had nowhere to live or stay and no one to split the cost of housing with. I didn't have enough money.

There was another looming problem. I did not have a major either. I had no idea what to major in. All my friends were majoring in business. It scared me to move into any field of business. I did not feel comfortable choosing a career. There was the possibility of teaching, but in talks with my counselor, I was told that there would be a lot of papers and a lot of writing and English. I knew this would never work for me. I was unable to express my deep frustration. The counselors all seemed aloof. They did not understand my plight. My family did not either, nor any of my aunts, uncles, or cousins. How could they? None of them had ever gone past high school.

In what felt like a great failure, I went home for the summer, hoping I would somehow figure out what to do.

# Travel School

With no major and nowhere to live, I privately decided not to return to Bowling Green. Telling my parents was the worst thing. I felt like a failure, and yet, if anyone understood what I was facing, they would have encouraged me to come home. Unfortunately, there was no encouragement, just an amplified silence and a return to my old duties.

By late summer, my decision, or rather ability to change it, was cemented as the deadline for signing up for classes had passed. I had heard about a travel school where one could learn to become a travel agent.

I signed up and started classes in mid-September.

Travel School was a breeze compared to Bowling Green, except for a few things. The first and most daunting was the use of computers. I had never been taught how to use a computer, and technology was something I had a hard time comprehending. I don't know if it was nerves or lack of confidence, but something frequently caused me to press the wrong button. After that, I don't know if it was my determination to always try again or hope I had simply pressed the wrong button the first time, but one of those two usually had me pressing the button again, or even a third time, and often a different button if that didn't work. This approach may have boded well in life, trying to be the mom to three brothers, but it did not bode well with computers.

The second problem was the return to my old life. I was twenty years old, and my brothers were sixteen, twelve, and nine. They needed me more than ever and listened to me less than ever. Papa, too, had only gotten worse in my two years away. He was now more vocal and violent with my brothers. He was constantly shouting and chasing them around the house, trying to hit them when they misbehaved during the long hours that stretched from after school until Mom came home sometime after 6:00 p.m.

The pressure was coming from family too. It was a pressure I put on myself, but the next several months were filled with constant explanations to my cousins, aunts, and uncles as to why I was not back at Bowling Green. Deep within, I knew I could never live it down. The spoken message from everyone was, *'It is OK, at least you tried.'* The unspoken message from everyone, and perhaps also the one running through my mind, was that *you failed. You were not smart enough to be the first one in the family to go to college. That as the oldest daughter of an Italian family, your job was to get married and have children. Husbands were the ones who provided for the family, not wives. Now you've learned your lesson.*

I wanted no part of it, and every time I had to explain, a little part of me died inside.

# Ohio State

## Columbus Ohio

Deep inside, I knew I could not quit college. If my brothers were going to go to college, I could not give up until I finished college and got my degree. So I began to think about what I could major in that would allow me to finish. One day, I found out that Ohio State had a program in Italian. The Italian language was something I loved. The Italian culture was something I understood. It would be my ideal major. Without telling anyone, I anxiously applied for the program and was accepted.

The news was accepted well by my family, which surprised me. Yet, the entire dynamic was a paradox, for as a girl in an Italian immigrant family, and indeed as the oldest girl, I was NOT expected to even be able to finish college. I was expected to become a wife and mother and keep the house. Yet, here I was. Somehow, I sensed that the entire family, myself included, silently understood that I would not quit. The announcement that I was returning to college seemed to galvanize a promise of future strength to come from our immigrant family. The promise of America was in my hands and suddenly well within our family's reach. We would not stop until we finished what we started, and I, Marisa, though I was the oldest daughter, laden with all the generational expectations surrounding what oldest daughters were supposed to do, was suddenly the one carrying the ball. I was not going down before the goal line.

Though my brothers were saddened again at my leaving, especially Ernesto, they also supported this silent momentum sweeping the entire family forward.

By early January, I had secured a small apartment on the corner of 13th Street and High Street. I began the winter quarter at the Ohio State University. It was a vast campus filled with students from all over the world. After a week of wandering and finding my way into daily routines, my new life in apartment Y settled in.

I went to my counselor's office to begin life at the university. My assigned counselor in the College of Arts and Sciences was Ann Wriggles. She welcomed me and gave me a map of the vast campus, pointing out the building where the Foreign Language Departments were housed. I was so excited.

The following day I walked over a half-mile from my apartment to my first class in my Italian Major, filled with excitement. The building was called the Compton Building, and the first two floors held about twenty classrooms of varying sizes. The Foreign Language Departments had their offices on the third through fifth floors. The Spanish and French Language Departments each had their own floor in the large building, full of officers for professors, administration personnel, and an accompanying small army of offices for student-teacher assistants.

And on the fifth floor was the Italian Department. It was one of the smallest departments and shared space with a handful of other smaller language departments. The Italian Professors, Klop, Mansini, and Farina, occupied three modest offices and two smaller offices shared by three student-teacher assistants.

So my time at Ohio State started with twice-weekly trips to the tutor lines to receive the needed help and monthly trips to my counselor, Ann Wriggles, for advice. Several nights a week, I could call home and talk with my brothers. I was proud of myself for returning to college and knew that my younger brother Crispino, now a junior in high school, would follow in my footsteps.

It was a lonely time for me, as I kept to myself. Across the street from my apartment were several frat houses. The most entertaining of which were the dentists and the doctors, or as everyone called them, the Gummies and the Docs. They were constantly at war.

The banter began between the two rivals every week around the same day and time. What was interesting and hilarious to me was that I was entertained without watching television. I could tell when they would begin their back and forth because the music would reach a high decibel. The running water in my apartment would shake and tremble as if it had been struck by lightning. The Docs would shout for at least two hours that the Docs are better than the Gummies because "we save lives."

The Gummies would provide rebuttal and say, "You don't save all lives. We are more important than Docs. Why? Because teeth are important for sustenance and overall heart health. Survival is found in us!"

"No," shouted the Docs, "we are more important than you, Gummies!"

This repetition of those two lines went on for a while. It was evident that each fraternity thought itself superior to the other, and each had their one-liners and competent quick wit traded until the designated time passed, when the back-and-forth outbursts died down as fast as the verbiage rivalry started.

I was bemused by all this and enjoyed the outdoor entertainment without leaving the balcony of my apartment.

Next door to me was the home of the leaders of Campus Crusade for Christ Ministry. I attended some of their meetings, and though I was raised Catholic, I valued their emphasis on having a personal relationship with Christ. This was something we were not really taught, and with my loneliness, the thought of Jesus being my Lord and Savior and Friend appealed to me.

They would all meet once a week and go out and evangelize or tell others about Jesus Christ. I did participate once and tried to share the "Four Spiritual Laws" tract with strangers or by knocking on doors.

I was introduced to these laws, and it was good. I had a hard time stopping strangers and speaking to them, but that is exactly how I was reached. So, I went with another person, and they paired us two by two. We would return and discuss how our visits went with the strangers we met. Mine never went that well because I did not have confidence. But I was kindly told by the other students not to worry that "I am a lamb and one day would be a sheep." I got it. I did commit to myself to evangelize one person, and I prayed that one day I would reach another.

One of the main struggles I faced, and indeed I had always faced, was how to meet someone. In high school, I was not allowed out. At Bowling Green, it was such a party school that the only place to meet anyone would have been in bars like all my dorm roommates did. I would never do this.

At Ohio State, the campus was so vast, everyone so busy, and the classes so large and impersonal that it seemed impossible to meet anyone. I was a waitress for the football players, but they were too big and athletic for me. I was just an unassuming petite woman who kept her head down and did her job. How could one of these stars of the campus possibly notice me? And so I prayed, trusting God would help me someday.

Some of the guys in Campus Crusade for Christ wanted to go out with me, and indeed I did date one or two of them a couple of times. But the problem was my Catholic faith. They did not believe in the things I held dear. When I told them I believed in the Blessed Mother, they told me that was not right. That ended those possibilities, as I would never marry someone who did not believe as I did.

It was too important to me.

A year and a half passed quickly at Ohio State. I bought a box turtle I called Iggy, and he became my friend during the long months away from home. I stayed for summer classes and visited my counselor nearly every month to make sure I was on track. It was a marvelous time, and a lonely time, a time of wonder about where I was going, and a time I grew closer to God.

## Scholarship

While attending Ohio State, I earned scholarships to spend my summer in Urbino, Italy. Unfortunately, Urbino was in the North of Italy, far from the home of my Nonno and Nonna. But I knew at the first chance I got I would travel south to be reunited with my beloved grandparents.

Going to Italy by myself was one of the most amazing trips of my life. For the first time ever, I felt like I was truly a grown woman, free to live her life however she pleased. In addition, the host family in Urbino was exceptional. They spoke to me in Italian, and we ate dinner together.

The food was portioned, filled the plate in its entirety, and was delicious. I would often buy a piece of pizza and grapefruit juice for lunch. The home of Raphael, the artist, was now a museum up on a big hill. I savored the evenings, the coffee bars, the classes, and the atmosphere. It all seemed surreal.

During my summer session, there was no time to travel south. Finally, the end came, and I was free to travel. I took the train to Scauri, Latina, where my Nonna and Nonno would be. They knew I would be visiting near the end of summer, but I decided to surprise them. Once I got off the train, I took a taxi to their home. My heart was racing with the thought of seeing my real mom, my Nonna Rosa. It had been many years since she left me to return to Italy. They were hard years in my life and years I had to endure with the broken heart of losing her, my best friend.

The taxi dropped me off, and I walked with my small bag in hand from the road down the short dirt drive to the side door of the large home situated on the Via Appia. I knocked on the door and called out, "Is anyone home?"

I heard some clanging in the kitchen, then the warm, familiar voice said, *"Espet, un momento."*

I smiled and wiped the tears forming in my eyes. In the next moment, Nonna opened the wide door, and her eyes grew wider than I had ever seen. "Marisa!" she shouted, and she immediately hugged me and began crying profusely. "I missed you, Marisa."

"I missed you too, Nonna," I said as we embraced tighter.

She grabbed my arms and held me at arm's length. "Look at you. You are a beautiful young woman."

I blushed and started nodding, my tears washing the corners of my wide smile.

"Come in! Come in!"

I went in and could already smell the old familiar smells of Nonna's cooking. A pot of sauce was on the stove, and the oven was warm with bread. She grabbed a large pot and filled it with water. "I will make some pasta. You go into the farm and find Nonno Ernesto. He is working on the grapevines."

I could not wait to see him, so I put my bag down and went outside. Then I walked for a while down the dirt drive to a fenced-in area. I entered and walked into a vast garden of countless rows of grapevines meticulously pruned, all burgeoning with clusters of nearly ripened red grapes. A cool breeze caressed my forehead from just over the small mountain, which fell dramatically into the nearby Mediterranean Sea.

I took in the air and smells, and understood the magic of this land, with all its sunshine and hope. It was this land, his land, that my Nonno Ernesto, the master farmer, had come home to ten years earlier. To be among his olive trees, his grape vineyards, and his vast farm he maintained with his bare hands, day in and day out, with all his strength and vigor. The immensity of who he was as a person to do all this struck me, and I was in awe of him all over again.

I kept walking along the path until, finally, I saw him. He was standing with his legs straight and slightly apart, like angled legs to a strong workbench. His back was perfectly bent forward, like a broad tabletop. His arms jutted ahead with a pruning tool in his hands, methodically trimming and moving right, trimming and moving again, like a machine.

"Nonno!" I cried.

He paused, glanced behind, and stood up straight, then turned to me, smiling. *"Marisella, vienne qua."*

I ran to him and fell into his broad, strong arms. His enormous hands held me tight. "Mari, it is good to see you."

"I love you, Nonno," I said, not feeling the tears I had before with Nonna. Somehow, I knew that with Nonno Ernesto, I had to show my strength, the strength he had exhibited for me my whole life.

*"Heh*, Mari. I love you too."

He pulled out a large bandana from a basket. "Here, Mari. Put this on your head to keep you cool. Then you can help me for a while."

I felt so honored. Suddenly I was catapulted back to Cleveland, to our family farm, to when I was just a little girl, helping him in our garden.

After an hour, we finished up and went into the house to round off our joyful reunion with a wonderful dinner.

My evening alone with my Nonno and Nonna was filled with deep satisfaction. I was here with the people who raised me and formed me with their lives. There was no one to take their attention away. It was just us.

After two days, I had an important trip to attend to. It was only a short trip away, but it was something I had wanted to do my whole life.

# The Investigator

I had heard rumors from one of my aunts that there was something going on with the land in Italy, something we were not supposed to know about. Something that Uncle Joe and his family were keeping very tight-lipped about. I remembered back to Uncle Italo's death, to the uneasy feelings I had. I remembered the phone call Uncle Italo had made to my dad the night before he died, telling him he had something important to tell him. I remembered too, about the troubled feelings I had when Uncle Joe and his wife got my dad and all his brothers and sisters to sell over their right to the land to him for a measly $2,000 each.

I knew something was wrong then, and now that I was here in Italy, I was going to investigate things for myself.

The trip to Coreno, Ausonio, took one train ride and two buses to reach the downtown main city hall. There was a home in the city and the original farmhouse in the country. It was in the country land where the rumors I needed to check out were. But I also wanted to see the home in the city, as I was already there. The name I was searching for was the one who owned my dad's property. I found that both properties were in my uncle's wife's maiden name. Emmanuela Costanzo. I immediately knew this must be for reasons of secrecy.

I asked where the city home was, and someone showed me. Some of the townspeople were taking their aprons off, closing their shops, and following me to see where I was headed. It was as if an alarm had sounded in the town, setting people in motion to keep an eye out. As I walked up the narrow street of Coreno, up a hill toward the home in the city, I was stopped. Out of nowhere, a man appeared. He said, "My name is Mariano. I am your uncle's brother-in-law. What are you looking for?"

"I want to see the house where my father was born."

"OK, I have the keys. Come with me."

We walked a ways further and reached the house. He reluctantly opened the place for me, and I entered the ghost-like, eerie surroundings. The rooms were bare walls and slab floors. The first I saw was the fireplace, abandoned and cold. I could picture my grandma Maria pregnant and with an apron on stirring the broth or stew on the cauldron-pot suspended in mid-air from the hook that I saw sticking out from the chimney near the hearth.

My insides felt as though they were turning inside out. Immediately, I saw what the rest of my family could never experience. I was seeing into the past. Seeing my ancestors and my ancestry, seeing where Papa was raised. I pictured him as shy and quiet and a good young boy needing his mom and her meeting those basic needs.

She was practical, poor, and kind.

After looking around, I asked, "I am going to go see the house in the country now. Is it far?"

"There is nothing there anymore. Just some ruins," he replied, adding, "It is a waste of time."

"That's OK," I said. "I want to see where the family was born."

"Well, I will have to call your uncle. He does not want anyone visiting there."

"OK, let's go call him now."

Mariano seemed bothered, but he led me away, and we walked several blocks to his house. His wife was there, and she greeted me as Mariano picked up the phone and called my Uncle Joe.

"Hey, Joe, yes, good. Joe, your niece is here, Marisella. Yes, she is here at my house. She wants me to take her to the house in the country. Hold on."

He turned and handed me the phone.

"Hello?" I said.

"Hey, Marisella. You are in Coreno. How come?"

"I am studying here this summer, Uncle Joe. So I decided to take a bus here to see Papa's house."

"OK, OK. That sounds good. Put Mariano back on the phone."

I handed the phone to Mariano. His eyes looked worried, and I wondered why.

He nodded and said, "OK, Joe. Bye."

He turned to me and smiled. "OK, I will take you."

We got in his car and drove up a winding road up the side of one of the many small mountains Coreno was situated near. Finally, we turned onto a level plain and soon stopped. In a large field to my right, I saw a few rolling acres of beautiful land, with the ruins of an old farmstead in the middle. Behind the field was a looming mountain. I got out and walked toward the ruins. As I neared them, I imagined Papa's family, with ten children, living in poverty, tending sheep and pigs, growing whatever foods they could. It felt like a place of honor until I saw the mountain behind. There were massive holes in the side of the mountain, as if explosives had been set, and mining had been going on. All at once, I comprehended that the rumors were true.

My Uncle Joe and his wife had realized there was a mountain of marble on the property. That was why they bought it from their brothers and sisters. That was why they moved to California. That was why they were so secretive about their life out there, as well as what was happening on the land in Italy. They had a mountain of marble worth millions and millions of dollars, and they took it all for themselves. They stole it from the rest of the family.

The place of honor had suddenly become a place of dishonor.

And I wondered again what was so important that Uncle Italo said he had to talk to my dad on the night before he was killed. Was it that he too, had found out there was marble? Uncle Italo would have shared it with the entire family. He would have set up a family trust, and let all of us cousins and our future families profit from the mountain that stood behind the poor farmhouse of my poor father's family.

I cried inside when I thought of the wrong done to us all. I turned to Mariano and asked, "What is going on back there?"

"Oh, nothing. They were moving dirt, that is all."

I knew in that instant he was in on it.

They were all in on it.

The townspeople, too, probably knew what was going on.

I had Mariano take me back to town, and after a short visit to the town church, where I cried out to God for what had been done, I walked back to the bus stop, and took the bus back to the train station and returned to the home of my grandparents in Scauri, Latina.

~ ~ ~ ~

For the next two weeks, I labored next to both of them by day and relished the quiet of the evening meal and talks by the fireplace at night.

When it was time to go back to Urbino for a final few days before heading back to America, I said goodbye. It was a tearful goodbye, for I did not know when I would see them again, but it was different now. They were here and happy in their lives. I, too, had grown and was strong, loving them as much as ever and yet not needing them as I once did. Nevertheless, their roots stood strong within me, and this goodbye felt like a belonging.

# The Rolling Stones

When I arrived back in Urbino, the final stopover before I would return to America, a once-in-a-lifetime event came along. The Rolling Stones were playing outside in Turin, Italy. I bought my ticket and went with a busload of other students, mainly those studying abroad with me. I felt this rock 'n' roll experience was a reward I had somehow earned by my faithfulness to my values. I was happy.

I was excited because I was never allowed to go to a concert at home. My parents knew drugs were at rock concerts, and even though I grew up in the sixties, I wasn't part of that slice of America.

At the time, whatever my parents told me, I adhered to their rules pretty much because I trusted them.

So, as we got closer to the place where the Rolling Stones would play, I was so excited.

We got off the bus and had to walk a long distance before getting there with the hot sun beaming on us. Many had already arrived and sat on the cement concrete Greek amphitheater. We sat and waited.

Quite a few were passing out, and ambulances were taking them away for dehydration. We did get sprinkled with these hoses set up for us to refresh and cool ourselves. The timing was perfect, and we sang the song "Angie" together in a group surrounded by all nationalities, races, and creeds. I felt the unity of human kindness and the unity of human nature and how we all got along with the famous international song "Angie."

On the way home, the bus driver had a tv monitor screen of the soccer game. The world soccer tournament was on, and Italy had won the cup. We saw people waving shirts in the streets, Italians honking their car horns, and others dancing in fountains. I saw the spirit of Italy with my own eyes. I saw a moment of triumph, joy, and happiness expressed in a nation that was proud of winning. The Italians are fanatics when it comes to sports, especially soccer.

And so my trip to Italy, the greatest adventure of my life, ended. I packed my bag and took the train to the airport. But a sadness hung over me because I was going back home.

My graduation date would be in a mere five months. I was tired, burned out, and mentally exhausted from going every quarter for five years consecutively without taking summer breaks. Looming in the distance was a decision about my career choice, which meant getting a job. I felt lost, confused, and uncertain about where my major would take me— a BA in Italian from the College of Arts and Sciences. I worked hard for this degree, and I wasn't going to give up until I finished what I began five years ago. I was trained to begin what I finished.

But what would I do after? Get a job as an interpreter? It did not seem like any standard career, and it might require me to go to New York. How could I possibly do that by myself? My mind raced with many questions, and there were so few answers, yet I trusted that somehow God would help me. I just couldn't see how, and deep down, it scared me.

## Blow Up

After I returned from Italy, it was late summer, and my family home felt like chaos. My brothers were wild, it was hot, and Papa seemed extra anxious. He was nervous that I had been gone and that I was no longer his little girl. Deep down, he knew our relationship would be changing dramatically, and somehow, this angered him.

The long trip through the airports and planes had left me very constipated. I had not gone to the bathroom in two days. Finally, when it was time, my brother was in the upstairs bathroom, so I went and used my parents' bathroom off of their bedroom. The parental bathroom was off-limits. No one ever used it except for my parents.

When I flushed the toilet, anxious to get out of there, it was somewhat plugged, so I flushed again. My heart sank within moments as the water rose and began overflowing.

I ran out of their room and downstairs, screaming and yelling as I reached the kitchen. The water flowed into the kitchen from my parents' restroom.

Papa was on the couch, his legs curled under him, reading the newspaper. When he heard the commotion, he exploded—jumping up instantly, screaming, hollering, and swearing. He ran upstairs to view the mess, and he exploded even more. Instantly, he vaulted into a fit of rage that sent us all running. I hid in the closet of my younger brother's room between two old dusty mattresses in the closet. Barely able to breathe, I listened, tears in my eyes, fear racing through my heart, hoping against hope he would not find me and kill me. It took over half an hour, but finally, the yelling stopped, and there was a long period of dead silence. My pounding heart began to slow. Was it safe to leave the closet? Was it safe to come out of my hiding place?

Was I going to live through this awful day?

The violence of my dad's reaction to the over-flooded toilet left me angry and hopeless.

When I came downstairs, my brothers were hiding in the living room. Papa was sitting on the couch with a belt strapped over his shoulder. Suddenly, Mom walked in from work, and the tense scene changed as my brothers came out of hiding in an instant.

"What's going on?" Mom asked.

And suddenly, Papa exploded again. I ran through the dining room, with Papa chasing me, Mom screaming for him to stop, and my brothers chasing after us all.

Finally, Mom stopped him by standing in his way. She ordered us all to get into the car.

Moments later, Mom came out to the car, and we drove in complete silence to a nearby park.

I was badly shaken and unable to stop crying. The tensions in my life were so high that coming home to such a traumatic event shook me to the core.

That night, Uncle Tony came over and unblocked the toilet. An uneasy peace descended on the home. The next day, I drove back to Ohio State to let things cool off.

# Ohio State

Back on campus, it was the quiet days of August. I had little to do, as classes would not begin for another four weeks. So, I decided to find a part-time job. I would go home on weekends until school started. I felt best that it would give my dad the space that he seemed to need.

There were people in love all around me, and I wondered again how I would ever meet someone. It seemed that there was no real opportunity. All my life I had been largely alone. Yes, I was part of a large Italian family, and who could ever be alone in one, but I was so very different from my cousins, or my brothers, who were part of American life and American ways. I was raised by old-world Europeans, and their imprint upon me was pronounced. Was I so different from most of those around me that I would never meet a person who would find me interesting or attractive? I wondered about this often, and dreamed, and hoped, and yet part of me knew I might have to settle for a life alone.

~ ~ ~ ~

A few weeks after returning to Ohio State, I ran into a Danish guy I had seen in my classes the previous year. He was handsome with straight blond hair neatly parted. He asked me out on a date and I agreed. I was not sure why I did, as I really did not have feelings for him. But I decided that perhaps this was part of the process, to go on dates like this, and give time for the rest to develop. He took me to a theater, and we watched a movie. Afterward, we went to get pizza, then he took me home. I went inside before he could kiss me, and I spent the night wondering if I should have let him kiss me. I did not expect a call back. But he did call.

The following week, we went on our second date. Again, he took me to a movie. After that, he took me to a nice Greek restaurant. I was beginning to enjoy myself as we talked over dinner and wondered if perhaps this man who was Danish might be someone I could grow close to. Before dinner ended, the subject of his living arrangements came up. He told me he lived off campus with two friends, two female friends. I could not comprehend this, so when he dropped me off, I exited quickly, and politely said good night.

~ ~ ~ ~

When he called a few days later, I told him I would not be able to go on any more dates with him. He asked why, but I just said it was not a good time for me to be dating. He didn't understand, but as I hung up the phone, I felt relieved I had broken it off. It was not the right person or the right time.

The following day was Friday. I went to my part-time job and on my way home to my apartment, I could see the stirrings. Campus life and all the surrounding houses and dorms were coming alive. Lovers, groups of girls, and groups of guys were coming out of their houses, hanging out on the porches and lawns, all getting ready for the party weekend. Though surrounded by thousands of people, I felt so alone. I just didn't fit in. I could not adapt to this lifestyle. As soon as I reached my apartment, I sat on the couch looking out the window, feeling so sad for myself. I knew if I stayed, it would be nothing by a depressing weekend, so I decided to go home.

Within the hour, I was turning onto the freeway, heading home to Cleveland for the weekend. A deep sadness came over me, because I did not fit in behind me, and going home was going back to my old life—as the slave and babysitter for my brothers. I did not fit in there either.

For the first half hour I was torn, considering turning around at nearly every exit, but something told me to keep going.

When I arrived, the news came. Uncle Mario, Aunt Theresa, Aunt Rose, and Uncle Ernie were all en route. The preparations and the commotion began. It was a marvelous weekend, as, during the afternoon meal, I heard a new family had moved in next door.

On Monday morning, as I walked out to my car to return to Ohio State, a tall, thin, young man in khaki shorts, a golf shirt, and wearing only socks was walking to his car. We were both walking down our drives at the same time, and we glanced at each other. I reached my car and noticed he was now walking toward me, as his car was nearby in the street. He smiled and asked, "Hi. Do you know how to get to Lakewood Country Club?"

I was very startled, as I had never seen him before. I realized that he must be part of the family that had just moved in. He had red curly hair and looked very athletic.

I was not good with directions, because I had never been allowed to go anywhere, but I did not want to appear dumb. So, I put my finger on my chin, and turned around slightly, looking down the street as if looking might show I really was thinking about how to help him. The truth was, I had no clue where Lakewood Country Club was. I turned back to him and replied, "No, I'm sorry."

He then asked, "Do you live here?"

I frowned. "No, I live in Columbus."

He kept looking at me, so I asked, "Do you live here?"

He shook his head. "No, I live in Cleveland."

"OK, well… bye," I said politely and got in my car, wondering about this man.

~ ~ ~ ~

The following weekend, when I returned home, I saw my other neighbor Jan Henry out on the sidewalk. "Oh, hi, Marisa. Hey, did you see the new family that moved in?" Jan lived on the other side of the new neighbor's house.

"No, I haven't yet."

"Well, they have a nice-looking son. He doesn't live here, though."

"Oh, *hmmm*…. I think I met him."

"Maybe you should introduce yourself."

"Jan, I don't know. I am tired of men. They all disappoint me. The last one I dated lived with two girls."

"What?"

"It's a long story, Jan. I just don't think I'm cut out for dating."

"Oh, I understand."

But despite my reservations and determinations, I wondered about the family and about the young man I had met. In the few times I was outside of the house, I looked for his car, or for any sign of him. But there was none.

Monday morning came, and it was time to return to Ohio State. Papa got me up early and said it was time to change the oil in the car. "Can't it wait, Papa? I have to get back to school."

Papa raised his hand in the air. "No, Mari, if we don't changa the oil, the car will break!"

I nodded. "Si, Papa." I knew he was right. I was just sad about a lot of things and torn between two worlds, neither of which I belonged in. We went outside and opened the garage. We brought the stool, the bucket, the oil cans, and the tools. I was handed an apron reserved for garage work and a big pair of yellow gloves.

I donned the apron and gloves as Papa sat on the stool and jacked up the car. I was to watch and hand him the needed tools. All of a sudden, the man next door pulled up in the street. My heart leaped for a moment. He was shouting something at me. He called out from his rolled-down window, "Hi, there."

I turned to wave and heard Papa say, "Mari, don't talka to him."

I stood still, embarrassed at what I was wearing, trying a half turn to hide my big shop apron, and at the same time hide my big yellow rubber gloves behind my back. I could not wave, so I half-smiled.

"What ya doing?" he asked.

"Mari, don't talka to him."

I pulled my hand out of the yellow rubber glove and waved. The man paused, smiled, and waved back, then drove off, racing down the street. Had I just blown any chance of really meeting him? Of course I had. I looked like a goof, changing the oil in my driveway wearing shorts, an apron, and big yellow gloves, and not willing to say even one word.

~ ~ ~ ~

I returned to Ohio State, very sad. This man would go the way of all the others who would never understand who I was, or why I was the way I was. It bothered me because I knew I was a good person who would love the right person with my whole heart. If only I could find him, or if only he would find me.

The week dragged on. I was growing very tired of my life at Ohio State. My final semester was coming, but what would that bring with it? Where would I go? Where would I work? I had no idea or prospect of any career. I really did not know where to start.

The following week, I returned home on Thursday evening, as I had no work on Friday. To my surprise, the man who was the son of my new neighbor was out washing his truck. I parked in my drive and gave him a subtle wave. He waved back and started to walk over. My heart sank into my stomach. What would I say to him? I hoped I could say the right words.

"Hi," he said.

"Hello," I replied pleasantly.

"My name is Dan."

"Hi, my name is Marisa." I was suddenly stuck. Oh, why did I not know what to say? I smiled, as we were both quiet for a moment, and I wondered what he was thinking.

He said, "It's funny, isn't it?"

"What?"

"That our parents live right next door to each other."

I had no reply and only smiled.

He then asked, "Hey, do you like to play tennis?"

"Not really." My reply sounded standoffish, and yet I'd never played tennis in my life. I would look dumb trying to.

I could see his thoughts scramble. "Well, do you ever work out?"

I had gone to the gym a few times in college, and my parents had just gotten a family pass to Scandinavian Health Spa. I had only gone there once or twice. I replied, "Yes, sometimes."

"Really, where?" he asked.

"*Umm*, my parents just bought a pass at Scandinavian Health Spa."

"No kidding," he said. "I just got a pass there, too."

Again, there was quiet for a moment when he asked, "Would you like to go there with me tomorrow?"

I was unsure of what to say. I wanted to, but I was not an athlete, and I was afraid I would look dumb. How do you go to work out with someone? I did not know. I smiled and replied, "I'll think about it."

I turned and slowly began to walk away, unsure of what else to say. I had blown it again. I was sure.

When I was near the door, I heard him call out, "Hey... how am I supposed to know what you're thinking?"

I smiled without turning, then turned and raised my chin, saying, "Pick me up at 1:00 p.m."

I could not believe it. I had just made a date with the boy next door.

All night long, I lay in my bed imagining my wedding and who my maids of honor would be. Somehow, I was sure I had just met Mr. Wonderful. But there was only one more obstacle, and it was perhaps the biggest.

My dad.

***

The following day, I carefully picked out my outfit for Scandinavia Health Spa. I put on a pair of sweats, white socks, and a shirt from Huntington Bank. It said "Electronically Yours" on the front and "Check it Out" on the back. I packed a small towel and change of clothes and waited at the top of the steps.

As one o'clock neared, I began to get nervous. My brothers were outside playing, and Papa was downstairs in the living room reading the paper. Suddenly, there was a knock at the door.

I went to the top of the stairs, knelt, and peered down. There was the neighbor, standing tall in the doorway. A long minute later, Papa walked from the living room, down the hall, and slowly to the door. I braced myself.

There was silence for an awkward moment, until Papa said in a thick Italian accent, "Whadda you want?"

The neighbor said, "I'm here for Marisa."

I could not see Papa's face, but I did not have to. I could tell by the way he stood, with one hand perched on the back of his hip and the other on the back of the door, ready to close it, that he was glaring.

The neighbor was staring down at him, not flinching. I was witnessing a modern-day David and Goliath in a standoff to see who would make the first move.

Finally, Papa raised his hand in the air and shouted, "Mareeeee!"

I did not need to be called twice.

I ran down the steps and said to the neighbor, "Oh, hi."

I kissed Papa, then went out the door.

As I walked away, I glanced back and saw Papa standing in the doorway, watching me leave. It was probably the first time ever he saw me leaving on a date, and I could feel the sadness reaching out the door. His little girl was leaving.

We drove to the gym, went in, and met up on the track. After a few minutes of talking, I launched onto the track first, wanting him to see my T-shirt from the bank that said, "Check it out."

We ran for a little while, did a few weight machines together, then hit the respective locker rooms to shower and met in the lobby. We then walked outside and sat on the grass outside.

We were quiet, as we did not know each other at all, really. I figured I better get right to the heart of things. I was not going to waste time with this young man if he did not respect my values. I said to him, "I wanted you to know that I read the Bible a lot. My faith is very important to me."

"Really," he replied. "I have just started doing that, too."

"You have?"

"Yes, I started just recently."

"Well, that's nice," I said, lowering my glance. I liked what I heard, but I needed to tell him more. "I am Catholic too, and that is very important to me."

"Oh, me too," he replied.

"You are?"

"Yes, I sure am," he replied.

I felt really happy. This young man seemed smart, and he was certainly good-looking. And he had a light in his eyes that told me he was sincere about the Bible and about his faith.

"Well, I have to go home now," I said.

"Sure, let's go."

When we got in his car to go home, he looked over at me and asked if we could go out again. "Yes," I said, trying not to show my elation too much. He surprised me by exclaiming a line from a hit song, "I feel good!"

I didn't know how to respond, but I only knew that I was really excited. Within the week, we had gone on two more dates. He then came down to Ohio State to see me. I took him to all my favorite places and favorite spots to eat. It was obvious to us both that we were falling in love.

We kissed and caressed in my little apartment, but I would not allow anything more. I was still a virgin and vowed to remain one until I was married. Daniel was OK with that.

Our first date had been on September 6. In that month, we had seen each other almost ten times. I was busy with my classes and needed to go see my counselor about how graduation worked. On October 3, twenty-seven days after we met, Daniel and I went to dinner at a restaurant called *Street Scene*. Coming home, it started to pour down. We laughed and ran through the rain, getting very wet, barely avoiding getting completely soaked.

We went into my apartment, laughing and drying our hair and clothing with towels. We made some hot chocolate and sat on the couch, planning on watching a movie. Before we could turn on the TV, Daniel stood up, and turned, then got down on one knee. He took my hand in his and asked, "Will you marry me?"

I was taken aback. It was so soon, and so sudden, and I had only known him for twenty-seven days. Yet here I was, needing to answer him. So, with all that in mind, I gave him the only answer that I could.

I exclaimed, "Yes!"

Our life together had begun, and we began making plans for our future. I was no longer alone, but now I had a companion to journey through life with me. Now we had to tell my parents.

## Ann Wriggles

My life was suddenly moving in a wonderful direction I could never have imagined. I was about to graduate. I had met the love of my life. I would be getting married soon. Everything else would take care of itself. I went to see Ann Wriggles, my counselor. She told me I had to petition for graduation.

"I don't understand. I thought once I finished the classes, I could graduate."

"No, you have to make a formal petition."

It felt so difficult, but I got the form and had it signed by my professors in the Italian Department. I returned it to Ann Wriggles' office.

For the next several weeks, Daniel and I were spending as much time as we could together. We attended Bible Studies together and went to Mass during the week in Cleveland and Ohio State. We were in the midst of a whirlwind romance, with Daniel coming down to visit on weekends, and returning home to attend his Senior Year classes at Cleveland State during the week.

It was on a Tuesday morning when I got a call from Ann Wriggles asking me to come to her office.

When I arrived, she seemed normal and busy, but something was different. She didn't look up at me, but only said, "Hi, Marisa. Please sit down."

"Okay," I said, as I sat down, wondering why the mood in the room felt so suddenly chilled.

Ann looked up, her eyes bearing heaviness I had never seen. "I have to talk to you about your petition."

"Is everything all right?"

"No, everything is not all right. There's a problem with your petition to graduate."

"What do you mean?"

"The Arts and Sciences College said they cannot approve you. They said it is because you took too many classes in your major."

"What! What does that mean?"

"It means you have a whole additional year of classes to take before you can graduate. Two more semesters."

I sat there in complete shock. I had come to her office almost every month for two years. I had been with my Italian professor's offices constantly. I had already told everyone at home that I was graduating, including all my aunts, uncles, cousins, and brothers. Everyone was proud of me. Worst of all, I had told Daniel. I was supposed to come home, and we were going to marry and begin our life.

I started to cry.

Ann leaned forward. "Marisa, I am sorry. It is between the college and your department. There is nothing I can do."

"But it's not fair," I said, between sobs.

"I'm sorry," she said, as she looked away, signaling there was nothing more to be said.

After getting up from my chair, I gathered my books and walked out of her office. I exited the building and wandered the campus for hours, lost, thinking. I did not have the strength to go on. This was going to kill me. It was going to end everything.

Daniel wanted to get married. How could I tell him I had a whole year left? Who knew how long it would last?

My parents were going to kill me, and this was going to be a huge embarrassment to my family, as my aunts, uncles, and cousins would not understand. They had been so proud of me.

I made it home before dark, went to my room, and cried myself to sleep.

# I Can't

I spent the next day in my apartment, alone, crying and praying, trying to figure out what I should do.

I was afraid to call Daniel.

I knew that he loved me, but we had only met two months ago. Now, I was delaying our plans for at least a year, and knowing me, probably more. Was he going to be OK with this?

Deep down, I doubted it.

Another of life's great disappointments had found me.

Later that day, I decided to call him.

"Hello?" he said.

"Dan, hi."

"Hi, Marisa. How are you?"

"I am not doing too good."

"What's wrong?" he asked tenderly.

"I just got back from my counselor's office. They said I cannot graduate. They said I have to stay here for another whole year."

"What! Why?"

"They said I took too many classes in my major."

I started to cry.

"I'm sorry," he said. "Are you going to be OK?"

"No, I am not. I cannot do this anymore. I don't know how I am going to find the strength."

"I'm sorry."

"We are supposed to get married. I feel so lost," I said.

There was quiet on the phone. He should have said something.

After a few moments of uncomfortable silence, he said, "I have to go now. But I will call you back later today."

I could tell by the tone in his voice that something had changed. This was not in his plans. Maybe I was suddenly no longer in his plans.

I hung up, stared at the phone for a few minutes in disbelief, then went to my room and cried until I fell asleep.

***

When I woke up it was evening. I glanced over at my answering machine. There were no messages. He had not called. I waited until almost 7:30 p.m., then decided to go for a walk.

I went to Mirror Lake, to the place where Daniel and I used to visit and talk about our plans for the future. I sat by the park lights, staring at the still water. My life had just careened into a brick wall. Daniel was not coming back. I would never find anyone again. I thought about my options. Maybe I would just become a teachers assistant here in the Italian Department. I would get a little apartment off campus and lead a quiet life.

I knew one thing for sure. I could never go home again.

I returned to my tiny apartment after 9:00 p.m. I was silent and sad, and the answering machine displayed the same. I went to bed and lay awake until somehow, I drifted off.

# The Door

I don't know how long I was asleep, but it was the middle of the night when there was a knock at my door. I anxiously got up, put on my robe, and walked to the door. "Who is it?" I called out.

"It's Daniel."

I glanced at the clock. It was 4:00 a.m. I opened the door. I was ready to hear whatever news he had decided to bring to me in the middle of the night, all the way to Columbus from Cleveland.

He stepped in and said, "I love you."

I hugged him tighter than I had ever hugged anyone in my life.

"What are you doing here in the middle of the night?" I asked.

"I've come to take you home."

I started to cry.

Yes. He was right. It was time to come home and begin my life. It mattered not that they said I had another year to finish.

"But what about graduating?" I asked.

"I will bring you back someday to finish your degree. Let's go home and start our life."

I hugged him again, and we kissed for the longest time. Finally, we curled up on the bed together, and in the morning, we packed all my belongings and left for Cleveland.

I had a great deal of explaining to do, but it did not matter. My life with the one I loved was about to begin, and God was with us, and that was all we needed.

# The Wedding

The wedding was scheduled for August, but in January, while attending a weekday Mass, Daniel and I talked and asked each other why we were waiting. We loved each other and were anxious to begin life together. So we asked the priest and moved the wedding up to the end of March.

This caused immediate rumors among the entire Italian community, but I did not care. All that mattered was that my future husband and I would be married very soon.

My mom sat us down and asked, "Is there a reason you are moving up the wedding?"

"No," we said, not even understanding the concerns. People thought we "had to get married" because I was pregnant. But Daniel and I had vowed to wait until marriage, so we weren't worried about what others thought. My wider family was in shock, too. I have about sixty cousins, as my dad came from a family of ten siblings. Many cousins said, "You were in college for five years, quiet, and now you're resurrected from the dead and getting married. To who?"

But the planning began in earnest. It was mid-January, and at the end of March, I was getting married.

## My Wedding Day

The morning of my wedding was mass confusion. Uncle Mario, Aunt Theresa, Aunt Rose, and Uncle Ernie were all staying with us. From the moment I woke up, there was chaos and anxiety as everyone was trying to get ready.

My aunt from Connecticut was a hair stylist, and was supposed to arrive at 9:30 a.m. to do my hair. Nine-thirty came and went, and we started trying to call her. Apparently, she had gone out drinking with my wild cousins the night before and was nowhere to be found. Finally, by 11:00, Mom said, "I will fix your hair. Go get showered and dressed, Mari."

Frustrated, I went upstairs. It seemed all eyes were on every move I made, which made me very embarrassed. I gathered up my wedding dress, white stockings, and underclothes, and went into the bathroom, locking and bolting the door because there were so many people in the house.

As I stepped into the shower, the water was ice cold. Everyone else had used up all the hot water. I made the best of it and took a quick shower, put on my clothing and wedding dress, and came out of the bathroom fully dressed, as I had been trained to do my entire life.

"Mom," I called down.

"What is it, Mari?" came the reply.

"I'm ready to do my hair!"

I waited and waited in my room. Finally, Mom and Aunt Theresa came in. They both smiled widely. Aunt Theresa hugged me tightly. "Oh, my beautiful Padina, you look so special."

"Thank you, Aunt Theresa."

Mom had a small tear in her eye. She hugged me and said, "Mari, you are going to be a beautiful wife."

"Thanks, Mom."

Mom and I never really talked too much, so this was a special moment for me. They had me sit down and fixed my hair. Last, I donned the hat that I had chosen and put on the white elbow-length gloves.

Aunt Theresa led me downstairs, and all grew quiet. My brothers, Papa, and my aunts and uncles all looked at me with awe. I felt like crying, and I also felt a bit embarrassed that I was the center of attention. The knock on the door broke the moment. It was the photographer.

Throughout the photo sessions, my brothers were strangely quiet. It was as if there was a sadness about the day. They had never seen me in such a light and they also knew I was leaving the home for good.

Papa was stoic, not speaking, but just standing like a statue for all the pictures. He was happy, I knew, but he just did not know how to say anything.

We got to the church, Old St. Patrick's in Cleveland. Hundreds of people from both sides of the family were there, anxiously waiting to see this young couple, both only twenty-three years old, who had just recently met.

Papa walked me down the aisle.

It took a very long time. I kept whispering out of the side of my mouth, hoping no one saw me, "Papa, we have to go faster." But it was as if he were in some trance, resolutely marching slow short step, by slow short step. I believe it was the first time he was ever on stage, and it must have frozen him to a degree. Halfway down the aisle, he was beginning to list to one side, keeping his slow, short pace forward. I could see everyone's faces slightly tilting. I helped him right himself, and we kept going, but ever so slowly. When we reached the front, he passed my hand to Daniel. Daniel and I turned and walked toward the altar.

I heard Mom yell under her breath, "Cresenz! Sit down!" I glanced back to see Papa standing in the same spot. He had forgotten he was supposed to return to his seat. Mom stepped into the aisle and pulled him over.

The wedding was the magical moment of my life I had always dreamed of. Near the end of the service, Daniel and I went to kneel in front of an altar dedicated to Mary, as Rocco Scotti sang *Ave Maria*. The entire church was touched.

The reception was a gala event with over 400 people attending. It was a chance for the Italians and the Irish to get to know each other. The highlight of the night was when Daniel's cousins, who were world champion Irish Dancers, performed to a mesmerized crowd, who erupted in wild applause when it was over.

And so that night, as we left for our honeymoon, Daniel and I began our life together.

~ ~ ~ ~

The last chapter of this book was reserved for my wedding. My wedding day was the beginning and the end. It was the beginning because I chose to marry the boy next door and vow to him before God and family and friends the popular vows. The popular vows are "I take you, Daniel, for better or for worse, richer or for poorer, in sickness or in health, until death do us part."

The sickness part of this vow is difficult for me to vow to. My mom had to live with an emotionally ill spouse for her whole life, which was difficult for her. I understood what that vow could mean.

My wedding day was like Rapunzel letting down her long hair and climbing down from the castle. I, in a sense, was leaving the old Italian tutelage from my immediate family and beginning my own family.

My wedding day was the end, too, in many ways. It was the end of all these stories. It was the end of my life with my brothers and parents. It was the end of all the days, struggles, and a lifetime of being misunderstood. The joys and sorrows of immigrant life were now over. When I took my fiancé's hand and said those vows, I was getting out of one boat and entering another. A new life was beginning without them and mysteries of what lay ahead were held by fate on the distant horizon.

This day was the end of all things that came before. And in a way, though difficult, saying goodbye to them saddens me, because it was such a part of me. The days are not lost, though. They are here in the pages of this book.

The End?
No, it is only the beginning.

# Epilogue and Reflections

I am fifty-eight as I write the last pages of this book. I had begun four years ago writing capsulized stories of my life, mainly so my children and grandchildren could know my history.

My husband, who is a writer, recognized that they belonged together in a novel. He said my story was too meaningful not to be presented for what it is: a Cinderella Story.

Dan and I just celebrated our 35th wedding anniversary. We were blessed with four children together, all born within three and a half years. Colleen, Bridget, Patrick, and Christopher are all a year apart. Colleen is married with two beautiful daughters of her own, our little Aubrey and our little Avery.

We lost Papa twenty years ago. His life of being misunderstood will continue in the place where he WILL be understood and loved. My mom is still in the same house, and I walk around the block with her every day. My brother Cris is married with kids but does take time to speak with me. Danny is married with kids, and I see him often. Ernesto has been gone for two years now. He was diagnosed in high school with severe schizophrenia, and I now understand his lifelong difficulty. I am only glad I got to love him and take care of him. His life, like Papa's, was very hard, and in the end, I think he gave up.

Late in life, Mom had another baby, born two months after my first child. Rosanna was raised like one of mine.

We stayed friends with the Valentinis, and they even moved to live across the street from us in the suburbs. The friendship ended shortly after mom had Rosanna.

I don't know who killed my Uncle Italo, but whoever pulled that trigger killed a wife and five daughters along with him on that day. Italo's wife stayed in Cleveland, for whatever reason, not having the courage to move. Her beautiful daughters, my dear cousins, all more or less became victims of the ravenous wolves that prey on fatherless girls in inner cities like Cleveland. Two of them are tragically gone and I can only imagine what life may have been had Italo stayed alive and taken them out of the city when they were younger. I daydream often as to why they could not have lived a vibrant, abundant life, but it seems that is what the inner city can take from you.

Uncle Joe and his wife and his sons truly stole and squandered the land in Italy. They were always the wealthy ones in California. None of us understood why they were so wealthy. Until, that is, we found out the poor DiRuggiero family with ten children living in the Italian countryside during World War II, was actually living with a mountain of marble in their backyard.

Uncle Joe died right after I married, and his oldest son died of a heart attack a few years later. One son remains, and I cannot really blame him for the selfishness of his father and mother. But I often think what would have been had Uncle Italo been in charge. Family trust perhaps? With all the children and grandchildren having their college paid for. Wow, what could that have meant for the DiRuggiero family. Wow, what was taken away...

My husband, Dan, was true to his word as he took me back to Ohio State to get permission to finish my last six classes in Cleveland. So today, I am a proud graduate of the Ohio State University.

My husband and I go dancing often and are faithful members of the Catholic Church. God has given us much grace and the strength to endure the hardships life inevitably brings.

I am honored to have been raised as I was, and though there are a lot of tears as well as joys as I look back at all the years, the one thing that stands out is the wonderful gift that life is.

May God Bless You Richly

*Marisa DiRuggiero Conway*

If you would be kind enough to review this book,
you can leave a review here:
<u>Amazon</u>


Visit Marisa's websites to
learn more and share your own stories.


<u>www.lessonsfromnonna.com</u>
<u>www.marisadi.com</u>


**Also by D.P. Conway**
Twelve Days
The Ghost of Christmas to Come
Nava
Starry Night
The Wancheen
Las Vegas Down
Parkland

Coming Soon by D. P. Conway

Game of Lords, the Series.
Mary Queen of Hearts
Salem
The Great Bowersville Bank Robbery!

Find out more at <u>www.dpconway.com</u>

Published by Day Lights Publishing House, Inc
5498 Dorothy Drive * North Olmsted Oh 44070

Cover by Nate Myers and Colleen Conway Cooper
Editing Team: Caroline Knecht, Jacqui Corn-Uys
Thanks to Books Go Social for their Beta Reader Support.

Send your inquiries or comments to conwaycpa@gmail.com

Print V 1.1 10.16.22

Made in the USA
Columbia, SC
05 March 2024

32727962R00181